DIVERTICULITIS COOKBOOK

A 3-STAGE DIET WITH 500+ RECIPES FOR YOUR GUT HEALTH. PREVENT PAINFUL FLARE-UPS AND ENJOY A STRESS-FREE LIFE AGAIN | SYMPTOM-SPECIFIC MEAL PLANS + 100 EXTRA RECIPES

SHONA FOULGER

© Copyright 2022 - All rights reserved.

This document is geared towards providing exact and reliable information in regard to the topic and issue covered.

- From a Declaration of Principles which was accepted and approved equally by a Committee of the American Bar Association and a Committee of Publishers and Associations.

In no way is it legal to reproduce, duplicate, or transmit any part of this document in either electronic means or in printed format. All rights reserved.

The information provided herein is stated to be truthful and consistent, in that any liability, in terms of inattention or otherwise, by any usage or abuse of any policies, processes, or directions contained within is the solitary and utter responsibility of the recipient reader. Under no circumstances will any legal responsibility or blame be held against the publisher for any reparation, damages, or monetary loss due to the information herein, either directly or indirectly.

Respective authors own all copyrights not held by the publisher.

The information herein is offered for informational purposes solely and is universal as so. The presentation of the information is without contract or any type of guarantee assurance.

The trademarks that are used are without any consent, and the publication of the trademark is without permission or backing by the trademark owner. All trademarks and brands within this book are for clarifying purposes only and are owned by the owners themselves, not affiliated with this document.

TABLE OF CONTENTS

TABLE OF CONTENTS 1
INTRODUCTION 9
DIFFERENCE BETWEEN DIVERTICULOSIS AND DIVERTICULITIS 10
   Diverticulosis 10
   Diverticulitis 10
RISK FACTORS FOR DIVERTICULITIS 10
   Family History 10
   Low-Fiber Diet 11
   Low Levels of Vitamin D 11
   Obesity 11
   Physical Inactivity 11
   Use of Non-Steroidal Anti-Inflammatory Drugs (NSAIDs) or Smoking 11
HOW TO DIAGNOSE DIVERTICULITIS 11
   Blood Tests 11
   Colonoscopy 11
   Examining Your Lower GI (Gastrointestinal) Arrangement 11
   CT Scans (Mechanized Tomography) ... 11
TREATMENT FOR DIVERTICULITIS 12
   When Is Surgery for Diverticulitis Considered? 12
   Surgery and Diverticulitis 12
PREVENTING DIVERTICULOSIS 12
   Eat More Fiber 12
   Drink Plenty of Water 12
   Exercise Daily 13
   How Much Fiber Should You Eat? 13
   What Foods Are High in Fiber? 13
EXPLANATION & DECLINATION OF THE 3 PHASES OF THE DIVERTICULITIS DIET 13
   Stage 1: The Clear Liquid Diet 13
      Goals 13
      Easy Excretion 13
      Maintenance of Hydration 13
   Stage 2: Low-Fiber, Low-Residue Diet ... 14

   Stage 3: The High-Fiber Diet 14
      Goals 14
      Guidelines for High-Fiber Diet 14
      Foods to Include and Exclude in High-Fiber Diet 14
FOODS TO AVOID AND RECOMMENDED FOODS FOR EACH OF THE 3 PHASES OF THE DIVERTICULITIS DIET 15
   Food to Avoid 15
      Vegetables with Small Particles or Seeds 15
      Seeds 15
      Sweets with Small Particles or Seeds 15
      Fruits with Small Particles or Seeds 16
      Starches (Refined) 16
ESSENTIALS SHOPPING LIST 16
   Fruits 16
   Juices 16
   Vegetables 16
   Beans & Peas 16
   Grains, Breads & Other 16
   Meats 16
   Dairy 17
   Spices, Herbs & Oils 17
   Condiments 17
   Starches 17
BASIC TIPS AND NATURAL REMEDIES TO AVOID RELAPSE 18
   Maintaining Bacterial Balance 18
   Probiotics 18
   Probiotic-rich foods: 18
   Do Not Overdose on Medications 18
   Lean Meats 18
   Colloidal Silver 18
   Alcohol Renunciation 19
   Behavioral Tips 19
CLEAR LIQUID DIET: BREAKFAST 20
   Apple-Cinnamon Tea 20
   Blueberry Green Tea 20

Citrus Sports Drink	20
Homemade Orange Gelatin	20
Raspberry Lemonade Ice Pops	20
Homemade No Pulp Orange Juice	21
Apple Orange Juice	21
Pineapple Mint Juice	21
Celery Apple Juice	21
Homemade Banana Apple Juice	21
Tropical Fruit Smoothie	21
Sweet Detox Juice	22
Fruit Julius	22
Vanilla Shake	22
Blueberry Gut Healing Protein Shake	22
Banana Oat Shake	22
Detoxifying Beet Juice	22
Blueberry Smoothie	23
Banana Smoothie	23
Lime and Kale Smoothie	23
Soothing Arugula and Apple Smoothie	23
Breakfast Boost With Apple and Berries	23
Aru-Avocado Detox Smoothie	23
Revitalizer Kale Smoothie	24
Cleansing Apple and Avocado Smoothie	24
Kale Green Smoothie	24
Papaya and Quinoa Smoothie	24
Avocado and Cucumber Smoothie	24
Orange and Banana Drink	24
Lettuce, Banana, and Berries Smoothie	25
Papaya-Mango Smoothie	25
Cantaloupe Smoothie	25
Cantaloupe-Mix Smoothie	25
Applesauce-Avocado Smoothie	25

LUNCH 26

Cranberry Smoothie	26
Sparkling Pineapple Mint Juice	26
Decaf Peppermint Tea	26
Sugar-Free Root Beer Ice Pops	26
Syrup	26
French Lavender Lemonade	26
Frozen Lemonade with Pineapple	27
Healthier Apple Juice	27

Citrus Apple Juice	27
Richly Fruity Juice	27
Delish Grape Juice	27
Lemony Grape Juice	27
Holiday Special Juice	28
Vitamin C Rich Juice	28
Incredible Fresh Juice	28
Favorite Summer Lemonade	28
Ultimate Fruity Punch	28
Thirst Quencher Sports Drink	29
Pineapple Ginger Juice	29
Carrot Orange Juice	29
Strawberry Apple Juice	29
Autumn Energizer Juice	29
Asian Inspired Wonton Broth	30
Mushroom, Cauliflower and Cabbage Broth	30
Indian Inspired Vegetable Stock	30
Ginger, Mushroom and Cauliflower Broth	30
Fish Broth	31
Clear Pumpkin Broth	31
Pork Stock	31
Slow Cooker Pork Bone Broth	31

DINNER 32

Chicken Bone Broth	32
Homemade Beef Stock	32
Three-Ingredient Sugar-Free Gelatin	32
Homey Clear Chicken Broth	32
Oxtail Bone Broth	33
Chicken Bone Broth with Ginger and Lemon	33
Beef Bone Broth	33
Ginger and Mushroom broth	33
Banana tea	33
Vegetable Stock	34
Strawberry Popsicles	34
Lemon Jello	34
Ginger Root Tea	34
Strawberry Gummies	34
Orange Gelatin	35
Refreshing Sports Drink	35
Perfect Sunny Day Tea	35
Nutritious Green Tea	35

Simple Black Tea	36
Lemony Black Tea	36
Metabolism Booster Coffee	36
Best Homemade Broth	36
Clean Testing Broth	36
Healing Broth	37
Veggie Lover's Broth	37
Brain Healthy Broth	37
Minerals Rich Broth	37
Holiday Favorite Gelatin	38

LOW RESIDUE DIET: BREAKFAST 39

Baked Banana-Nut Oatmeal Cups	39
Oatmeal Pumpkin Raisin Pancakes	39
Pumpkin Pie Oatmeal	39
Sante Fe Omelet	39
Sunrise Burrito Wrap	40
Green Smoothie	40
Muesli with Raspberries	40
Peanut Butter Protein Overnight Oats	40
Fruit & Yogurt Smoothie	40
Everything Bagel Avocado Toast	40
Creamy Blueberry-Pecan Overnight Oatmeal	41
Spinach-Avocado Smoothie	41
Blueberry Almond Chia Pudding	41
Green Bean Potato Salad	41
Spinach Frittata	41
Banana and Pear Pita Pockets	42
Pear Pancakes	42
Ripe Plantain Bran Muffins	42
Easy Breakfast Bran Muffins	42
Apple Oatmeal	43
Breakfast Burrito Wrap	43
Zucchini Omelet	43
Coconut Chia Seed Pudding	43
Spiced Oatmeal	44
Breakfast Cereal	44
Cajun Omelet	44
Strawberry Cashew Chia Pudding	44
Peanut Butter Banana Oatmeal	44
Overnight Peach Oatmeal	44
Coconut Pancakes	45

Lemon Baked Eggs	45
Banana Pancakes	45
Deviled Egg	45
Crunchy Maple Sweet Potatoes	46
Banana Cake	46
Apple Pudding	46
Super-Food Scramble	47
Family Favorite Scramble	47
Tasty Veggie Omelet	47
Fluffy Pumpkin Pancakes	47
Sper-Tasty Chicken Muffins	48
Classic Zucchini Bread	48

LUNCH 49

Barbecue Beef Stir-Fry	49
Chicken Saffron Rice Pilaf	49
Green Bean Tuna Salad	49
Sweet Potato Hash with Sausage and Spinach	49
Grilled Shrimp and Bean Salad	50
Grilled Steak and Mixed Greens Salad	50
Lentil Tomato Salad	50
Light Shrimp and Barley Salad	50
Mango Black Bean Salad	50
Mediterranean Salmon and Potato Salad	51
Celery Soup	51
Pea Tuna Salad	51
Vegetable Soup	51
Carrot and Turkey Soup	52
Creamy Pumpkin Soup	52
Mixed Bean Salad	52
Quick Spinach and Black Bean Salad	52
Shrimp, Pasta and Spinach Salad	53
Stir-Fry Ground Chicken and Green Beans	53
Stewed Lamb	53
Pulled Chicken Salad	53
Lemongrass Beef	54
Beetroot Carrot Salad	54
Veggie Bowl	54
Pomegranate Salad	54
Dijon Orange Summer Salad	55
Pulao Rice Prawns	55
White Radish Crunch Salad	55

Apple And Mushroom Soup 55
Spring Watercress Soup 56
Oyster Sauce Tofu 56
Potato and Rosemary Risotto.............................. 56
Cheesy Baked Tortillas 57
Smoky Rice 57
Zucchini Lasagna 57
Greek Chicken Skewers 58
Roast Beef 58
Grilled Fish Steaks 58
Lamb Chops 58
Eggplant Croquettes 59
Cucumber Egg Salad 59
Garden Veggies Quiche 59
Greek Inspired Cucumber Salad 59
Light Veggie Salad 60
Eastern European Soup 60
Citrus Glazed Carrots 60
Braised Asparagus 60
Spring Flavored Pasta 60
Versatile Mac 'n Cheese 60
Gluten-Free Curry 61
New Year's Luncheon Meal 61
Entertaining Wraps 61
Amazing Chicken Platter 61
Colorful Chicken Dinner 62
Easiest Tuna Salad 62
Lemony Salmon 62
Spinach and Apple Salad 62
Tuna and Bean Salad 63
Veggie and Rice Salad 63
Zesty Bean and Tomato Salad 63

DINNER 64

Ground Beef Tostada 64
Delicious Combo Dinner 64
Beef Barley Soup 64
Ground Beef and Rice Bowls 64
Fish Sticks 65
Beet Soup 65
Chicken Burgers 65
Pumpkin Waffles 65

Bean Soup 66
Carrot Cucumber Salad 66
Lemon Chicken and Rice 66
Peachy Pork with Rice 67
Skillet Ham and Rice 67
Honey Chicken Kabobs 67
Baked Chicken Breasts 67
Loaded Pumpkin Chowder 67
Fish Stew 68
Mushroom Soup 68
Chicken Soup 68
Pumpkin Casserole 69
Fresh Tomato Juice 69
Chicken Cutlets 69
Slow Cooker Salsa Turkey 69
Sriracha Lime Chicken and Apple Salad 70
Pan-Seared Scallops with Lemon-Ginger Vinaigrette
.... 70
Roasted Salmon and Asparagus 70
Cod with Ginger and Black Beans 70
Halibut Curry 71
Chicken Cacciatore 71
Chicken and Bell Pepper Sauté 71
Chicken Salad Sandwiches 71
Rosemary Chicken 71
Crystallized Ginger 72
Scrambled Eggs and Smoked Salmon Croissants 72
Sango de Choclo and Green Plantains with Shrimp 72
Mini Paleo Salmon Cakes and Lemony Herb Aioli 73
Low Fodmap One Pan Chicken Dinner Bake 73
Friendly Chicken Fingers 73
Best Low Fodmap Chocolate Chip Cookies 74
Low Fodmap Mediterranean Grilled Cheese 74
Low Fodmap Banana Nut Oatmeal Muffins 74
Pumpkin Oatmeal Muffins with Chocolate Chips 75
Flavorful Shrimp Kabobs 75
Pan-Seared Scallops 75
Mediterranean Shrimp Salad 75
Health-Conscious People's Salad 76
Italian Pasta Soup 76
Pure Comfort Soup 76

Goof-for-You Stew 76
Zero-Fiber: Chicken Dish 77
Carrot Ginger Soup 77
Zucchini, Cashew, Thyme Soup 77

HIGH-FIBER DIET: BREAKFAST 78

Cocoa Almond French Toast 78
Cherry Smoothie 78
Ham & Egg Breakfast Burrito 78
PB & J Oats 78
Artichoke & Egg Tartine 79
Strawberry-Pineapple Smoothie 79
Peach-Blueberry Parfaits 79
Southwest Breakfast Quesadilla 79
Raspberry Yogurt Cereal Bowl 80
Bean & Bacon Breakfast Tacos 80
Peanut Butter & Fig Crispbreads 80
Strawberry-Ricotta Waffle Sandwich 80
Make-&-Take Breakfast Sausage Sandwich 80
Loaded Pita Pockets 80
West Coast Avocado Toast 81
Mango Raspberry Smoothie 81
Peanut Butter & Chia Berry Jam English Muffin 81
Green Eggs & Ham Bagel Breakfast Sandwich 81
Pumpkin Pie Smoothie 81
Peanut Butter-Chocolate Chip Overnight Oats with Banana 82
Baked Banana Cups 82
Peanut Butter-Banana English Muffin 82
White Bean & Avocado Toast 82
Berry-Almond Smoothie Bowl 82
Avocado Toast with Burrata 83
Baked Oatmeal 83
Homestyle Pancake Mix 83
Multigrain Pancakes 83
Cinnamon-Oat Bran Pancakes 83
Whole-Wheat Buttermilk Pancakes 84
Cornmeal Pancakes 84
Oven-Baked Pancake 84
Baked Pancake 84
Wheat Waffles 85
Oatmeal Waffles 85

Bran Applesauce Muffins 85
Oat Bran Muffins 85
Orange Bran Muffins 86
Pasta Fritters 86
Cinnamon Honey Scones 86
Oatmeal Raisin Scones 86
Whole Grain Scones 87
Granola 87
Toasty Nut Granola 87
Breakfast Bars 87
Whole-Wheat Coffee Cake 88
Black Beans and Avocado Toasts 88
Apples N' Oats Breakfast Smoothie 88
Crunchy Breakfast Topping 88
Vegetables and Fruits Breakfast 89
Blueberry Coconut Smoothie Bowl 89
No-Bake Apricot Oat Protein Bars 89
Cinnamon Apple Omelet 90
Mango Ginger Smoothie 90
Cinnamon and Vanilla Cantaloupe Smoothie 90
Wild Blueberry and Cherry Smoothie 90
Peanut Butter Chia Overnight Oats 90
Pumpkin Pie Chia Pudding 91
2 Minute Flourless English Muffin 91
Blueberry Muffins 91

LUNCH 92

Packed Burrito 92
Blood Orange Chia Pudding 92
Avocado & Caper Flagel 92
Springtime Tofu Scramble 92
Date-Sweetened Banana Bread 93
Blueberry Chia Jam 93
Pumpkin Pie Butter 93
Spiced Pumpkin Granola 93
Coconut Almond Protein Bars 94
Grain-Free Granola Clusters 94
Toasted Coconut and Berry Grain 94
Berry Soft Serve & Vanilla Chia Pudding Parfait 95
Creamy Raspberry, Coconut & Chia Shake 95
Raw Cherry-Apple Pie 95
Jacket Potatoes with Home-Baked Beans 96

- Pea & Broad Bean Shakshuka 96
- Lentil Fritters 96
- Summer Pistou 97
- Winter Vegetable & Lentil Soup 97
- Pea Soup 97
- Guacamole 97
- Cabbage Soup 98
- Cauliflower And Potato Curry Soup 98
- Sweet Potato and Black Bean Chili 98
- White Bean Chili 99
- Chickpea Stew 99
- Veggie Sandwich 99
- Bean and Veggie Taco Bowl 100
- Cobb Salad 100
- Asparagus Soup 100
- Creamy Carrot Soup 100
- Mushroom Barley Soup 101
- Broccoli Soup 101
- Chicken and Asparagus Pasta 101
- Red Beans and Rice 101
- Beef Stir Fry 102
- Black Bean Nacho Soup 102
- Butternut Squash Soup 102
- Broccoli Salad 102
- Beef and Bean Sloppy Joe 103
- LEMONY MEDITERRANEAN CHICKEN 103

DINNER 104

- Spinach and Artichoke Dip Pasta 104
- Grilled Eggplant 104
- Stuffed Potatoes with Salsa and Beans 104
- Mushroom Quinoa Veggie Burgers 104
- Sweet Potato Soup 105
- Minestrone Soup 105
- Lentil Soup 105
- Grilled Corn Salad 106
- Kale Soup 106
- Pasta Fagioli 106
- Sweet Potato Gnocchi 107
- Bean and Ham Soup 107
- Grilled Pear Cheddar Pockets 107
- Chicken and Apple Kale Wraps 107
- Cauliflower Rice Pilaf 108
- Fresh Herb and Lemon Bulgur Pilaf 108
- Corn Chowder 108
- Strawberry and Rhubarb Soup 108
- Chicken Sandwiches 109
- Tex-Mex Bean Tostadas 109
- Fish Tacos 109
- Cucumber Almond Gazpacho 109
- Pea and Spinach Carbonara 110
- Sautéed Broccoli with Peanut Sauce 110
- Edamame lettuce wraps burgers 110
- Pizza stuffed Spaghetti Squash 111
- One-Pot Dinner Soup 111
- 3-Beans Soup 112
- Heavenly Tasty Stew 112
- Thanksgiving Dinner Chili 112
- Meatless Monday Chili 113
- Beans Trio Chili 113
- Staple Vegan Curry 113
- Fragrant Vegetarian Curry 114
- Omega-3 Rich Dinner Meal 114
- Weekend Dinner Casserole 115
- Family Dinner Pilaf 115
- Very Berry Fruit Leather 115
- Strawberry Lemon Bars 115
- Dill Potato Salad with Radishes and Peas 116
- Wildflower Honey Berries 116
- Watermelon Sparklers 116
- Wild Blueberry Soup 117
- Baked Zucchini Tater Tots 117
- Watermelon Strawberry Ginger Lemonade 117
- Potato Nests with Spinach Salad 117
- Ground Beef & Pasta Skillet 118
- Slow-Cooker Vegetable Soup 118
- Roasted Vegetable & Black Bean Tacos 118
- Chicken & Vegetable Penne with Parsley-Walnut Pesto 118
- Turmeric-Roasted Cauliflower 119
- Cucumber and Avocado Salad 119
- Salmon Cakes 119

GET YOUR BONUS! 120

EXTRA RECIPES READY IN 30 MINS 121

- Smoothie with Mixed Berries 121
- Applesauce 121
- Fruit Punch 121
- Chocolate Pudding 121
- Soup with Mushroom 121
- Soup with Broccoli 121
- Wonton Broth 122
- Cauliflower Broth 122
- Ginger Juice 122
- Lemon Tea 123
- Soup with Red Lentils and Coconut 123
- Soup with Asparagus 123
- Mashed Sweet Potatoes 123
- Zucchini Soup 124
- Ginger and Mushroom Broth 124
- Ginger Root Tea 124
- Gummies Made with Strawberries 124
- Smoothie with Creamy Cherries 124
- Lemon Baked Eggs 124
- Pancakes with Banana 125
- Deviled Egg 125
- Muesli Muffins with Pears 125
- Shakshuka 126
- Salmon Fritter 126
- Vanilla Almond Hot Chocolate 126
- Frittata with Spinach 126
- Smoothie with Banana 127
- Muffins with Banana 127
- Omelet with Mushrooms 127
- Omelet with Zucchini 127
- Fluffy Pancakes 127
- French Toast 128
- Waffles with Peaches 128
- Muffins with Pumpkin 128
- Cookies with Peanut Butter 128
- Barbecue Beef Stir-Fry 129
- Chicken Salad 129
- Lemongrass Beef 129
- Veggie Bowl 129
- Pomegranate Salad 130

- White Radish Crunch Salad 130
- Spring Watercress Soup 130
- Potato & Rosemary Risotto 130
- Cucumber Egg Salad 131
- Loaded Pumpkin Soup 131
- Simple Fish Stew 131
- Homemade Chicken Soup 131
- Easy Ground Beef Bowl 132
- Homemade Pumpkin Waffles 132
- Lemon Chicken and Rice 132
- Peachy Pork with Rice 132
- Skillet Ham and Rice 133
- Mango and Ginger Smoothie 133
- Spinach & Cherry Smoothie 133
- Banana & Cacao Smoothie 133
- Spinach and Egg Scramble with Raspberries 133
- Blackberry Smoothie 134
- Vegetable Frittata 134
- Smoothie with Chocolate and Banana 134
- Cocoa Almond French Toast 134
- Muesli with Raspberries 134
- Baked Banana-Nut Oatmeal Cups 134
- Banana Bran Muffins 135
- Dark Chocolate Raspberry Oatmeal 135
- Pineapple-Raspberry Parfaits 135
- Green Smoothie 135
- Peach-Blueberry Parfaits Recipe 136
- Raspberry Yogurt Cereal Bowl 136
- Avocado toast 136
- Fully-Loaded Pita Pockets 136
- Creamy Pea Soup 136
- Guacamole 137
- Cabbage Soup 137
- The Best Veggie Sandwich 137
- Quick Veggie Taco Bowl 137
- Cobb Salad 137
- Cream of Asparagus Soup 138
- Carrot Soup 138
- Mushroom-Barley Soup 138
- Penne with Chicken and Asparagus 138
- Red Beans and Rice Recipe 139

Black Bean Nacho Soup 139
Best Butternut Squash Soup 139
Easy Broccoli Salad 139
Beef & Bean Sloppy Joes Recipe 139
Peanut Soup with Sweet Potato 140
Cheddar & Pear Panini 140
Chicken & Apple Kale Wraps 140
Easy Cauliflower Rice Pilaf 140
Strawberry & Rhubarb Soup 141
Chicken Pesto Sandwich 141
Bean Tostadas 141
Perfect Fish Tacos 141
Easy Pea & Spinach Carbonara 141
Broccoli with Peanut Sauce 142
Spinach Artichoke Dip Pasta 142
Stuffed Potatoes with Salsa & Beans 142
Classic Minestrone Soup 142
Vegan Carrot Cake Energy Balls 143
Skillet Lemon Chicken with Spinach 143
Tomato Basil Pasta 143

30 DAYS MEAL PLAN 144
CONCLUSION 146

INTRODUCTION

Diverticulitis generally affects the large intestine and concerns the inflammation/infection of one or even several (balloon-like) sacs that may develop in the large intestine: namely, diverticula. Before analyzing diverticulitis, it is essential to know about its earlier and non-serious forms. Diverticula are persistent joint disorder, and estimates show us that about 65% of adults, particularly women, have diverticulosis. Infection (diverticulitis) does not constantly develop from this condition but only affects 10-25% of people with diverticulosis.

However, what are the risk factors for the development of diverticulosis? It is essential to point out that diverticulosis is not a pathology but an anatomical alteration. Most people with this condition have no symptoms; it is rarely necessary to go to the emergency room. The risk factors that play a leading role in the development are:

- Age
- Female sex
- Poor eating habits
- Obesity
- An excessively sedentary lifestyle
- High intake of anti-inflammatory drugs

It is defined as "the pathology of the elderly" because its frequency progressively increases with age, from the age of forty onwards. In case of diverticulosis, there are some dietary recommendations: drink water, consume fruits and vegetables and, therefore, take fiber to facilitate the mobility of the intestine. These measures are to avoid constipation. It is often reported not to eat fruits with seed (for example, kiwi) in the presence of diverticula, but it is not valid. These are old beliefs. A study was carried out on a sample of fifty thousand patients that shows precisely the opposite: reducing the consumption of vegetables, fruits, and foods containing seeds brings the subject at risk of diverticulitis. For some time now, doctors have also abandoned the hypothesis that diverticulitis is caused by the consumption of nuts, seeds, corn, or popcorn.

Diverticulosis, as already mentioned, implies the presence of diverticula, but it is asymptomatic. Instead, we mean "diverticular disease" when symptoms disturb the patient, such as bloating, abdominal pain, and alteration of his bowel regularity. The patient often has pain in the lower quadrants, especially on the left side, where the diverticula are more present. When subject to diverticular disease, one should follow a diet based on fiber.

The scenario changes when diverticulitis occurs. Diverticulitis, as specified initially, is an actual inflammation of the diverticula, and the patient complains of extreme pain. The most systemic symptoms associated with diverticulitis are:

- Abdominal pain
- Pain associated with constipation/diarrhea
- Meteorism
- Reduced appetite
- Nausea

The first practical intervention for the patient is often to follow a liquid diet, but it depends on the severity of inflammation. This diet is usually maintained for a maximum of 15 days, but it depends on how the symptoms resolve and whether complications occur. At a later date, he is given antibiotics. With these steps and diligence in the diet often, in about 90% of cases, the inflammation of the diverticulum is eliminated permanently. Rarely in cases of diverticulitis is surgical intervention required, only in 1% of cases.

DIFFERENCE BETWEEN DIVERTICULOSIS AND DIVERTICULITIS

DIVERTICULOSIS

Diverticulosis is the presence of several small pockets or bulges in the colon known as diverticula. These bulges are quite harmless and do not require any form of treatment. Neither do they present symptoms. But, if care is not taken, diverticulosis could spiral into a more dangerous condition. Put simply, if diverticula are neither inflamed nor infected, the condition is known as diverticulosis. Research reveals that 80 percent of patients with diverticulosis present with no symptoms (Persons, 2019). Thus, since there is no symptom, treatments are unnecessary. However, in worse cases, diverticulosis is known to trigger gastrointestinal symptoms such as abdominal pain and bloating. When this occurs, the condition is termed SUDD (symptomatic uncomplicated diverticular disease). When diverticulosis develops into SUDD, there's a 4% chance that it might further worsen into diverticulitis.

Once diverticula appear, they never really disappear again unless they are removed through surgery. As a result, diverticulosis could last a lifetime if untreated. Albeit, the condition is manageable with some dietary adjustments. With adequate treatment, symptoms of diverticulosis, including bleeding and pain, could abate within a couple of days. But it's worth noting that symptoms could persist or worsen in the event of severe illnesses or complications. People who consume lots of fiber in their day-to-day diets have a lower susceptibility to developing diverticular diseases. The American Dietetic Association posits that the daily recommended intake of fiber borders between 20 to 35 grams. But not all fibers are good for the body. For diverticulosis, you are better off getting your fiber from grains, fruits, and veggies. To improve your daily intake of fiber, undergo the process gradually. Additionally, you should take lots of water to help bowel movements by improving bulk. Doing this will help to reduce pressure when passing the bowel.

DIVERTICULITIS

Diverticulitis only occurs due to infection and inflammation (swelling) in one or multiple diverticula. Meaning, that for diverticulitis to occur, one must already have diverticulosis. Unlike diverticulosis, diverticulitis is a graver condition with the potential to become dangerous over time. This condition, however, is treatable. For mild diverticulitis, antibiotics, changes in diet, and enough rest can help to cure symptoms. But recurring or severe diverticulitis may require surgical procedures. In simpler terms, diverticulitis is a pretty serious condition, which could range from micro-perforations in the diverticula to more severe occurrences. When micro-perforations occur, the diverticula develop tiny holes, which can potentially empty the contents of the colon into the abdominal cavity.

These perforations stem from the constant strain and pressure caused by the movement of stool via the colon. Sometimes, the diverticula could be outrightly ruptured in the process, leading to graves entering and contaminating the peritoneum—the membrane encasing the abdominal cavity. Ruptures could also stem from abscesses, which are infected diverticula with pus, which could grow and ruin the tissues of the colon. If the abscesses that appear on the colon are tiny and do not exceed the region, they could be cleared up with some antibiotic treatment. Otherwise, they might have to be drained to prevent further complications.

Another complication of diverticulitis is peritonitis, which demands immediate surgical intervention to clean out the abdominal cavity and remove the damaged areas of the colon. Fistula is another such condition, presenting as the abnormal connection of tissues between different organs. When a damaged tissue touches a different organ, it could stick there. And when it heals that way, it results in a fistula. When diverticulitis infections spread outside the colon, the tissue of the organ could stick to another nearby organ (bladder, skin, or small intestine). Fistulas commonly form between the bladder and the colon and are more prevalent in men than women. They can result in chronic infections in the urinary tract, which require surgery to remove the affected area of the colon and the fistula.

Infected diverticula could also lead to scarring, which may result in total or partial blockage of the large intestine. When such intestinal obstruction occurs, it becomes difficult for the colon to manage bowel movement effectively. Hence, emergency surgical interventions are imperative. Partial blockages aren't as dire and won't be treated as emergencies, so surgical interventions can be planned.

RISK FACTORS FOR DIVERTICULITIS

One of the major risk factors for diverticulitis is advanced age. Diverticulitis is more common in older people than in younger people. It is most common in men under 50 and women between 50 and 70. Conversely, diverticulitis is more likely to occur in people who develop diverticula at a young age. Other potential risk factors for diverticulitis, as per a review published in 2018, include:

FAMILY HISTORY

Diverticular disease is linked to genetics, according to

two large twin studies. The authors estimate that hereditary factors account for 40 to 50 percent of the risk of diverticular disease.

LOW-FIBER DIET

In some studies, low-fiber diets have been associated with a higher risk of diverticulitis. Other research, on the other hand, has found no link between dietary fiber and this condition.

LOW LEVELS OF VITAMIN D

According to one study, people with higher vitamin D levels may lower the risk of developing diverticulitis.

OBESITY

Diverticulitis is more common in people with a higher BMI and larger waistlines. Obesity may increase the risk of diverticulitis by altering the bacterial balance in the gut.

PHYSICAL INACTIVITY

According to some studies, diverticulitis is less common in physically active people than in inactive people.

USE OF NON-STEROIDAL ANTI-INFLAMMATORY DRUGS (NSAIDS) OR SMOKING

Regular use of aspirin, ibuprofen, or other nonsteroidal anti-inflammatory drugs (NSAIDs) may increase your risk of developing diverticulitis. Diverticular disease, including diverticulitis, is more common in smokers than nonsmokers.

HOW TO DIAGNOSE DIVERTICULITIS

Medicinal services suppliers regularly discover diverticulosis amid a normal X-ray or a colonoscopy, a test used to peer inside the rectum and whole colon.

Because of the side effects and seriousness of the disease, a man might be assessed and analyzed by an essential consideration doctor, a crisis division doctor, a specialist, or a gastroenterologist—a specialist who works in digestive diseases.

BLOOD TESTS

A blood test includes drawing a man's blood at a medicinal services supplier's office, a business office, or a healing facility and sending the example to a lab for examination. The blood test can demonstrate the nearness of irritation or paleness—a condition in which red platelets are less or littler than ordinary, which keeps the body's cells from getting enough oxygen.

COLONOSCOPY

The colonoscopy is performed at a healing facility or an outpatient focus by a gastroenterologist. Before the test, the individual's social insurance supplier will give composed entrails prep directions to take after at home. The individual may need to take after an unmistakable fluid eating routine for 1 to 3 days before the test.

The individual may likewise need to take intestinal medicines and bowel purges the night before the test. By and large, light anesthesia, and perhaps torment pharmaceutical, people groups unwind for the test.

While the gastroenterologist inserts an adjustable tube into the patient's intestines, the patient will be positioned on a table. A little camera on the tube sends a video picture of the intestinal coating to a PC screen. The test can demonstrate diverticulosis and diverticular sickness.

EXAMINING YOUR LOWER GI (GASTROINTESTINAL) ARRANGEMENT

A lower GI arrangement is an X-ray exam that is utilized to take a gander at the digestive organ. The test is performed at a doctor's facility or an outpatient focus by an X-ray specialist, and the pictures are translated by a radiologist. Anesthesia is not required.

The medicinal services supplier may give composed inside prep guidelines to take after at home before the test. The individual might be requested to take after a reasonable fluid eating regimen for 1 to 3 days before the strategy. A diuretic or douche might be utilized before the test. A purgative is a pharmaceutical that extricates stool and expands solid discharges.

A bowel purge includes flushing water or purgative into the rectum utilizing a unique squirt bottle. These drugs cause the runs, so the individual ought to remain nearby to a restroom amid the inside prep. While the radiologist puts an adjustable tube into the back of the patient's neck, the patient will lie down on a table.

The colon is loaded with barium; making indications of diverticular illness appear entire more plainly on x beams.

CT SCANS (MECHANIZED TOMOGRAPHY)

A CT sweep of the colon is the most widely recognized test used to analyze Diverticular infection. CT filters utilize a mix of x beams and PC innovation to make three-dimensional (3-D) pictures. For a CT sweep, the individual might be given a beverage and an infusion of exceptional color called contrast medium. CT checks require the individual to lie on a table that slides into a passage molded gadget where the x beams are taken.

The technique is performed in an outpatient focus or a doctor's facility by an x-beam expert, and the pictures are deciphered by a radiologist—a specialist who represents considerable authority in medicinal imaging. Anesthesia is not required. CT sweeps can distinguish diverticulosis and affirm its analysis.

TREATMENT FOR DIVERTICULITIS

If your diverticulitis is moderate, your doctor may prescribe an antibiotic. Rest, over-the-counter pain relievers, and a low-fiber or liquid diet may be advised until the symptoms improve. Once your symptoms have improved, you can gradually return to soft foods, followed by a more normal diet containing plenty of high-fiber foods. The specifics of the treatment plan will be discussed between you and the healthcare provider. You could be admitted to the hospital for intravenous (IV) antibiotics, IV fluids, or surgery if the diverticulitis is severe, you have rectal bleeding, or you are having a repeat bout of diverticulitis.

WHEN IS SURGERY FOR DIVERTICULITIS CONSIDERED?

Surgery may be considered in the presence of:

- Abscesses

An abscess is an infection in the abdomen that is contained or "walled off." Surgery is required if the fluid in an abscess cannot be drained with a needle or catheter. The abscess is cleaned out during surgery, and the affected part of the colon is removed.

- Perforation/Peritonitis

Peritonitis is caused by a tear (perforation) in your colon that allows pus or stool to leak into the abdominal cavity. This life-threatening infection necessitates immediate surgery to clean the cavity and remove the colon's damaged section.

- Blockages or Strictures

Scars from previous infections in your colon can form, resulting in a partial or complete blockage or strictures. A total blockage necessitates surgery, whereas partial blockage does not.

- Fistulas

A fistula is an abnormally formed passageway or tunnel that connects one organ to another. These passageways are formed by an abscess that erodes into the surrounding tissue. Because most fistulas do not heal on their own, surgery is required.

- Continued Rectal Bleeding

Diverticular bleeding occurs when a tiny blood artery near the diverticula rupture. Mild bleeding usually goes away on its own, but about 20% of cases require medical attention. If the bleeding is severe and uncontrollable, emergency surgery is required.

- Having Multiple Attacks on a High-Fiber Diet

The surgeon may decide to remove the colon's diseased part as the best option to prevent future attacks.

- Severe Diverticulitis Failed to Respond to Other Treatment Methods

SURGERY AND DIVERTICULITIS

During surgery, a portion of the colon is routinely removed. The diseased section of the colon is removed during surgery, and the colon is reattached to the rectum. Depending on the extent and severity of the disease, surgery can be done in one operation, two operations, an open procedure (traditional surgery involving a large incision), or a minimally invasive laparoscopic procedure. A colostomy may or may not be required. A colostomy is a procedure that involves bringing the healthy end of the colon to the skin's surface through a hole in your abdominal wall. A colostomy bag is attached to the colon on the skin's surface to collect colon waste. While your colon heals, you may need to use the colostomy bag for several months. The colon is reattached to the rectum after it has healed.

PREVENTING DIVERTICULOSIS

Diverticular disease can be prevented and its complications reduced by having regular bowel movements and avoiding constipation and straining. To do so, follow these steps:

EAT MORE FIBER

Fiber draws more water into your stool, making it bulkier, softer, and easier to move through your colon—and move faster.

DRINK PLENTY OF WATER

Because eating more fiber results in more water absorption, you'll need to drink more water to keep your stool soft and moving. Many doctors recommend that you drink half your body weight in oz.

EXERCISE DAILY

Food passes more easily through your intestines when you move around and exercise for thirty minutes on most days.

HOW MUCH FIBER SHOULD YOU EAT?

14 grams of protein per 1,000 calories ingested daily is recommended by the National Institute of Diabetes and Digestive and Kidney Diseases. If you eat 2,000 calories per day, you should aim for 28 grams of fiber per day. Regardless of whether or not they have diverticula, everyone should try to eat this much fiber every day. Fiber is the percentage of plant foods that cannot be digested.

WHAT FOODS ARE HIGH IN FIBER?

High-fiber foods include:

- Pasta, bread, crackers, barley, brown rice, and oatmeal are whole grain foods.
- Berries and other types of fruit
- Vegetables: cabbage, broccoli, spinach, asparagus, carrots, squash, and beans.
- Brown rice is a good option.
- Rice, wheat, corn, oats, rye, barley, and millet bran products
- Dried beans and peas, cooked

A high-fiber diet not only prevents constipation but also lowers cholesterol, and blood pressure improves blood sugar and lowers the risk of developing specific intestinal disorders like colorectal cancer.

EXPLANATION & DECLINATION OF THE 3 PHASES OF THE DIVERTICULITIS DIET

There are three main phases of the Diverticulitis diet: eating during an active flare-up, eating while recovering from a flare and preventing a flare in the future. As with any other diet, you will need to listen to your body throughout each stage and adjust the diet slowly as you add new foods while closely monitoring your symptoms.

STAGE 1: THE CLEAR LIQUID DIET

Just as the name implies, a clear liquid diet is a diet that consists entirely of clear liquids.

These liquids include broth, water, juices with no pulp, and gelatin (the plain one). The liquid may be colored, but they're clear since you can see through them.

While going through an active flare, your symptoms can become extreme. Due to this, it's smart for you to give your bowel a period of rest. As you can imagine, the best way to do this is by sticking to a clear fluid diet. This will aid in your recovery as your body may outright reject solid foods.

It is vital to note that the clear fluid stage of the diet is NOT intended to be a long-term diet.

Restricting yourself to a clear fluid diet for an excessive amount of time may cause you to feel light-headed, weak, hungry, and fatigued. You can also experience muscle wasting, excessive weight loss, and depletion of vitamins and minerals.

This occurs because it's incredibly difficult to meet the body's daily caloric requirements for fat, protein, and carbohydrates through a clear fluid diet. If you struggle with low blood sugar, diabetes, or other blood sugar challenges, you may want to monitor your blood sugar levels during this stage.

GOALS

The following are the goals of adhering to a clear liquid diet:

- Giving proper rest to the intestinal region.
- By intake of cleared liquid foods, the abdomen is saved from so much stress. The digestion becomes quicker and smoother. This allows the intestine to be at rest while the operated region steps back to its original functioning.
- Strengthen the intestines for digestion.

A clear liquid diet acts as a cleanser that washes the abdominal and intestinal region of any undesired bacteria and enzymes that are causing the condition to persist. Regular intake of clear liquid diets will flush off all the toxicities and create a healing environment more acceptable to nutrition intake.

EASY EXCRETION

After the diverticulitis surgery, the colon and rectum are usually in bad shape. The pouches in the colon are still in recovery mode and hence passing of the stool becomes a problem. A clear liquid diet ensures the passing of excreta in the most painless way possible. Since most of it is liquid part and contains water, a substantial amount of excretion occurs through mostly effortless urination. And hence protects the patient from further damage.

MAINTENANCE OF HYDRATION

Most surgical treatments rely on heavy antibiotics post-treatment. These drain the hydration out of the body making it highly deficient in water content. One of the aims of liquid diets is to replenish the body with all the lost water content. Along with the water content, such diets also replenish the electrolyte and vitamin levels in the body bringing back sodium, and potassium levels to the required ranges.

STAGE 2: LOW-FIBER, LOW-RESIDUE DIET

Low-residue and low-fiber diets cause stool to move slowly down the intestines. It also decreases the amount of stool in the intestines. By so doing, it prevents blockage.

Plants are the major source of dietary fiber. Humans cannot digest fiber. Residue refers to the fiber, and other substances, present in the colon after digestion. A low-fiber diet does not contain up to 15 grams of fiber per day. It also does not contain foods that bulk your stool. Basically, a low-residue diet is a low-fiber diet with some restrictions.

You can get the Recommended Dietary Allowances from both low-residue and low-fiber diets if you choose the right foods. But note that long-term use of a low-residue or low-fiber diet may cause a folic acid or vitamin C deficiency.

A low-residue (or low-fiber) diet acts as the reintroduction phase, after your flare-up symptoms have mostly passed but before your body is ready for high-fiber foods.

STAGE 3: THE HIGH-FIBER DIET

This is the final stage where the diverticulitis condition has almost healed and the patient is on track to adopt a normal eating lifestyle. Though the diverticulitis condition has healed, it is still important that the patient monitors his diet for days to come. This will eliminate any possibility of reoccurrence of the disease.

GOALS

The goals of a high fiber diet are to bring back a patient to his normal and healthy eating routine. It aims at enabling the patient to resume his daily life post-treatment of diverticulitis. The fiber intake is advised to be monitored carefully to not overburden the intestine all of a sudden. Only when a low residue diet shows positive results, does a patient shift to a high fiber diet.

GUIDELINES FOR HIGH-FIBER DIET

A high-fiber diet should be started only after the body adapts to fiber intake through a low residue diet. High-fiber diets should be well complemented by the intake of water and other fluids. The water makes absorption of fiber easier and hence aids digestion.

The fibrous intake should be controlled in portion size. Just because the patient is allowed to take up an increased number of foods, does not mean the portion size does not matter. High-fiber diets should be well calculated in portions and only about 25-30 grams of fiber should be eaten on daily basis.

Since most of the diverticulitis condition is cured by this stage, it is quite likely that a patient will fall back to his previous eating habits. It is strongly advised that patients keep off anything that got them to have the disease in the first place.

FOODS TO INCLUDE AND EXCLUDE IN HIGH-FIBER DIET

- **Bread and starches**: High-fiber diets may include finely grounded whole grains like wheat, barley, etc. Pasta, noodles, and rice can be eaten normally as well starches from potatoes, wheat, graham, and rye can be included in the diet. It is still desirable to keep off refined flours that may cause indigestion.

- **Meat and protein:** soft tender meats like fish and slightly stiffer meats like chicken, eggs, proteins in the form of lentils, cheese particularly cottage cheese are advised to be eaten regularly. Red meat is to be avoided at all costs since it is very high in fat and causes severe indigestion.

- **Vegetables:** All vegetables can be included in the diet, especially the green leafy ones that have adequate fiber. However, avoid gas-inducing vegetables like cauliflower, broccoli, cabbage, radish, and kale.

- **Fruits:** A high-fiber diet may include all fruits like apples, oranges, peaches, pears, grapes, watermelon, melon, and papaya. Almost all fruits work pretty well since there is no restriction on fiber intake. Dried fruits, whether cooked or raw still remain an exception.

- **Dairy products:** Milk and milk products, especially yogurt is very good for the cure of diverticulitis. Yogurts blended with fruits are a good way to keep the gut function under control.

- **Fats:** Fats from red meats pose serious issues in a diverticulitis diet. Olive oils are denser forms of oil that again should be avoided until complete recovery. Any other kinds of fat like butter, margarine, cream fat, etc. are all fine to be used in a high-fiber diverticulitis diet.

- **Sweets and desserts:** All sweets can be eaten normally with a condition that they are free from nuts and dried fruits. Honey and sugar can be used for sweetness. Candies and fruit jellies are another way to satiate the sweet tooth while recovering from diverticulitis disease.

It is important to note, however, that you do not want to jump directly from a significantly low-fiber diet (such as a clear fluid diet) to a high-fiber diet, as this will do more harm to your colon than good. It is always best to ease into any stage of the plan that requires an increase in your fiber intake. Aim to increase your fiber intake by 2 to 4 grams per week until you reach the recommended amount for your age and biology. Bear in mind that as you increase your fiber, you also need to increase your water intake to help move the fiber through your intestinal tract.

FOODS TO AVOID AND RECOMMENDED FOODS FOR EACH OF THE 3 PHASES OF THE DIVERTICULITIS DIET

The diverticulitis diet is a special diet meant to heal any existing diverticulitis in the digestive system and prevent it from coming back.

The first step in healing diverticulitis is to eliminate all inflammatory foods from your diet. This means avoiding drinking milk. This will dramatically improve your digestive health and lead to a higher quality of life after diverticulitis is gone. Dairy products can also be reintroduced one at a time into your diet in small amounts to see how well you tolerate them. If you can accept it, go for it. If not, skip it.

Sugar is another inflammatory food that should be removed from your diet. Sugar can be contained in so many foods that you will have to start reading labels and learn how to spot it independently. It is also disguised under many names, including corn syrup, high fructose corn syrup, sucrose, and dextrose. However, if you stick with fresh fruits and vegetables, your sugar intake should be minimal or nonexistent.

Refined grains are a category of food that should also be tossed out of your diet for a while. This means that you should conduct clear white bread, rice, pasta, and pastries for as long as it takes to heal the inflammation in your digestive tract.

Dairy, sugar, and refined grains are inflammatory foods that must be avoided from your diet to get rid of diverticulitis.

Fiber, which is institute in foods like fruits, vegetables, and whole grains, is an integral part of staying healthy and can help protect the digestive tract from further attacks of diverticulitis.

FOOD TO AVOID

Patients with diverticulitis are often urged to be cautious when consuming seeds or anything with seeds (i.e., tomatoes, melons, berries, etc.). Small food particles such as seeds are theorized to potentially be able to get logged in the diverticulum and cause inflammation.

There are several reasons why certain foods should be avoided during the acute (symptomatic) phase of diverticulitis. Some of these reasons include:

- **Increase the bulk of the stool:** Some of these foods are high in fiber and, therefore, contribute to the consistency and bulk of the stool. In many cases, as a person already suffers from severe constipation, increased intake of such foods will only make it harder to defecate and will eventually result in more abdominal discomfort.

- **Some of these foods can get caught in the pouches called diverticula.**

- **Take a longer time for digestion:** Some of these foods take a longer time to digest. As the digestive system is already sore (inflamed), and under abnormally high-pressure during diverticulitis, more of such foods will only create more complications, and as a result, the stomach and intestines would not get the "rest" they need the most during diverticulitis.

- **Produce flatulence and bloating:** Intestinal gas and bloating are common side effects of a high fiber diet. The presence of such symptoms will increase the risk of more complications in diverticulitis attacks.

VEGETABLES WITH SMALL PARTICLES OR SEEDS

- Cucumber (only English is acceptable)
- Green Peppers (Acceptable if seeds are removed)
- Tomato (Acceptable if seeds are removed)
- Chili Peppers
- Corn

SEEDS

Avoid all types.

SWEETS WITH SMALL PARTICLES OR SEEDS

- Nutty Candy
- Fruit Jam with Seeds
- Nutty Desserts
- Raisins with Seeds

FRUITS WITH SMALL PARTICLES OR SEEDS

- Blackberries
- Blueberries
- Coconut (dried)
- Whole Cranberries (Cranberry Relish)
- Figs
- Grapes with seeds
- Kiwi
- Pomegranates
- Raspberries
- Strawberries
- Watermelon (Acceptable if seedless)

STARCHES (REFINED)

- Bread or rolls with seeds
- Popcorn
- Wild Rice

ESSENTIALS SHOPPING LIST

FRUITS

- Apple Sauce
- Apples
- Apricots
- Bananas
- Dates
- Mangoes
- Oranges
- Peaches
- Prunes

JUICES

- Apple Juice
- Lemon Juice
- Lime Juice
- Orange Juice
- Cranberry Juice

VEGETABLES

- Alfalfa Sprouts
- Artichoke Hearts
- Asparagus
- Avocados
- Black Olives
- Broccoli
- Butternut Squash
- Cabbage
- Carrots
- Celery
- Eggplants
- Garlic
- Green Bell Peppers (seedless)
- Green Olives
- Green Onions
- Leeks
- Mushrooms
- Lettuce
- Olives
- Onions
- Peas (frozen, cooked)
- Pimento
- Red Bell Peppers (seedless)
- Russet Potatoes
- Shallots
- Spinach
- Sugar Snap Peas
- Summer Squash
- Yellow Peppers (seedless)
- Tomatoes (seedless)
- Water chestnuts
- Zucchini
- Sweet Yams

BEANS & PEAS

- Black Beans
- Butter Beans
- Cannellini Beans
- Garbanzo Beans
- Canned Kidney Beans
- Lentils
- Canned Lima Beans
- Canned Navy Beans
- Canned Red Beans

GRAINS, BREADS & OTHER

- All-Bran Cereal
- Barley
- Brown Rice
- Fiber One Cereal
- Long Grain Rice
- Oat Bran
- Rolled Oats

MEATS

- Crab Meat, Cooked
- Ground Chicken, Lean
- Ground Turkey, Lean
- Lean Ham
- Shrimp, large, peeled
- Canned Tuna Fish
- Turkey Breast
- Chicken Breast

DAIRY

- Cheddar Cheese (low fat)
- Cottage Cheese (low fat)
- Cream Cheese (low fat)
- Feta Cheese
- Monterrey Jack Cheese (low fat)
- Parmesan Cheese
- Eggs
- Half and half cream
- Yogurt, low fat

SPICES, HERBS & OILS

- Baking Powder
- Basil (fresh or dried)
- Canola Oil
- Cilantro (fresh)
- Cinnamon powder
- Cumin
- Curry Powder
- Dill, (fresh or dried)
- Italian Seasoning
- Nutmeg
- Olive Oil
- Oregano, (fresh and dried)
- Parsley, Italian (fresh)
- Sage (fresh)
- Tarragon (fresh)
- Thyme (fresh and dried)
- Vanilla

CONDIMENTS

- Vegetable Stock
- Chicken Stock
- Coconut Milk
- Dijon Mustard
- Honey
- Light Ranch Dressing
- Maple Syrup
- Mayonnaise, low fat
- Red Wine Vinegar
- Rice Vinegar
- Soy Sauce
- Sweet Pickle Relish
- Tarragon Vinegar
- Tomato Paste
- Tomato Sauce
- Tomato Puree
- Canned Tomato, diced, seedless

STARCHES

- Whole Grains
- Whole Wheat Flour
- Whole Wheat Pasta
- Whole Wheat Pita
- Whole Wheat Tortillas
- Whole Wheat Bread

BASIC TIPS AND NATURAL REMEDIES TO AVOID RELAPSE

The actual well-being of our organism depends on knowing how much and how to rebalance the intestinal flora. The perfect coexistence of good and bad bacteria in the intestine is a deal for digestion, immune defenses, and physical and mental well-being. When we hear about intestinal "bacteria," we usually associate them with something harmful to health. In reality, there are bacteria necessary for the correct functioning of our organism, and they make up the so-called intestinal flora, the group of germs living inside the intestine. Its primary function is to regulate our immune system; moreover, it promotes digestion and the correct absorption of foods; it produces some vitamins; it helps prevent disorders such as diarrhea, constipation, and irritable colon syndrome; it intervenes in the metabolism.

MAINTAINING BACTERIAL BALANCE

Patients with diverticulitis have excessive intestinal bacterial overgrowth. Specifically, this is an overgrowth of harmful bacteria. These bacteria cause inflammation and make digestion less effective. Remaining mindful of nutrition is paramount. It is essential to start with eating habits to best treat this aspect. Dysregulated eating, excessive consumption of refined foods, sugary foods, highly seasoned foods, and alcoholic beverages are risk factors for the balance of the intestinal ecosystem, which needs a healthy and varied diet rich in fibers and probiotics.

Even stress, by affecting the mood, often influences the unbalance of the bacterial flora causing lousy digestion. The intestine is our second brain, and negative emotions directly affect it.

PROBIOTICS

Probiotics, essential in the balance of the intestine, are live microorganisms compatible with those contained physiologically in the intestine. Probiotics have three main functions: they promote digestive functions, help the body with intestinal inflammation/flu symptoms, and hinder and eliminate pathological bacteria. Feeding foods containing probiotics daily can prevent and reduce the risk of diverticulitis as they bring healthy bacteria to the digestive system and allow the colon to work more smoothly and efficiently. This process allows for less development of diverticular disease.

PROBIOTIC-RICH FOODS:

- Yogurt.

Yogurt contains numerous "good" bacteria that fight inflammation in the intestines. These favor intestinal flora development, facilitate the digestive process, and help fight abdominal bloating. The suggestion is to consume it far from meals to avoid the microorganisms that remain in the stomach for a long time because of long digestion.

- Tempeh.

It is a processed product obtained by the fermentation of yellow soybeans, typical of Indonesia. Rich in vitamins, fibers, proteins, and good bacteria, it regulates the balance of the intestinal flora and increases the production of antibodies. Fermentation also makes it highly digestible.

- Miso.

Miso is a product of Japanese origin. It has digestive properties and facilitates the reactivation of the intestinal peristalsis (that is, the regular contraction of the intestinal musculature)

- Sauerkraut.

Sauerkraut is the result of the fermentation of cabbage. Fermentation increases the number of probiotics and the resulting nutritional value while making them more digestible.

DO NOT OVERDOSE ON MEDICATIONS

Antibiotics eliminate pathogenic bacteria responsible for the infection and the "good" ones that keep in balance the intestinal microbiota. Therefore, it is essential not to overdo the dosage of medicines and take antibiotics only if strictly necessary. After the treatment, restore the intestinal flora by taking probiotics by mouth and trying to eat vegetables, preferably bitterish, which also help the liver to purify itself.

LEAN MEATS

If you are going to consume meat, make sure it is lean meat. Meats, having much fatty tissue, are not considered healthy for digestion. They are also responsible for carrying a disproportionate share of unhealthy bacteria in the colon. When consuming meat, the advice is to take white meats and lean fish to supplement noble proteins. Some meats to eat may be: Skinless poultry, selected lean cuts of steak, or pork loin. Instead, avoid sausages (such as sausage, salami, coppa and all processed meats in general) and fatty meats (such as a game, for example).

COLLOIDAL SILVER

Having properties that make it effective in fighting germs, viruses and bacteria can be used as a kind of home remedy. Colloidal silver is used to treat the most varied forms of inflammation and is particularly effective in case of gastrointestinal tract infections and, therefore, against bacterial infections from diverticulitis. Its use must be coordinated with a natural medicine practitioner. However, its use must not preclude a dietary discipline that is still fundamental.

ALCOHOL RENUNCIATION

If there is an inflammation of the diverticula, it is better to drink only natural water and avoid alcohol and carbonated or sugary drinks. Coffee and tea are allowed, but only if they are caffeine-free. Avoid milk.

BEHAVIORAL TIPS

- Diverticulitis should also be treated with bed rest

- Get regular physical activity (e.g., walking at least 20-30 minutes a day/exercise). Physical activity helps keep abdominal wall muscles toned, and this reduces stool stagnation in diverticula. Recommended guidelines are: a minimum of 150 minutes per week, optimal 300.

- Reach a bodyweight appropriate to your weight. In case of overweight or obesity, it is advisable to lose the extra kilos with regular physical activity and an adequate diet. To achieve this goal, it is first necessary to measure your body mass index (BMI) and the percentage of fat mass: in case of obesity (or overweight condition), you should consult a nutritionist doctor to agree on a specific diet.

- Whether you have diverticulosis or diverticulitis, it is important to stop smoking.

- Take adequate intakes of vitamin D. The role of this fat-soluble vitamin in diverticular disease has been studied for a long time and optimal values are necessary for prevention. Therefore, an adequate daily intake is recommended, and possible supplementation if a deficiency is found in the diet.

- During the evening meal, in order to increase the intake of fiber and water, it is good to get used to eating vegetable soups and purees. The increase in fiber consumption may temporarily cause an increase in meteorism, but this effect will disappear in a few weeks. Meteorism induced by fiber consumption can be reduced with the following 3 strategies: Gradually increasing fiber intake (limiting cauliflower and broccoli), simultaneously increasing water consumption and increasing physical activity.

- Broths can be of meat, as long as fat-free or vegetable but filtered.

- Meats should be lean and not very fibrous, chopping or mincing them to make them more digestible.

- In diverticulosis, it is an excellent dietary habit to reduce salt. It is an excellent rule to reduce the amount of salt added to food during and after cooking and limit the consumption of foods that naturally contain high quantities of salt.

CLEAR LIQUID DIET: BREAKFAST

APPLE-CINNAMON TEA
Prep Time: 5 minutes | **Cook Time:** 15 minutes
Servings: 4
Ingredients:
- 1 cup chopped apples
- 3 cinnamon sticks
- 1/4 water
- 2 bags tea
- 1/3 cup honey

Directions:
1. In a large saucepan over high heat, set the apples, cinnamon sticks, and water. Bring to a boil. Simmer for 15 minutes.
2. Remove from the heat and add the teabags. Steep for 10 minutes.
3. With a spoon, remove the tea bags, apples and cinnamon sticks. Add the honey.

Nutrition:
Calories: 101 | Fat: 1g | Carbs: 27g | Fiber: 1g | Protein: 1g

BLUEBERRY GREEN TEA
Prep Time: 5 minutes | **Cook Time:** 5 minutes
Servings: 4
Ingredients:
- 1/2 cup fresh or frozen blueberries
- 1/4 water
- 2 bags of green tea
- 1/3 cup honey

Directions:
1. In a saucepan over high heat, place the blueberries and water and bring to a boil. Set the heat to low and stir for 5 minutes.
2. Detach from the heat and add the green tea bags. Steep for 10 minutes.
3. Using a slotted spoon, set the tea bags and blueberries. Add the honey.

Nutrition:
Calories: 95 | Fat: 0 g | Carbs: 26g | Fiber: 1g | Protein: 1g

CITRUS SPORTS DRINK
Prep Time: 5 minutes | **Cook Time:** 0 minutes
Servings: 8
Ingredients:
- 4 cups coconut water
- 4 large oranges juice (about 1 1/2 cup), strained
- 2 tbsp lemon juice, strained
- 2 tbsp honey or maple syrup
- 1 tsp sea salt

Directions:
1. Place the coconut water, orange juice, lemon juice, honey, and salt in a jug or pitcher.
2. Stir until the salt is dissolved.
3. Serve cold.

Nutrition:
Calories: 59 | Fat: 1g | Carbs: 14g | Fiber: 1g | Protein: 1g

HOMEMADE ORANGE GELATIN
Prep Time: 4 hours 10 minutes | **Cook Time:** 3 minutes
Servings: 4
Ingredients:
- 3 cups oranges juice
- 2 tbsp unflavored gelatin
- 2 tbsp honey or maple syrup

Directions:
1. In a large bowl, pour in 1/2 cup of orange juice and sprinkle with gelatin. Whisk well and let sit until the gelatin begins to set but is not quite smooth.
2. In a saucepan over low heat, pour in the remaining 2 1/2 cups of orange juice and cook until just before boiling, 2-3 minutes.
3. Remove from the heat and pour the hot juice into the gelatin mixture. Add the honey or maple syrup and stir until the gelatin is dissolved.
4. Pour into an 8 x 8 inches baking dish and transfer to the refrigerator.
5. Cool for 4 hours to set. Serve cold.

Nutrition:
Calories: 127 | Fat: 1g | Carbs: 28g | Fiber: 1g | Protein: 6g

RASPBERRY LEMONADE ICE POPS
Prep Time: 4 hours 10 minutes | **Cook Time:** 0 minutes
Servings: 4 ice pops
Ingredients:
- 3 cups frozen raspberries
- 1 tsp lemon juice, strained
- 1/4 cup coconut water
- 1/4 cup honey or maple syrup

Directions:
1. In a blender, puree the raspberries, lemon juice and coconut water until smooth.
2. In a bowl, strain the mixture through a fine-mesh strainer. Add the honey.
3. Divide the mixture among 4 popsicle molds and freeze until solid.

Nutrition:
Calories: 120 | Fat: 0g | Carbs: 31g | Fiber: 7g | Protein: 2g

HOMEMADE NO PULP ORANGE JUICE

Prep Time: 5 minutes | **Cook Time:** 0 minutes
Servings: 1
Ingredients:
- 4 oranges

Directions:
1. Lightly squeeze the oranges on a hard surface to soften the exterior. Slice each in half.
2. Squeeze each orange over a fine-mesh strainer.
3. Gently, press the pulp to extract all possible liquid.
4. Serve over ice. Enjoy!

Nutrition:
Calories: 50 | Fat: 0.2g | Carbs: 11.5g | Protein: 0.8g

APPLE ORANGE JUICE

Prep Time: 5 minutes | **Cook Time:** 0 minutes
Servings: 2
Ingredients:
- 1 Gala apple, peeled, cored, and sliced
- 2 oranges, peeled, halved, and seeded
- 2 tsp honey (optional)
- 3/4 cup water

Directions:
1. Squeeze each orange over a fine-mesh strainer.
2. Gently, press the pulp to extract as much liquid as possible.
3. Add the apple, water, and orange juice to your blender and pulse.
4. Set a fine-mesh strainer in a bowl. Before transferring your juice into the strainer.
5. Once again, gently press the pulp to remove all possible liquid then discard it.
6. Stir in your honey then serve over ice.

Nutrition:
Calories: 180 | Fat: 1g | Carbs: 43g | Fiber: 1g | Protein: 2g

PINEAPPLE MINT JUICE

Prep Time: 5 minutes | **Cook Time:** 0 minutes
Servings: 4
Ingredients:
- 3 cups pineapple, cored, sliced and chunks
- 10-12 mint leaves, or to taste
- 2 tbsp sugar, or to taste (optional)
- 1 1/2 cup water
- 1 cup ice cubes

Directions:
1. Set all the ingredients into your blender, and pulse.
2. Set a fine-mesh strainer in a bowl. Before transferring your juice into the strainer.
3. Gently, press the pulp to extract all possible liquid then discard it.
4. Serve over ice. Enjoy!

Nutrition:
Calories: 78 | Fat: 1g | Carbs: 22g | Fiber: 2g | Protein: 1g

CELERY APPLE JUICE

Prep Time: 5 minutes | **Cook Time:** 0 minutes
Servings: 2
Ingredients:
- 12 celery stalks, peeled and chopped
- 3 Apple, peeled, cored, seeded and sliced
- 1-inch ginger root, peeled and chopped
- 1/4 lemon juice
- 2 cups water

Directions:
1. Set all the ingredients into your blender, and pulse.
2. Set a fine-mesh strainer in a bowl. Before transferring your juice into the strainer.
3. Gently, press the pulp to extract all possible liquid then discard it.
4. Serve over ice. Enjoy!

Nutrition:
Calories: 119 | Fat: 1g | Carbs: 29g | Fiber: 7g | Protein: 2g

HOMEMADE BANANA APPLE JUICE

Prep Time: 10 minutes | **Servings:** 2
Ingredients:
- 2 bananas, peeled and sliced
- 1 Gala apple, peeled, cored and chopped
- Water

Directions:
1. Blend all ingredients.
2. In a bowl, strain the mixture through a fine-mesh strainer.
3. Extract all the liquid. Serve.

Nutrition:
Calories: 132 | Fat: 2g | Carbs: 27g | Fiber: 3g | Protein: 4g

TROPICAL FRUIT SMOOTHIE

Prep Time: 5 minutes | **Cook Time:** 5 minutes
Servings: 2
Ingredients:
- 1 cup combination of pineapples, mangoes, & bananas
- 1 cup vanilla yogurt
- 1/2 cup all-Bran cereal
- 1 tsp vanilla
- 1 tbsp honey
- 1 cup almond

- 1/2 avocado
- 1 cup ice

Directions:
1. In a blender, mix all the ingredients & mix on high speed till smooth & creamy.

Nutrition:
Calories: 112 | Fat: 3 g | Carbs: 5 g | Protein: 2 g

SWEET DETOX JUICE

Prep Time: 10 minutes | **Cook Time:** 0 minutes
Servings: 2
Ingredients:
- 2 cups baby spinach, chopped
- 1 handful parsley, chopped
- 1 green apple, peeled, cored, seeded and sliced
- 1 large English cucumber, seeded and chopped
- 1-inch ginger, peeled
- 1 lemon, juiced

Directions:
1. Blend all ingredients.
2. In a bowl, strain the mixture through a fine-mesh strainer.
3. Extract all the liquid. Serve.

Nutrition:
Calories: 209 | Fat: 2g | Carbs: 48g | Fiber: 17g | Protein: 12g

FRUIT JULIUS

Prep Time: 5 minutes | **Cook Time:** 4 minutes
Servings: 4
Ingredients:
- 2 tsp tang powder
- 1/2 cup egg substitute
- 1/2 cup juice: orange, cranberry, grape or other
- 3 ice cubes, crushed

Directions:
1. Mix all ingredients except for ice until smooth.
2. Add ice. Blend till slushy.

Nutrition:
Calories: 87 | Fat: 7g | Carbs: 9g | Protein: 7g

VANILLA SHAKE

Prep Time: 5 minutes | **Cook Time:** 3 minutes
Servings: 1
Ingredients:
- 1/4 cup non-dairy yogurt
- 1/4 cup vanilla ice cream
- 1/4 cup prepared Jell-O

Directions:
1. Mix all of the ingredients in a blender.
2. Blend till smooth.

Nutrition:
Calories: 144 | Fat: 12 g | Carbs: 21g | Protein: 5g

BLUEBERRY GUT HEALING PROTEIN SHAKE

Prep Time: 5 minutes | **Cook Time:** 5 minutes
Servings: 2
Ingredients:
- 1/4-1/2 cup of organic frozen blueberries
- 1 tsp of organic cinnamon
- 1 cup of organic full-fat coconut milk in the can
- 2 scoops of protein powder of your choice.
- A scoop of organic greens powder.

Directions:
1. Collect all of the ingredients.
2. Remove the coconut milk from the can and blend until smooth and creamy. Transfer the whipped coconut milk to a glass mason jar.
3. Frozen organic blueberries, gut-healing protein, and cinnamon are added to the mix.
4. Serve and enjoy.

Nutrition:
Calories: 450 | Fat: 32g | Carbs: 19g | Protein: 28g

BANANA OAT SHAKE

Prep Time: 10 minutes | **Cook Time:** 7 minutes
Servings: 2
Ingredients:
- 1 tbsp of wheat germ
- 1/2 cup of chilled and cooked oatmeal
- 2/3 cup of non-dairy milk
- 1 1/2 tsp of vanilla extract
- 1/2 frozen banana, cut into chunks
- 2 tbsp of brown sugar

Directions:
1. The oatmeal should be put in a blender and blended for a few minutes.
2. Then milk, brown sugar, wheat germ, vanilla, and 1/2 banana should be added. Then it should be blended until thick and smooth.

Nutrition:
Calories: 172 | Fat: 19.7 g | Carbs: 33g | Protein: 6g

DETOXIFYING BEET JUICE

Prep Time: 10 minutes | **Cook Time:** 10 minutes
Servings: 4
Ingredients:
- 1 lb. beets, washed with ends cut off
- 2 lb. carrots, washed with ends cut off
- 1 bunch celery, washed and broken into ribs
- 2 lemons, peel cut off and quartered
- 1 lime, peel cut off and quartered
- 1 bunch flat-leaf parsley, washed
- 1 Fuji apple, chopped (optional)

Directions:
1. Wash the products and cut them.

2. Run the vegetable pieces through the juicer.
3. Serve immediately or store in the refrigerator.

Nutrition:
Calories: 58 | Fat: 0 g | Carbs: 13 g | Fiber: 17g | Protein: 2 g

BLUEBERRY SMOOTHIE

Prep Time: 5 minutes | **Cook Time:** 2 minutes
Servings: 4
Ingredients:
- 1 cup frozen blueberries
- 6 tbsp protein powder
- 8 packets Splenda
- 14 oz apple juice, unsweetened
- 8 cubes of ice

Directions:
1. Take a blender and place all the ingredients (in order) in it. Process for 1 minute until smooth.
2. Distribute the smoothie between four glasses and then serve.

Nutrition:
Calories: 162 | Fat: 0.5g | Carbs: 30g | Fiber: 3.6g | Protein: 8g

BANANA SMOOTHIE

Prep Time: 5 minutes | **Cook Time:** 0 minutes
Servings: 2
Ingredients:
- 1 burro banana, peeled
- 4 dates, pitted, chopped
- 1 cup milk
- 1 cup of soft-jelly coconut water

Directions:
1. Add all ingredients to a blender.
2. Cover the blender jar with its lid and then blend for 1 minute until smooth. Serve.

Nutrition:
Calories: 199 | Fat: 5g | Carbs: 34.7g | Fiber: 3.5g

LIME AND KALE SMOOTHIE

Prep Time: 5 minutes | **Cook Time:** 0 minutes
Servings: 2
Ingredients:
- 1 apple, peeled, cored, chopped
- 2 cups kale leaves
- 1 tsp key lime juice
- 1 1/4 cups orange juice
- 1/6 tsp cayenne pepper (Extra)

Directions:
1. Add all ingredients to a blender.
2. Cover the blender jar with its lid and then blend for 1 minute until smooth. Serve.

Nutrition:
Calories: 188 | Fat: 1 g | Carbs: 50 g | Fiber: 14g | Protein: 4.4 g

SOOTHING ARUGULA AND APPLE SMOOTHIE

Prep Time: 5 minutes | **Cook Time:** 0 minutes
Servings: 2
Ingredients:
- 2 cups arugula
- 1 burro banana, peeled
- 2 apples, cored
- 2 cups of soft-jelly coconut water
- 4 tbsp key lime juice (Extra)

Directions:
1. Add all ingredients to a blender.
2. Cover the blender jar with its lid and then blend for 1 minute until smooth. Serve.

Nutrition:
Calories: 180 | Fat: 0g | Carbs: 45g | Fiber: 8g | Protein: 0g

BREAKFAST BOOST WITH APPLE AND BERRIES

Prep Time: 5 minutes | **Cook Time:** 0 minutes
Servings: 2
Ingredients:
- 2 cups greens
- 1 cup mixed berries
- 1 apple, cored, diced
- 1 cup hemp milk, homemade

Directions:
1. Add all ingredients to a blender.
2. Cover the blender jar with its lid and then blend for 1 minute until smooth. Serve.

Nutrition:
Calories: 136.5 | Fat: 2.9g | Carbs: 23.4g | Fiber: 8.1g | Protein: 7.1g

ARU-AVOCADO DETOX SMOOTHIE

Prep Time: 5 minutes | **Cook Time:** 0 minutes
Servings: 2
Ingredients:
- 2 cups arugula
- 1/4 cup cranberries
- 1/2 avocado, peeled, pitted
- 1 apple, cored
- 1 kiwifruit

Extra:
- 1 tbsp key lime juice
- 1/2 cup spring water

Directions:
1. Add all ingredients to a blender.

2. Cover the blender jar with its lid and then blend for 1 minute until smooth. Serve.

REVITALIZER KALE SMOOTHIE
Prep Time: 5 minutes | **Cook Time:** 0 minutes
Servings: 2
Ingredients:
- 1 burro banana, peeled
- 2 cups chopped kale
- 1 mango, peeled, destoned, diced
- 1 cup of coconut water

CLEANSING APPLE AND AVOCADO SMOOTHIE
Prep Time: 5 minutes | **Cook Time:** 0 minutes
Servings: 2
Ingredients:
- 1 cup of soft-jelly coconut water
- 1 cup strawberries
- 1 apple, cored, diced
- 1/2 of avocado, peeled, pitted
- 1 cup Kale

Extra:
- 1 tbsp key lime juice

KALE GREEN SMOOTHIE
Prep Time: 5 minutes | **Cook Time:** 0 minutes
Servings: 2
Ingredients:
- 2 cups kale leaves
- 1 cup mango cubes
- 2 key limes, juiced
- 1 cup peaches

Extra:
- 1 1/2 cups spring water

PAPAYA AND QUINOA SMOOTHIE
Prep Time: 5 minutes | **Cook Time:** 10 minutes
Servings: 2
Ingredients:
- 2 cups papaya cubes
- 2 tbsp date
- 1 cup cooked quinoa or amaranth
- 2 tsp bromide + powder
- 2 cups hemp milk, homemade

AVOCADO AND CUCUMBER SMOOTHIE
Prep Time: 5 minutes | **Cook Time:** 0 minutes
Servings: 2
Ingredients:
- 1 burro banana, peeled
- 1/4 of an avocado
- 1/4 of a cucumber
- 1 tbsp agave syrup
- 1/2 cup herbal tea

Extra:
- 1 tbsp chopped walnuts

ORANGE AND BANANA DRINK
Prep Time: 5 minutes | **Cook Time:** 0 minutes
Servings: 2
Ingredients:
- 1/2 of a burro banana, peeled

Nutrition:
Calories: 192 | Fat: 4.9g | Carbs: 22g | Fiber: 4g | Protein: 5g

Directions:
1. Add all ingredients to a blender.
2. Cover the blender jar with its lid and then blend for 1 minute until smooth. Serve.

Nutrition:
Calories: 145 | Fat: 0.5g | Carbs: 36.5g | Fiber: 4.5g

- 1/8 tsp cayenne pepper

Directions:
1. Add all ingredients to a blender.
2. Cover the blender jar with its lid and then blend for 1 minute until smooth. Serve.

Nutrition:
Calories: 215 | Fat: 7.2g | Carbs: 39.3g | Fiber: 5.3g | Protein: 2.8g

- 1 tbsp agave syrup

Directions:
1. Add all ingredients to a blender.
2. Cover the blender jar with its lid and then blend for 1 minute until smooth. Serve.

Nutrition:
Calories: 117 | Fat: 0.8g | Carbs: 26.4g | Fiber: 3.5g | Protein: 2.5g

Directions:
1. Add all ingredients to a blender.
2. Cover the blender jar with its lid and then blend for 1 minute until smooth. Serve.

Nutrition:
Calories: 224.6 | Fat: 7.7g | Carbs: 33.7g | Fiber: 3.5g | Protein: 7g

- 1 cup soft-jelly coconut milk, homemade

Directions:
1. Add all ingredients to a blender.
2. Cover the blender jar with its lid and then blend for 1 minute until smooth. Serve.

Nutrition:
Calories: 103 | Fat: 4.5g | Carbs: 16.2g | Fiber: 2.5g | Protein: 1.6g

- 3 oranges, peeled
- 1 1/2 tbsp date
- 1/2 tsp bromide + powder
- 1 cup of soft-jelly coconut water

Directions:
1. Add all ingredients to a blender.
2. Cover the blender jar with its lid and then blend for 1 minute until smooth. Serve.

LETTUCE, BANANA, AND BERRIES SMOOTHIE

Prep Time: 5 minutes | **Cook Time:** 0 minutes
Servings: 2
Ingredients:
- 1/2 of a burro banana
- 1/4 cup blueberries
- 1 cup Romaine lettuce
- 2 tbsp key lime juice
- 1/2 cup soft jelly coconut water

PAPAYA-MANGO SMOOTHIE

Prep Time: 5 minutes | **Cook Time:** 0 minutes
Servings: 2
Ingredients:
- 1 cup mango, diced
- 1 cup papaya chunks
- 1 cup almond or lactose-free milk
- 1 tbsp honey or maple syrup

CANTALOUPE SMOOTHIE

Prep Time: 5 minutes | **Cook Time:** 0 minutes
Servings: 2
Ingredients:
- 1 cup cantaloupe, diced
- 1/2 cup vanilla yogurt or lactose-free yogurt
- 1/2 cup of orange juice
- 1 tbsp honey or maple syrup
- 2 ice cubes

CANTALOUPE-MIX SMOOTHIE

Prep Time: 5-10 minutes | **Cook Time:** 0 minutes
Servings: 2
Ingredients:
- 1 cup cantaloupe, diced
- 1/2 cup mango, diced
- 1/2 cup almond milk or lactose-free cow milk
- 1/2 cup of orange juice
- 2 tbsp lemon

APPLESAUCE-AVOCADO SMOOTHIE

Prep Time: 5-10 minutes | **Cook Time:** 0 minutes
Servings: 1
Ingredients:
- 1 cup unsweetened almond or lactose-free milk
- 1/2 avocado
- 1/2 cup applesauce
- 1/4 tsp ground cinnamon
- 1/2 cup ice

Nutrition:
Calories: 138.5 | Fat: 0.6g | Carbs: 35.1g | Fiber: 4.7g | Protein: 1.5g

Directions:
1. Add all ingredients to a blender.
2. Cover the blender jar with its lid and then blend for 1 minute until smooth. Serve.

Nutrition:
Calories: 147 | Fat: 0.8g | Carbs: 36g | Fiber: 4g | Protein: 3.3g

Directions:
1. Blend all ingredients in a blender and then pulse until smooth.
2. Pour into a large glass. Enjoy!

Nutrition:
Calories: 554 | Fat: 32g | Carbs: 14g | Fiber: 2g | Protein: 50g

Directions:
1. Merge all ingredients in a blender and then pulse until smooth.
2. Pour into a large glass. Enjoy!

Nutrition:
Calories: 179 | Fat: 13g | Carbs: 6g | Fiber: 1g | Protein: 10g

- 1 tbsp honey or maple syrup
- 2 ice cubes

Directions:
1. Merge all ingredients in a blender until smooth.
2. Pour into a large glass. Enjoy!

Nutrition:
Calories: 329 | Fat: 17g | Carbs: 9g | Fiber: 5g | Protein: 37g

- 1/2 tsp stevia or 1 tbsp honey, for sweetness (optional)

Directions:
1. Blend all ingredients in a blender. Pulse the mix until smooth.
2. Pour into a large glass. Enjoy!

Nutrition:
Calories: 270 | Fat: 11g | Carbs: 4g | Fiber: 1g | Protein: 39g

LUNCH

CRANBERRY SMOOTHIE
Prep Time: 5 minutes | **Cook Time:** 0 minutes
Servings: 1
Ingredients:
- 3/4 cup of frozen cranberries (75g)
- 1 large apple cored and chopped into chunks
- 1 small handful/about Two tbsp of raw pecans or walnuts
- 1 tbsp maple syrup
- 1 cup non-dairy milk (240 ml)
- 1/4 tsp ground cinnamon

Directions:
1. Add all the ingredients to a blender.
2. Blend until smooth.

Nutrition:
Calories: 424 | Carbs: 61g | Protein: 10g | Fat: 19g

SPARKLING PINEAPPLE MINT JUICE
Prep Time: 10 minutes | **Cook Time:** 10 minutes
Servings: 2
Ingredients:
- Peeled and sliced fresh pineapple
- 1/4 cup fresh mint (one tiny handful)
- A few tbsp of honey (optional)
- 1 l sparkling water or club soda bottle
- To serve, crushed ice

Directions:
1. Blend the pineapple, mint, and sweetener (if using) until smooth.
2. Add sparkling water. Serve garnishing with mint or pineapple chunks.

Nutrition:
Calories: 27 | Carbs: 10g | Protein: 2g | Fat: 2g

DECAF PEPPERMINT TEA
Prep Time: 5 minutes | **Cook Time:** 0 minutes
Servings: 1
Ingredients:
- 1 teabag peppermint tea
- 8 oz water
- 2 tbsp Artificial sweetener optional

Directions:
1. Fill a coffee cup halfway with teabags.
2. Place a teapot on the burner with the water. Wait for the whistle to blow. Pour it over the teabag.
3. Allow the tea to infuse for a few seconds in the water.
4. Stir in the artificial sweetener with a spoon until it dissolves.

Nutrition:
Calories: 220 | Carbs: 12g | Protein: 2g | Fat: 2g

SUGAR-FREE ROOT BEER ICE POPS
Prep Time: 5 minutes | **Cook Time:** 180 minutes
Servings: 4
Ingredients:
- Packet Sugar-free on-the-go drink mix
- 16 oz water, bottled

Directions:
1. Pour the drink mix into a 16.9 fluid ounce bottle of water.
2. Twist the cap back on securely and shake to mix.
3. Pour four oz of liquid into each ice pop mold.
4. Insert the ice pop sticks with caution.
5. Freeze for three hours or until firm.

Nutrition:
Calories: 172 | Carbs: 36g | Protein: 28g | Fat: 11g

SYRUP
Prep Time: 2 Minutes | **Cook Time:** 3 Minutes
Servings: 8
Ingredients:
- 1 cup water
- 1 cup granulated sugar or turbinado, demerara

Directions:
1. Preheat a small saucepot to high. Fill the saucepan with water and sugar.
2. Bring to a boil, stirring constantly. Stir once the water has reached a boil, then remove from the heat. (Add the herbs to the simple heated syrup if you're infusing them.)
3. Allow cooling to room temperature before storing in an airtight container.

Nutrition:
Calories: 97 | Carbs: 25g | Protein: 25g | Fat: 2g

FRENCH LAVENDER LEMONADE
Prep Time: 15 minutes | **Cook Time:** 5 minutes
Servings: 10
Ingredients:
- 10 cups of water, divided
- 3 cups of granulated sugar
- 1/2 cup lavender leaves, roughly chopped
- 2 cups freshly squeezed lemon juice, from 9-11 lemons
- Ice
- Fresh lavender sprigs for garnishing

Directions:
1. 5 cups of water, sugar, and lavender leaves in a

medium saucepan. Bring the water to a boil. When the water is boiling, mix it in and cover it. Remove from the heat and set aside to steep until the mixture comes to room temperature.
2. Squeeze the lemons, taking care to remove any stray seeds. Remove the lavender leaves when the simple lavender syrup has cooled. In a large pitcher, combine the syrup, lemon juice, and 5 cups of water.
3. Garnish with beautiful lavender sprigs and ice!

Nutrition:
Calories: 248 | Carbs: 65g | Protein: 1g | Fat: 1g

FROZEN LEMONADE WITH PINEAPPLE

Prep Time: 10 minutes | **Cook Time:** 10 minutes
Servings: 8
Ingredients:
- 6 cups of frozen pineapple chunks
- 3/4 cup of fresh lemon juice (about 5 lemons)
- 1/2 cup of granulated sugar or equivalent alternative sweetener
- 2-4 cups of cold water
- 2-4 cups of ice

Directions:
1. 2 lemons, zested. Then, squeeze roughly 5 lemons to get 3/4 cup of fresh juice.
2. In a blender, mix the lemon juice, lemon zest, sweetener of choice, and 2 cups of water until completely blended.
3. In tiny increments, add frozen pineapple pieces, mixing thoroughly between additions.
4. 2 cups of ice should be added at the end. To get the required thickness, taste the mixture and add additional ice or water as needed. Serve right away.

Nutrition:
Calories: 308 | Carbs: 80g | Protein: 2g | Fat: 0g

HEALTHIER APPLE JUICE

Prep Time: 5 minutes | **Cook Time:** 0 minutes
Servings: 2
Ingredients:
- 8 medium apples, cored and quartered

Directions:
1. Add the apples into a juicer and extract the juice.
2. Through a cheesecloth-lined sieve, strain the juice and transfer it into 2 glasses.
3. Serve immediately.

Nutrition:
Calories: 164 | Fat: 1.6g | Carbs: 123.6g | Fiber: 21.6g | Protein: 2.4g

CITRUS APPLE JUICE

Prep Time: 5 minutes | **Cook Time:** 0 minutes
Servings: 2
Ingredients:
- 5 large apples, cored and chopped
- 1 small lemon
- 1 cup fresh orange juice

Directions:
1. Add all the ingredients to a blender and pulse until well combined.
2. Through a cheesecloth-lined sieve, strain the juice and transfer it into 2 glasses.
3. Serve immediately.

Nutrition:
Calories: 148 | Fat: 1.3g | Carbs: 90.6g | Fiber: 14g | Protein: 2.4g

RICHLY FRUITY JUICE

Prep Time: 15 minutes | **Cook Time:** 0 minutes
Servings: 2
Ingredients:
- 5 large green apples, cored and sliced
- 2 cups seedless white grapes
- 2 tsp fresh lime juice

Directions:
1. Set all ingredients into a juicer and extract the juice.
2. Through a cheesecloth-lined sieve, strain the juice and transfer it into 2 glasses.
3. Serve immediately.

Nutrition:
Calories: 152 | Fat: 1.3g | Carbs: 92.8g | Fiber: 14.3g | Protein: 2.1g

DELISH GRAPE JUICE

Prep Time: 15 minutes | **Cook Time:** 0 minutes
Servings: 3
Ingredients:
- 2 cups white seedless grapes
- 1 1/2 cup filtered water
- 6-8 ice cubes

Directions:
1. Attach all the ingredients to a blender and pulse until well combined.
2. Through a cheesecloth-lined sieve, strain the juice and transfer it into 3 glasses.
3. Serve immediately.

Nutrition:
Calories: 41 | Carbs: 10.5g | Protein: 0.4g | Fat: 0.2g | Fiber: 10g

LEMONY GRAPE JUICE

Prep Time: 15 minutes | **Cook Time:** 0 minutes
Servings: 3

Ingredients:
- 4 cups seedless white grapes
- 2 tbsp fresh lemon juice

Directions:
1. Add all the ingredients to a blender and pulse until well combined.
2. Through a cheesecloth-lined sieve, strain the juice and transfer it into 3 glasses.
3. Serve immediately.

Nutrition:
Calories: 85 | Carbs: 21.3g | Protein: 0.9g | Fat: 0.5g | Fiber: 1.1g

HOLIDAY SPECIAL JUICE

Prep Time: 15 minutes | **Cook Time:** 0 minutes
Servings: 4
Ingredients:
- 4 cups fresh cranberries
- 1 tbsp fresh lemon juice
- 2 cups of filtered water
- 1 tsp raw honey

Directions:
1. Add all the ingredients to a blender and pulse until well combined.
2. Through a cheesecloth-lined sieve, strain the juice and transfer it into 4 glasses.
3. Serve immediately.

Nutrition:
Calories: 66 | Carbs: 11.5g | Protein: 0g | Fat: 0g | Fiber: 4g

VITAMIN C RICH JUICE

Prep Time: 15 minutes | **Cook Time:** 0 minutes
Servings: 2
Ingredients:
- 8 oranges, peeled and sectioned

Directions:
1. Add the orange sections into a juicer and extract the juice.
2. Through a cheesecloth-lined sieve, strain the juice and transfer it into 2 glasses.
3. Serve immediately.

Nutrition:
Calories: 146 | Fat: 0.9g | Carbs: 86.5g | Fiber: 17.7g | Protein: 6.9g

INCREDIBLE FRESH JUICE

Prep Time: 15 minutes | **Cook Time:** 0 minutes
Servings: 4
Ingredients:
- 2 pounds carrots, trimmed and scrubbed
- 6 small oranges, peeled and sectioned

Directions:
1. Add the carrots and orange sections into a juicer and extract the juice.
2. Through a cheesecloth-lined sieve, strain the juice and transfer it into 4 glasses.
3. Serve immediately.

Nutrition:
Calories: 152 | Fat: 1.3g | Carbs: 92.8g | Fiber: 14.3g | Protein: 2.1g

FAVORITE SUMMER LEMONADE

Prep Time: 15 minutes | **Cook Time:** 0 minutes
Servings: 8
Ingredients:
- 8 cups of filtered water
- 1/2 cup fresh lemon juice
- 1/4 tsp pure stevia extract
- Ice cubes, as required

Directions:
1. In a pitcher, place the water, lemon juice and stevia. Mix well.
2. Through a cheesecloth-lined sieve, strain the lemonade into another pitcher.
3. Refrigerate for 30-40 minutes.
4. Set ice cubes in serving glasses and fill with lemonade.
5. Serve chilled.

Nutrition:
Calories: 4 | Fat: 0.1g | Carbs: 0.3g | Fiber: 0.1g | Protein: 0.1g

ULTIMATE FRUITY PUNCH

Prep Time: 15 minutes | **Cook Time:** 0 minutes
Servings: 12
Ingredients:
- 3 cups fresh pineapple juice
- 2 cups fresh orange juice
- 1 cup fresh ruby red grapefruit juice
- 1/4 cup fresh lime juice
- 2 cups seedless watermelon, cut into bite-sized chunks
- 2 cups fresh pineapple, cut into bite-sized chunks
- 2 oranges, peeled and cut into wedges
- 2 limes, quartered
- 1 lemon, sliced
- 2 (12 oz) cans of diet lemon-lime soda
- Crushed ice, as required

Directions:
1. In a large pitcher, add all ingredients except for soda cans and ice. Stir to combine.
2. Set aside for 30 minutes.
3. Through a cheesecloth-lined sieve, strain the punch into another large pitcher.
4. Set the glasses with ice and top with punch about 3/4 of the mixture.
5. Add a splash of the soda and serve.

Nutrition:
Calories: 95 | Fat: 0.3g | Carbs: 23.4g | Fiber: 1.8g | Protein: 1.3g

THIRST QUENCHER SPORTS DRINK

Prep Time: 15 minutes | **Cook Time:** 0 minutes
Servings: 8
Ingredients:
- 7 cups of spring water
- 1 cup fresh apple juice
- 2-3 tsp fresh lime juice
- 2 tbsp honey
- 1/4 tsp sea salt

Directions:
1. In a large pitcher, add all ingredients and stir to combine.
2. Through a cheesecloth-lined sieve, strain the punch into another large pitcher.
3. Refrigerate to chill before serving.

Nutrition:
Calories: 30 | Carbs: 7.8g | Fiber: 0.1g | Protein: 0.1g

PINEAPPLE GINGER JUICE

Prep Time: 35 minutes | **Cook Time:** 0 minutes
Servings: 7
Ingredients:
- 10 cups pineapple, chopped
- 6 cups water
- 3 Fuji apples, chopped
- 4-inch ginger root, peeled and chopped
- 1/4 cup lemon juice
- 1/4 cup sugar

Directions:
1. Set all the ingredients into your blender, and pulse.
2. Set a fine-mesh strainer in a bowl. Before transferring your juice into the strainer.
3. Gently, press the pulp to extract all possible liquid then discard it.
4. Serve over ice. Enjoy!

Nutrition:
Calories: 71 | Fat: 1g | Carbs: 20g | Fiber: 3g | Protein: 1g

CARROT ORANGE JUICE

Prep Time: 15 minutes | **Cook Time:** 0 minutes
Servings: 2
Ingredients:
- 1 medium yellow tomato, cut into wedges
- 1 orange, peeled and quartered
- 1 apple, peeled, cored and chopped
- 4 jumbo carrots, peeled and chopped
- 2 cups water

Directions:
1. Set all the ingredients into your blender, and pulse.
2. Set a fine-mesh strainer in a bowl. Before transferring your juice into the strainer.
3. Gently, press the pulp to extract all possible liquid then discard it.
4. Serve over ice. Enjoy!

Nutrition:
Calories: 111 | Fat: 1g | Carbs: 24g | Fiber: 1g | Protein: 2g

STRAWBERRY APPLE JUICE

Prep Time: 5 minutes | **Cook Time:** 0 minutes
Servings: 8
Ingredients:
- 2 cups strawberries (tops removed)
- 1 red apple, peeled, seeded, and chopped
- 1 tbsp chia seeds
- 1 cup water

Directions:
1. Set all the ingredients into your blender, and pulse.
2. Set a fine-mesh strainer in a bowl. Before transferring your juice into the strainer.
3. Gently, press the pulp to extract all possible liquid then discard it.
4. Add in your chia seeds then leave to sit for at least 5 minutes.
5. Serve over ice. Enjoy!

Nutrition:
Calories: 245 | Fat: 5g | Carbs: 52g | Fiber: 7g | Protein: 4 g

AUTUMN ENERGIZER JUICE

Prep Time: 10 minutes | **Cook Time:** 0 minutes
Servings: 2
Ingredients:
- 2 pears, peeled, seeded and chopped
- 2 Ambrosia apples, peeled, cored and chopped
- 2 Granny Smith apples, peeled, cored, chopped
- 2 mandarins, juiced
- 2 cups sweet potato, peeled and chopped
- 1-pint cape gooseberries
- 2 inches ginger root, peeled

Directions:
1. Set all the ingredients into your blender, and pulse.
2. Set a fine-mesh strainer in a bowl. Before transferring your juice into the strainer.

3. Gently, press the pulp to extract all possible liquid then discard it.
4. Serve over ice. Enjoy!

Nutrition:
Calories: 170 | Fat: 3g | Carbs: 33g | Fiber: 9g | Protein: 4g

ASIAN INSPIRED WONTON BROTH

Prep Time: 5 minutes | **Cook Time:** 1 hour 30 minutes
Servings: 2
Ingredients:
- 1 chicken thigh, skin on
- 1 carrot, coarsely chopped
- 1 celery stalk, coarsely chopped
- 1 small onion, quartered
- 3 dime-sized ginger pieces
- 2 tbsp kosher salt
- 1/4 tsp turmeric
- 1/8 tsp MSG (don't leave it out)
- 5 white peppercorns
- 1 l water

Directions:
1. Transfer all the ingredients to your stockpot. Top with enough water to cover then allow to slowly come to a boil on high heat.
2. Switch to low heat and simmer for at least 1 hour and 30 minutes.
3. Set and pour the mixture through a fine-mesh strainer into a large bowl.
4. Taste and season with salt.
5. Serve hot.

Nutrition:
Calories: 182 | Fat: 7g | Carbs: 14g | Fiber: 1g | Protein: 14g

MUSHROOM, CAULIFLOWER AND CABBAGE BROTH

Prep Time: 10 minutes | **Cook Time:** 50 minutes
Servings: 2
Ingredients:
- 1 large yellow onion
- 1 cup celery stalks, chopped
- 2 carrots, diced or cubed
- 10 French beans
- 1/2 cabbage, diced
- 1-2 stalks of celery leaves
- 1 1/2 cup mushrooms, sliced
- 8 florets cauliflower
- 1 tsp garlic, chopped
- 1 tsp ginger, chopped
- 1 tbsp oil
- 1 scallion stalk
- 1/2 tsp pepper, crushed

Directions:
1. Transfer all the ingredients to your stockpot. Top with enough water to cover then allow to slowly come to a boil on high heat.
2. Switch to low heat and simmer for 50 minutes.
3. Strain the mixture through a mesh strainer. Serve hot!

Nutrition:
Calories: 141 | Fat: 5g | Carbs: 22g | Fiber: 7g | Protein: 5g

INDIAN INSPIRED VEGETABLE STOCK

Prep Time: 10 minutes | **Cook Time:** 11 minutes
Servings: 3
Ingredients:
- 3/4 cup onions, roughly chopped
- 3/4 cup carrot, roughly chopped
- 3/4 cup tomatoes, roughly chopped
- 3/4 cup potatoes, roughly chopped
- 1 tsp turmeric
- Salt to taste

Directions:
1. Transfer all the ingredients to your stockpot. Top with enough water to cover then allow to slowly come to a boil on high heat.
2. Switch to low heat and simmer for 11 minutes.
3. Strain the mixture through a mesh strainer. Serve hot!

Nutrition:
Calories: 103 | Fat: 0.2g | Carbs: 23.3g | Fiber: 3.1g | Protein: 2.2g

GINGER, MUSHROOM AND CAULIFLOWER BROTH

Prep Time: 10 minutes | **Cook Time:** 50 minutes
Servings: 3
Ingredients:
- 1 large yellow onion
- 1 cup celery stalks, chopped
- 2 carrots, diced or cubed
- 10 French beans
- 1 ginger root, peeled, diced or grated
- 1-2 stalks celery leaves or coriander leaves
- 1 1/2 cup mushrooms, sliced
- 8 florets cauliflower
- 1 tsp garlic, chopped
- 1 tbsp oil
- 1 stalk of spring onion greens or scallions
- 1/2 tsp crushed pepper or ground pepper

Directions:
1. Transfer all the ingredients to your stockpot. Top with enough water to cover then allow to slowly come to a boil on high heat.

2. Switch to low heat and simmer for at least 50 minutes.
3. Strain the mixture through a mesh strainer. Serve hot!

FISH BROTH

Prep Time: 15 minutes | **Cook Time:** 45 minutes
Servings: 3
Ingredients:
- 1 large onion, chopped
- 1 large carrot chopped
- 1 fennel bulb and fronds, chopped (optional)
- 3 celery stalks, chopped
- Salt
- 2-5 pounds of fish bones and heads
- 1 handful of dried mushrooms (optional)
- 2-4 bay leaves
- 1-star anise pod (optional)

CLEAR PUMPKIN BROTH

Prep Time: 15 minutes | **Cook Time:** 30 minutes
Servings: 6
Ingredients:
- 6 cups water
- 2 tbsp ginger, minced
- 2 cups potatoes, peeled and diced
- 3 cups kabocha, peeled and diced
- 1 carrot, peeled and diced
- 1 onion, diced
- 1/2 cup scallions, chopped

PORK STOCK

Prep Time: 15 minutes | **Cook Time:** 12 hours
Servings: 8
Ingredients:
- 2 Pounds pork bones, roasted
- 1 onion, chopped in quarters
- 2 celery stalks, chopped in half
- 2 carrots, chopped in half
- 3 whole garlic cloves
- 2 bay leaves
- 1 tbsp salt
- Filtered water (enough to cover bones)

SLOW COOKER PORK BONE BROTH

Prep Time: 15 minutes | **Cook Time:** 24 hours
Servings: 12
Ingredients:
- 2 pounds pork bones, roasted
- 1/2 onion, chopped
- 2 medium carrots, chopped
- 1 stalk celery, chopped
- 2 whole garlic cloves
- 1 bay leaf
- 1 tbsp sea salt
- 1 tsp peppercorns
- 1/4 cup apple cider vinegar

Nutrition:
Calories: 141 | Fat: 5g | Carbs: 22g | Fiber: 7g | Protein: 5g

- 1-2 tsp thyme, dried or fresh
- 3-4 pieces of dried kombu kelp (optional)

Directions:
1. Transfer the bones and vegetables to your stockpot. Top with enough water to cover then allow to slowly come to a boil on high heat.
2. Set to low heat and simmer for 45 minutes.
3. Strain the mixture through a mesh strainer. Serve hot!

Nutrition:
Calories: 29 | Fat: 1g | Carbs: 2g | Fiber: 1g | Protein: 1g

Directions:
1. Transfer the bones and vegetables to your stockpot. Top with enough water to cover then allow to slowly come to a boil on high heat.
2. Switch to low heat and simmer for at least 30 minutes.
3. Strain the mixture through a mesh strainer. Serve hot!

Nutrition:
Calories: 216 | Fat: 1g | Carbs: 37g | Fiber: 4g | Protein: 8g

Directions:
1. Transfer the bones and vegetables to your stockpot. Top with enough water to cover then allow to slowly come to a boil on high heat.
2. Set to low heat and simmer for 12 hours.
3. Strain the mixture through a mesh strainer. Serve hot!

Nutrition:
Calories: 69 | Fat: 4g | Carbs: 1g | Fiber: 0.1g | Protein: 6 g

- Filtered water (enough to cover bones)

Directions:
1. Transfer all the ingredients to your slow cooker. Top with enough water to cover then allow to slowly come to a boil on high heat.
2. Switch to low heat and simmer for at least 24 hours.
3. Strain the mixture through a mesh strainer. Serve hot!

Nutrition:
Calories: 65 | Fat: 2g | Carbs: 7g | Fiber: 4g | Protein: 6g

DINNER

CHICKEN BONE BROTH
Prep Time: 10 minutes | **Cook Time:** 90 minutes
Servings: 8
Ingredients:
- 3-4 pounds of bones (from 1 chicken)
- 4 cups water
- 2 large carrots, cut into chunks
- 2 large stalks of celery
- 1 large onion
- 2 cups fresh rosemary sprigs
- 3 fresh thyme sprigs
- 2 tbsp apple cider vinegar
- 1 tsp kosher salt

Directions:
1. Put all the ingredients in your pot and allow to sit for 30 minutes.
2. Pressure cook and adjust the time to 90 minutes.
3. Set the release naturally until the float valve drops and then unlock the lid.
4. Strain the broth and transfer it into a storage container. The broth can be refrigerated for 3-5 days or frozen for up to 6 months.

Nutrition:
Calories: 140 | Fat: 2.6g | Carbs: 0.6g | Fiber: 0.1g | Protein: 25g

HOMEMADE BEEF STOCK
Prep Time: 10 minutes | **Cook Time:** 2-12 hours
Servings: 6
Ingredients:
- 2 pounds of beef bones (preferably with marrow)
- 5 celery stalks, chopped
- 4 carrots, chopped
- 1 white or Spanish onion, chopped
- 2 garlic cloves, crushed
- 2 bay leaves
- 1 tsp dried thyme
- 1 tsp dried sage
- 1 tsp black peppercorns
- Salt

Directions:
1. Preheat the oven to 425°F.
2. On a baking sheet, spread out the beef bones, celery, carrots, onion, garlic, and bay leaves. Sprinkle the thyme, sage, and peppercorns over the top.
3. Roast until the vegetables and bones have a rich brown color.
4. Transfer the roasted bones and vegetables to a large stockpot. Cover with water and slowly bring to a boil over high heat.
5. Simmer for at least 2 hours and up to 12 hours.
6. Pour the mixture through a fine-mesh strainer into a large bowl. Serve hot.

Nutrition:
Calories: 37 | Fat: 1g | Carbs: 3g | Fiber: 0g | Protein: 4g

THREE-INGREDIENT SUGAR-FREE GELATIN
Prep Time: 5 minutes | **Cook Time:** 0 minutes
Servings: 6-8
Ingredients:
- 1/4 cup room temperature water
- 1/4 cup hot water
- 1 tbsp gelatin
- 1 cup orange juice, unsweetened

Directions:
1. Combine your gelatin and room temperature water, stirring until fully dissolved.
2. Stir in hot water then leave to rest for about 2 minutes.
3. Add in the juice and stir until combined.
4. Transfer to serving size containers then place on a tray in the refrigerator to set for about 4 hours.
5. Enjoy!

Nutrition:
Calories: 17 | Fat: 0g | Carbs: 4g | Fiber: 0g

HOMEY CLEAR CHICKEN BROTH
Prep Time: 10 minutes | **Cook Time:** 2-12 hours
Servings: 6
Ingredients:
- 2 pounds of chicken neck
- 2 celery ribs with leaves, cut into chunks
- 2 medium carrots, cut into chunks
- 2 medium onions, quartered
- 2 bay leaves
- 2 quarts of cold water
- Salt to taste

Directions:
1. Transfer the bones and vegetables to your stockpot. Top with enough water to cover then allow to slowly come to a boil on high heat.
2. Switch to low heat and simmer for at least 2 hours and up to 12 hours.
3. Set and pour the mixture through a fine-mesh strainer into a large bowl.
4. Taste and season with salt. Serve hot.

Nutrition:
Calories: 245 | Fat: 14g | Carbs: 8g | Fiber: 2g | Protein: 21 g

OXTAIL BONE BROTH

Prep Time: 15 minutes | **Cook Time:** 12 hours
Servings: 8
Ingredients:
- 2 pounds oxtail
- 1 onion, chopped in quarters
- 2 celery stalks, chopped in half
- 2 carrots, chopped in half
- 3 whole garlic cloves
- 2 bay leaves
- 1 tbsp salt
- Filtered water (enough to cover bones)

Directions:
1. Transfer the bones and vegetables to your stockpot. Top with enough water to cover then allow to slowly come to a boil on high heat.
2. Switch to low heat and simmer for at least 2 hours and up to 12 hours.
3. Set and pour the mixture through a fine-mesh strainer into a large bowl.
4. Taste and season with salt. Serve hot.

Nutrition:
Calories: 576 | Fat: 48g | Carbs: 48g | Fiber: 0g | Protein: 24g

CHICKEN BONE BROTH WITH GINGER AND LEMON

Prep Time: 10 minutes | **Cook Time:** 90 minutes
Servings: 8
Ingredients:
- 3-4 pounds of bones (from 1 chicken)
- 8 cups water
- 2 large carrots, cut into chunks
- 2 large stalks of celery
- 1 large onion
- 3 fresh rosemary sprigs
- 3 fresh thyme sprigs
- 2 tbsp apple cider vinegar
- 1 tsp kosher salt
- 1 (1/2 inches) piece of fresh ginger, sliced
- 1 large lemon, cut into quarters

Directions:
1. Put all the ingredients in your pot and allow to sit for 30 minutes.
2. Pressure cook and adjust the time to 90 minutes.
3. Set the broth using a fine-mesh strainer and transfer it into a storage container.

Nutrition:
Calories: 44 | Fat: 1g | Carbs: 0g | Fiber: 0g | Protein: 7g

BEEF BONE BROTH

Prep Time: 15 minutes | **Cook Time:** 24 hours
Servings: 4
Ingredients:
- 1 1/2 pounds beef oxtails
- 2 pounds of beef marrow bones
- 3 carrots, washed and sliced
- 3 celery stalks, rinsed and thickly sliced
- 1 onion, quartered, unpeeled
- 8 garlic cloves, halved
- 1 leek, white and green parts only, sliced and halved lengthwise
- 2 tbsp apple cider vinegar
- 1/2 tsp salt
- 1/2 tsp Black peppercorns
- 4 cups water
- 2 bay leaves

Directions:
1. Preheat the oven to 375°F.
2. Line a rimmed baking sheet with foil.
3. Place garlic, onion, celery, carrots, bones, and oxtail onto the baking sheet.
4. Bake it for thirty minutes.
5. Then, add this baked content into the slow cooker. Add peppercorns, salt, leek, and apple cider vinegar. Then, add water to cover the content. Cook on low for twenty-two hours.
6. After that, add bay leaves and cook for two hours more.
7. Strain broth through a strainer. Serve and enjoy!

Nutrition:
Calories: 481 | Fat: 23.1g | Carbs: 15 g | Protein: 53.8g

GINGER AND MUSHROOM BROTH

Prep Time: 3 minutes | **Cook Time:** 6 minutes
Servings: 4
Ingredients:
- 1/2 cup oyster trimmed mushrooms
- 1 tbsp fresh ginger, grated and peeled
- 28 oz low-sodium chicken broth, fat-free
- 1 tsp soy sauce, low-sodium
- 1/2 cup green onions
- 2 tbsp fresh basil

Directions:
1. Add ginger and mushroom into the saucepan and heat it over medium-high flame for 2 minutes. Add soy sauce and chicken broth and boil it.
2. Add onion and basil and heat it.
3. Pass the soup through a strainer and serve!

Nutrition:
Calories: 76 | Carbs: 14.6g | Protein: 4.2g

BANANA TEA

Prep Time: 2 minutes | **Cook Time:** 8 minutes
Servings: 1

Ingredients:
- 1 banana, peeled, ends trimmed off

- 1 1/4 cup of water
- 1 cinnamon stick, optional
- 1/4 tsp vanilla extract

Directions:
1. Add banana, water, and cinnamon stick into the pot and boil it.
2. Cover with a lid and simmer on low for 10 minutes.
3. When done, remove from the flame.
4. Pass the mixture through a strainer. Add vanilla extract and sweetener if desired. Serve.

VEGETABLE STOCK

Prep Time: 15 minutes | **Cook Time:** 35 minutes
Servings: 12
Ingredients:
- 1 tbsp olive oil
- 1 onion
- 2 celery stalks
- 2 carrots
- 1 green onions bunch, chopped
- 8 garlic cloves, minced
- 8 fresh parsley sprigs
- 6 fresh thyme sprigs
- 2 bay leaves
- 1 tsp salt
- 2 quarts water

Directions:
1. Firstly, chop scrubbed vegetables into chunks.
2. Add oil into the pot and heat it. Then, add bay leaves, thyme, parsley, garlic, scallions, carrots, celery, and onion, and cook on high for five to ten minutes. Add water and salt and boil it.
3. Reduce the flame and simmer for thirty minutes.
4. Then, strain the stock through a strainer and remove the vegetables. Serve!

Nutrition:
Calories: 37 | Fat: 1.4g | Carbs: 5.9g | Protein: 1.3g

STRAWBERRY POPSICLES

Prep Time: 5 minutes | **Cook Time:** 0 minutes
Servings: 8
Ingredients:
- 2 1/2 cups strawberries, chopped
- 2 tbsp honey
- 1 cup water

Directions:
1. Firstly, slice strawberries into chunks.
2. Add it into the blender with water and honey.
3. Blend until smooth.
4. Pour the mixture into the molds.
5. Add Popsicle sticks and freeze them for 4 hours.

Nutrition:
Calories: 8 | Fat: 3g | Carbs: 17g | Protein: 0g

LEMON JELLO

Prep Time: 10 minutes | **Cook Time:** 7 minutes
Servings: 12-15
Ingredients:
- 1/2 cup lemon, squeezed
- 1 1/2 cups sparkling water
- 2 tbsp gelatin, grass-fed
- 2 tbsp honey

Directions:
1. Firstly, rinse and slice the lemon in half. Then, place a strainer over the mixing bowl. Squeeze the lemon until you get a half cup of lemon juice.
2. Add water and lemon juice into the saucepan. Add gelatin into the lemon juice. Stir well. Let stand for two to three minutes.
3. Cook it over low flame for 7 minutes.
4. When done, remove from the flame. Then, add honey and stir well.
5. Place mixture into the Jello mold.
6. Place it in the refrigerator for three to four hours.

Nutrition:
Calories: 18 | Fat: 9g | Carbs: 4g | Protein: 1g

GINGER ROOT TEA

Prep Time: 5 minutes | **Cook Time:** 20 minutes
Servings: 2
Ingredients:
- 2 tbsp fresh ginger root
- 4 cups water
- 1 tbsp fresh lime juice, optional
- 1-2 tbsp honey

Directions:
1. Peel the ginger and cut it into pieces.
2. Add sliced ginger and water into the pot and boil it for ten minutes.
3. When done, remove from the flame.
4. Pass tea through a strainer and then add lime juice and honey. Serve!

Nutrition:
Calories: 42 | Fat: 0g | Carbs: 2.9g | Protein: 0g

STRAWBERRY GUMMIES

Prep Time: 10 minutes | **Cook Time:** 5 minutes
Servings: 30-40
Ingredients:
- 1 cup strawberry puree
- 2-3 tbsp honey
- 1/2 tsp vanilla extract
- 1/3 cup water
- 4 tbsp gelatin powder, un-flavored, grass-fed

Directions:
1. Add vanilla extract, honey, and strawberry puree into the saucepan and simmer for 3 minutes over medium-low flame.

2. During this, add water into the bowl and then add gelatin powder to it. Stir well.
3. Turn off the flame and add the gelatin mixture into the saucepan and whisk it well.

ORANGE GELATIN

Prep Time: 10 minutes | **Cook Time:** 5 minutes
Servings: 6
Ingredients:
- 4 1/2 tsp unflavored gelatin
- 1/4 cup cold water
- 1 cup boiling water
- 1 3/4 orange juice
- 2 tsp orange zest, grated
- 1 tsp lemon zest, grated
- 3/4 white sugar
- 1/2 lemon juice
- 1 pinch salt

REFRESHING SPORTS DRINK

Prep Time: 15 minutes | **Cook Time:** 0 minutes
Servings: 9
Ingredients:
- 8 cups fresh cold water, divided
- 3/4 cup fresh orange juice
- 1/4 cup fresh lemon juice
- 1/4 cup fresh limes juice
- 3 tbsp honey
- 1/2 tsp salt

PERFECT SUNNY DAY TEA

Prep Time: 15 minutes | **Cook Time:** 3 minutes
Servings: 6
Ingredients:
- 5 cups of filtered water
- 5 green tea bags
- 1/4 cup fresh lemon juice, strained
- 1/4 cup fresh lime juice, strained
- 1/4 cup honey
- Ice cubes, as required

Directions:
1. Pour 2 cups of water into a pot and bring to a boil.

NUTRITIOUS GREEN TEA

Prep Time: 15 minutes | **Cook Time:** 4 minutes
Servings: 4
Ingredients:
- 4 cups of filtered water
- 4 orange peel strips
- 4 lemon peel strips
- 4 green tea bags
- 2 tsp honey

Directions:
1. In a medium pan, add the water, orange, and lemon peel strips over medium-high heat and bring to a boil.

4. Place the mixture into the molds and put it into the refrigerator for two to four hours.

Nutrition:
Calories: 6.9 | Fat: 0.01g | Carbs: 1.2g | Protein: 0.5g

Directions:
1. Add gelatin into the cold water and soak it for five minutes. Then, add boiling water and stir it well.
2. Add lemon zest, orange, and 3 tbsp orange juice and keep it for five minutes.
3. Pass orange juice through the strainer and discard the zest.
4. Add salt, lemon juice, sugar, and orange to the gelatin and stir well.
5. Place the mixture into the mold and put it into the refrigerator. Serve and enjoy!

Nutrition:
Calories: 141 | Fat: 0.1g | Carbs: 34.5g | Protein: 2.1g

Directions:
1. In a large pitcher, add all ingredients and stir to combine.
2. Through a cheesecloth-lined sieve, strain the punch into another large pitcher.
3. Refrigerate to chill before serving.

Nutrition:
Calories: 33 | Fat: 0.1g | Carbs: 8.1g | Protein: 0.2g | Fiber: 0.1g

2. Insert the tea bags and turn off the heat. Cover the pot and let steep for 3-4 minutes.
3. Remove and discard the tea bags.
4. Add the honey and stir.
5. Place tea, lemon, and lime juice in a large pitcher and stir to combine. Add the remaining cold water and stir.
6. Chill in the refrigerator before serving.

Nutrition:
Calories: 46 | Fat: 0.1g | Carbs: 12g | Protein: 0.1g | Fiber: 0.1g

2. Set the heat to low and stir, uncovered, for about 10 minutes.
3. With a slotted spoon, remove the orange and lemon peel strips and discard them.
4. Add in the tea bags and turn off the heat.
5. Immediately, cover the pan and steep for 3 minutes.
6. With a large spoon, gently press the tea bags against the pan to extract the tea completely.
7. Detach the tea bags from the pan and discard them.
8. Add honey and stir until dissolved.
9. Strain the tea in mugs and serve immediately.

Nutrition:
Calories: 11 | Fat: 0g | Carbs: 3g | Protein: 0g | Fiber: 0.1g

SIMPLE BLACK TEA

Prep Time: 10 minutes | **Cook Time:** 3 minutes
Servings: 2
Ingredients:
- 2 cups of filtered water
- 1/2 tsp black tea leaves
- 1 tsp honey

Directions:
1. In a pan, add the water and bring to a boil.
2. Stir in the tea leaves and turn off the heat.
3. Immediately, cover the pan and steep for 3 minutes.
4. Add honey and stir until dissolved.
5. Strain the tea in mugs and serve immediately.

Nutrition:
Calories: 11 | Fat: 0g | Carbs: 2.9g | Protein: 0g | Fiber: 0g

LEMONY BLACK TEA

Prep Time: 10 minutes | **Cook Time:** 3 minutes
Servings: 6
Ingredients:
- 1 tbsp black tea leaves
- 1 lemon, sliced thinly
- 1 cinnamon stick
- 6 cups boiling water

Directions:
1. In a large teapot, place the tea leaves, lemon slices and cinnamon stick.
2. Pour hot water over the ingredients and immediately cover the teapot.
3. Set aside for about 5 minutes to steep.
4. Strain the tea in mugs and serve immediately.

Nutrition:
Calories: 1 | Fat: 0g | Carbs: 0.2g | Protein: 0g | Fiber: 0.1g

METABOLISM BOOSTER COFFEE

Prep Time: 5 minutes | **Cook Time:** 4 minutes
Servings: 1
Ingredients:
- 1/4 tsp coffee powder
- 1 1/4 cup filtered water
- 1 tsp fresh lemon juice
- 1 tsp honey

Directions:
1. In a small pan, add the water and coffee powder. Bring it to boil.
2. Cook for about 1 minute.
3. Detach from the heat and pour into a serving mug.
4. Add the honey and lemon juice then stir until dissolved
5. Serve hot.

Nutrition:
Calories: 23 | Fat: 0g | Carbs: 6g | Protein: 0.1g | Fiber: 0g

BEST HOMEMADE BROTH

Prep Time: 15 minutes | **Cook Time:** 2 hours 5 minutes
Servings: 8
Ingredients:
- 1 (3 pounds) chicken, cut into pieces
- 5 medium carrots
- 4 celery stalks with leaves
- 6 fresh thyme sprigs
- 6 fresh parsley sprigs
- Salt to taste
- 9 cups of cold water

Directions:
1. In a large pan, add all the ingredients over medium-high heat and bring to a boil.
2. Set the heat to medium-low and stir, covered for about 2 hours, skimming the foam from the surface occasionally.
3. Through a fine-mesh sieve, strain the broth into a large bowl.
4. Serve hot.

Nutrition:
Calories: 275 | Fat: 5.2g | Carbs: 4g | Protein: 49.7g | Fiber: 1.2g

CLEAN TESTING BROTH

Prep Time: 5 hours 50 minutes | **Cook Time:** 15 minutes
Servings: 10
Ingredients:
- 4 pounds of chicken bones
- Salt to taste
- 10 cups of filtered water
- 2 tbsp apple cider vinegar
- 1 lemon, quartered
- 3 bay leaves
- 3 tsp ground turmeric
- 2 tbsp peppercorns

Directions:
1. Preheat the oven to 400°F.
2. Arrange the bones onto a large baking sheet and sprinkle with salt.
3. Roast for about 45 minutes.
4. Detach from the oven and transfer the bones into a large pan.

5. Add the remaining ingredients and stir to combine.
6. Put the pan over medium-high heat and bring to a boil.
7. Set the heat to low and stir, covered for about 4-5 hours, skimming the foam from the surface occasionally.

HEALING BROTH

Prep Time: 10 hours 25 minutes | **Cook Time:** 15 minutes
Servings: 12
Ingredients:
- 3 tbsp extra-virgin olive oil
- 2 1/2 pounds of chicken bones
- 4 celery stalks, chopped roughly
- 3 large carrots, peeled and chopped roughly
- 1 bay leaf
- 1 tbsp black peppercorns
- 2 whole cloves
- 1 tbsp apple cider vinegar
- Warm water, as required

Directions:
1. In a Dutch oven, heat the oil over medium-high heat and sear the bones until browned.

VEGGIE LOVER'S BROTH

Prep Time: 2 hours 5 minutes | **Cook Time:** 15 minutes
Servings: 10
Ingredients:
- 4 carrots, peeled and chopped roughly
- 4 celery stalks, chopped roughly
- 3 parsnips, peeled and chopped roughly
- 2 large potatoes, peeled and chopped roughly
- 1 medium beet, trimmed and chopped roughly
- 1 large bunch of fresh parsley
- 1 (1 inch) piece of fresh ginger, sliced
- Filtered water, as required

BRAIN HEALTHY BROTH

Prep Time: 12 hours 5 minutes | **Cook Time:** 10 minutes
Servings: 6
Ingredients:
- 12 cups of filtered water
- 2 pounds of non-oily fish heads and bones
- 1/4 cup apple cider vinegar
- Sea salt to taste

Directions:
1. In a large pan, add all the ingredients over medium-high heat.
2. Add enough water to cover the veggie mixture

MINERALS RICH BROTH

Prep Time: 15 minutes | **Cook Time:** 2 hours 25 minutes
Servings: 8
Ingredients:
- 5-7 pounds non-oily fish carcasses and heads
- 2 tbsp olive oil
- 3 carrots, scrubbed and chopped roughly
- 2 celery stalks, chopped roughly

8. Through a fine-mesh sieve, strain the broth into a large bowl.
9. Serve hot.

Nutrition:
Calories: 140 | Fat: 2.6g | Carbs: 0.6g | Protein: 25g | Fiber: 0.1g

2. Transfer the bones into a bowl.
3. In the same pan, add the celery stalks and carrots. Cook for about 15 minutes, stirring occasionally.
4. Add browned bones, bay leaf, black peppercorns, cloves and vinegar. Stir to combine.
5. Add enough warm water to cover the bones mixture completely and bring to a gentle boil.
6. Set the heat to low and stir, covered for about 8-10 hours, skimming the foam from the surface occasionally.
7. Strain the broth into a large bowl. Serve hot.

Nutrition:
Calories: 67 | Fat: 4.1g | Carbs: 2g | Protein: 5.7g | Fiber: 0.5g

Directions:
1. In a pan, add all the ingredients over medium-high heat.
2. Add enough water to cover the veggie mixture and bring to a boil.
3. Set the heat to low and simmer, covered for about 2-3 hours.
4. Through a fine-mesh sieve, strain the broth into a large bowl.
5. Serve hot.

Nutrition:
Calories: 82 | Fat: 0.2g | Carbs: 19g | Protein: 1.9g | Fiber: 3.7g

and bring to a boil.
3. Set the heat to low and simmer, covered for about 10-12 hours, skimming the foam from the surface occasionally.
4. Through a fine-mesh sieve, strain the broth into a large bowl.
5. Serve hot.

Nutrition:
Calories: 75 | Fat: 1.7g | Carbs: 0.1g | Protein: 13.4g | Fiber: 0g

Directions:
1. In a pan, heat the oil over medium-low heat and cook the carrots and celery for about 20 minutes, stirring occasionally.
2. Add the fish bones and enough water to cover by 1-inch and stir to combine.
3. Set the heat to medium-high and bring to a boil.
4. Set the heat to low, covered, for about 1-2 hours,

skimming the foam from the surface occasionally.
5. Through a fine-mesh sieve, strain the broth into a large bowl.
6. Serve hot.

Nutrition:
Calories: 113 | Fat: 5.2 g | Carbs: 2.5 g | Protein: 13.7g | Fiber: 0.7g

HOLIDAY FAVORITE GELATIN

Prep Time: 15 minutes | **Cook Time:** 2 hours 25 minutes
Servings: 6
Ingredients:
- 1 tbsp grass-fed gelatin powder
- 1 3/4 cup fresh apple juice, warmed
- 1/4 cup boiling water
- 1-2 drops of fresh lemon juice

Directions:
1. In a medium bowl, pour in the tbsp of gelatin powder.
2. Add just enough warm apple juice to cover the gelatin and stir well.
3. Set aside for about 2-3 minutes or until it forms a thick syrup.
4. Add 1/4 cup of the boiling water and stir until gelatin is dissolved completely.
5. Add the remaining juice and lemon juice then stir well.
6. Transfer the mixture into a parchment paper-lined baking dish and refrigerate for 2 hours or until the top is firm before serving.

Nutrition:
Calories: 40 | Fat: 0.1g | Carbs: 8.2g | Protein: 1.9g | Fiber: 0.2g

LOW RESIDUE DIET: BREAKFAST

BAKED BANANA-NUT OATMEAL CUPS
Prep Time: 10 minutes | **Cook Time:** 40 minutes
Servings: 12
Ingredients:
- 3 cups rolled oats
- 1 1/2 cups water
- 2 mashed ripe bananas
- 1/3 cup packed brown sugar
- 2 lightly beaten eggs
- 1 tsp baking powder
- 1 tsp ground cinnamon
- 1 tsp vanilla extract
- 1/2 tsp salt
- 1/2 cup toasted minced pecans

Directions:
1. Oven Preheated to 375°F. With cooking spray, coat the muffin tin.
2. Combine water, oats, brown sugar, bananas, baking powder, eggs, vanilla, salt & cinnamon in the bowl. Fold in the pecans.
3. Split the combination around 1/3 cup each b/w the muffin cups. Bake till the toothpick injected in the middle gets out clean, around 25 minutes.
4. Let it cool in the skillet for ten minutes, then put it on the wire rack. Now serve it.

Nutrition:
Calories: 176 | Fat: 6g | Carbs: 26g | Fiber: 1.9g | Protein: 5g

OATMEAL PUMPKIN RAISIN PANCAKES
Prep Time: 10 minutes | **Cook Time:** 10 minutes
Servings: 8
Ingredients:
- 1 1/2 cup rolled oats
- 1/2 cup whole-wheat flour
- 1 tbsp baking powder
- 1 tsp cinnamon
- 1 tsp nutmeg
- 1 egg
- 1 mashed banana,
- 1 tbsp honey
- 1/2 cup canned pumpkin puree
- 1 1/2 cup cereal milk
- 1/2 cup seedless raisins
- Cooking spray (Non-stick)

Directions:
1. Combine whole-wheat flour, oats, cinnamon, nutmeg & baking powder in the large bowl. Put aside.
2. Combine banana, pumpkin puree, honey, raisins & milk in the different bowls. Mix the wet combination into a dry combination.
3. Heat the skillet over medium heat. Spray with non-stick cooking spray.
4. Put around or less than 1/4 cup of batter into a warm pan for each pancake. Cook the pancakes till puffed & dry around corners. Flip & cook the other side till its color changes to golden.

Nutrition:
Calories: 175 | Fat: 5g | Carbs: 8g | Protein: 2g

PUMPKIN PIE OATMEAL
Prep Time: 5 minutes | **Cook Time:** 5 minutes
Servings: 1
Ingredients:
- 1/2 cup rolled oats
- 3/4 cups water
- 1/2 cup pumpkin puree
- 1 tsp brown sugar
- 1 tsp pumpkin spice

Directions:
1. Combine water, pumpkin puree & oats in the microwave-safe bowl.
2. Microwave it for 45 seconds. Whisk & microwave it again for 30 seconds.
3. Drizzle with pumpkin spice & brown sugar.

Nutrition:
Calories: 115 | Fat: 5g | Carbs: 3 g | Protein: 2 g

SANTE FE OMELET
Prep Time: 5 minutes | **Cook Time:** 10 minutes
Servings: 2
Ingredients:
- 4 eggs
- 2 tbsp water
- 1/4 tsp salt
- 1 1/2 tbsp butter
- 1/2 cup drained & rinsed red beans
- 1 chopped & seeded tomato
- 1/2 cup seeded & chopped green bell pepper
- 2 tbsp grated cheddar cheese
- 2 pieces of whole-wheat tortillas

Directions:
1. Whisk together water, salt & eggs in a med bowl.
2. In a med skillet, Heat the butter & put in red beans. Now Cook it for three minutes, put green peppers & tomatoes.
3. Cook for additional five minutes till veggies soften. Put in egg combination and drizzle the cheese on the eggs.
4. Cover it till the cheese melts. Enjoy it with the whole-wheat tortillas.

Nutrition:
Calories: 145 | Fat: 1g | Carbs: 4g | Protein: 4g

SUNRISE BURRITO WRAP

Prep Time: 10 minutes | **Cook Time:** 20 minutes
Servings: 1
Ingredients:
- 1 tbsp olive oil, 1 Tbsp
- 2 slices turkey, 2 Slices
- 1/4 cup seeded & chopped green bell pepper
- 1/4 cup black beans
- 2 eggs
- 2 tbsp milk
- 1/4 tsp salt
- 2 tbsp grated Monterrey Jack cheese
- 1 wheat tortilla

Directions:
1. Heat olive oil in a nonstick skillet and cook the turkey for about 2 minutes until slightly crispy.
2. Put beans & bell peppers, then keep on cooking till warmed fully.
3. Beat together the egg with salt & milk in a small bowl. Put beaten eggs & whisk till eggs are fully cooked.
4. Put grated cheese & reduce the heat. Cover & carry on cooking till the cheese has fully melted. Put the combination on a wheat tortilla & turn it into the burrito.

Nutrition:
Calories: 190 | Fat: 5g | Carbs: 2g | Protein: 3g

GREEN SMOOTHIE

Prep Time: 5 minutes | **Cook Time:** 5 minutes
Servings: 1
Ingredients:
- 1 ripe banana
- 1 cup packed baby kale
- 1 cup vanilla almond milk (unsweetened)
- 1/4 ripe avocado
- 1 tbsp chia seeds
- 2 tsp honey
- 1 cup ice cubes

Directions:
1. Blend all the ingredients till smooth & creamy.
2. Put ice & process till smooth.

Nutrition:
Calories: 343 | Fat: 14g | Carbs: 54g | Fiber: 4g | Protein: 6g

MUESLI WITH RASPBERRIES

Prep Time: 5 minutes | **Cook Time:** 0 minutes
Servings: 1
Ingredients:
- 1/3 cup muesli
- 1 cup raspberries
- 3/4 cup low-fat milk

Directions:
1. Garnish muesli with the raspberries & enjoy with the milk.

Nutrition:
Calories: 288 | Fat: 6g | Carbs: 51g | Fiber: 8.4g | Protein: 13g

PEANUT BUTTER PROTEIN OVERNIGHT OATS

Prep Time: 5 minutes | **Cook Time:** 8 hours
Servings: 1
Ingredients:
- 1/2 cup soymilk
- 1/2 cup rolled oats (old-fashioned)
- 1 tbsp pure maple syrup
- 1 tbsp chia seeds
- 1 tbsp powdered peanut butter
- Salt to taste
- 1/2 sliced banana

Directions:
1. In the two-cup mason jar, whisk soymilk, oats, salt, chia, syrup & powdered peanut butter together. Put it in the refrigerator overnight.
2. Top it with banana/berries. Now serve it.

Nutrition:
Calories: 368 | Fat: 9g | Carbs: 62g | Fiber: 3.9g | Protein: 13g

FRUIT & YOGURT SMOOTHIE

Prep Time: 5 minutes | **Cook Time:** 5 minutes
Servings: 1
Ingredients:
- 3/4 cup plain yogurt
- 1/2 cup pure fruit juice
- 1 1/2 cups frozen fruit, like raspberries, blueberries, pineapple/peaches

Directions:
1. In the blender, Puree yogurt with juice till smooth. Put the fruit thru the hole in the lid while the motor blender is running & process till smooth.

Nutrition:
Calories: 279 | Fat: 2g | Carbs: 56g | Fiber: 0.1g | Protein: 11g

EVERYTHING BAGEL AVOCADO TOAST

Prep Time: 5 minutes | **Cook Time:** 5 minutes
Servings: 1

Ingredients:
- 1/4 medium mashed avocado
- 1 slice of toasted whole-grain bread
- 2 tsp bagel seasoning
- Pinch flaky sea salt

Directions:
1. On toast, spread the avocado. Sprinkle with salt & seasoning.

Nutrition:
Calories: 172 | Fat: 9g | Carbs: 17g | Protein: 5g | Fiber: 10.4g

CREAMY BLUEBERRY-PECAN OVERNIGHT OATMEAL

Prep Time: 10 minutes | **Cook Time:** 8 hours
Servings: 1
Ingredients:
- 1/2 cup rolled oats (old-fashioned)
- 1/2 cup water
- A pinch of salt
- 1/2 cup thawed blueberries
- 2 tbsp plain Greek yogurt
- 1 tbsp toasted minced pecans
- 2 tsp pure maple syrup

Directions:
1. In the jar/bowl, combine water, salt & oats. Cover & put it in the refrigerator for a night. If required, in the morning, heat it & garnish it with yogurt, blueberries, syrup & pecans.

Nutrition:
Calories: 291 | Fat: 8g | Carbs: 48g | Protein: 9g | Fiber: 9.3g

SPINACH-AVOCADO SMOOTHIE

Prep Time: 5 minutes | **Cook Time:** 5 minutes
Servings: 1
Ingredients:
- 1 cup non-fat plain yogurt
- 1 cup fresh spinach
- 1 frozen banana
- 1/4 avocado
- 2 tbsp water
- 1 tsp honey

Directions:
1. In the blender, put spinach, yogurt, avocado, banana, honey & water. Process it till smooth.

Nutrition:
Calories: 357 | Fat: 2g | Carbs: 457g | Protein: 17g | Fiber: 4g

BLUEBERRY ALMOND CHIA PUDDING

Prep Time: 10 minutes | **Cook Time:** 8 hours
Servings: 1
Ingredients:
- 1/2 cup unsweetened almond milk
- 2 tbsp chia seeds
- 2 tsp pure maple syrup
- 1/8 tsp almond extract
- 1/2 cup divided fresh blueberries
- 1 tbsp divided toasted slivered almonds

Directions:
1. In the small bowl, whisk together the chia, almond milk, almond extract & maple syrup. Cover & put it in the refrigerator for a minimum of 8 hours & it can be kept for up to 3 days.
2. Whisk the pudding well once it is ready to serve. Put the pudding half into the serving bowl & garnish with the almonds & blueberries half. Put the remaining pudding & serve.

Nutrition:
Calories: 229 | Fat: 10g | Carbs: 30g | Protein: 5g | Fiber: 2.2g

GREEN BEAN POTATO SALAD

Prep Time: 10 minutes | **Cook Time:** 8 minutes
Servings: 5
Ingredients:
- 1 1/2 pound fresh green beans
- 6 cubed & unpeeled red potatoes
- 1 thinly sliced onion
- 1/3 cup olive oil
- 1/4 cup red wine vinegar
- 1/4 cup rice vinegar
- 1 tbsp garlic powder
- 1 tsp sugar

Directions:
1. Cook green beans and potatoes in a big pot of simmering water for around seven minutes.
2. To stop the cooking process, Drain & put the beans in chilled water. Drain & put aside.
3. Combine potatoes, onions & green beans in a big salad bowl.
4. Stir together vinegar, olive oil, sugar, & garlic powder in the small bowl for the dressing.
5. Put the dressing on veggies & toss to cover well. Refrigerate it for one hour before serving.

Nutrition:
Calories: 210 | Fat: 3g | Carbs: 5g | Protein: 2g | Fiber: 1.5g

SPINACH FRITTATA

Prep Time: 10 minutes | **Cook Time:** 30 minutes
Servings: 4
Ingredients:
- 2 tsp olive oil
- 1 cup red pepper, seeded and chopped

- 1 garlic clove, minced
- 3 cups spinach leaves, chopped
- 4 large eggs, beaten
- 1/2 tsp salt
- 1/4 cup Parmesan cheese, freshly grated

Directions:
1. Preheat the oven to 350°F. In a non-stick oven pan, heat 1 tsp of olive oil over medium heat.
2. Cook red peppers and garlic until vegetables are soft (about 10 minutes). In a medium bowl, combine the eggs, spinach and salt; set aside.
3. Add the remaining 1 tsp of olive oil into the pan with vegetables and add to the egg mixture.
4. Set the heat and cook for 15 minutes. Sprinkle Parmesan cheese over the mixture and broil for an additional 4 minutes.

Nutrition:
Calories: 106 | Fat: 8g | Carbs: 7g | Protein: 3g | Fiber: 2g

BANANA AND PEAR PITA POCKETS

Prep Time: 10 minutes | **Cook Time:** 0 minutes
Servings: 1
Ingredients:
- 1/2 small banana, peeled and sliced
- 1 round of pita bread, made with refined white flour
- 1/2 small pear, peeled, seedless, cored, cooked and sliced
- 1/4 cup low-fat Cottage cheese

Directions:
1. Combine the banana, pear, and Cottage cheese in a small bowl. Slice the pita bread to make a pocket.
2. Fill it with the mixture.
3. Serve.

Nutrition:
Calories: 402 | Fat:2g | Carbs: 87g | Protein: 14g | Fiber: 11g

PEAR PANCAKES

Prep Time: 10 minutes | **Cook Time:** 15 minutes
Servings: 4
Ingredients:
- 2 eggs
- 1 cup pear, peeled mashed
- 1 tsp cinnamon
- 2 tsp sugar
- 1 1/2 cup refined white flour
- 1/2 cup flour, whole-wheat
- 2 tsp baking powder
- 2 tsp vanilla
- Non-stick cooking spray

Directions:
1. In a bowl, beat the eggs until fluffy. Add baking powder, cinnamon, vanilla, sugar, flours, and pear, then continue to stir just until smooth.
2. Sprinkle with non-stick cooking spray. Pour a sizeable amount of the batter that you want your pancake to be into the hot pan.
3. Cook the pancakes until puffy and dry around the edges. Turn and cook another side until golden.
4. Serve pancakes with additional pear if desired.

Nutrition:
Calories: 174 | Fat: 2g | Carbs: 34g | Protein: 95g | Fiber: 2g

RIPE PLANTAIN BRAN MUFFINS

Prep Time: 10 minutes | **Cook Time:** 20 minutes
Servings: 12
Ingredients:
- 1 1/2 cup refined cereal
- 2/3 cup low-fat milk
- 4 large eggs, lightly beaten
- 1/4 cup canola oil
- 2 medium ripe plantains, mashed
- 1/2 cup brown sugar
- 1 cup refined white flour
- 2 tsp baking powder
- 1/2 tsp salt

Directions:
1. Preheat the oven to 400°F. In a bowl, combine the bran cereal and milk; set aside.
2. Add eggs and oil; stir in brown sugar and mashed ripe plantain. In another bowl, combine salt, flour, and baking powder.
3. Dissolve the dry ingredients into the ripe plantain mixture, and stir until combined.
4. Pour the batter evenly into paper-lined muffin tins; bake for 18 minutes or until golden brown and firm. Allow cooling before serving.

Nutrition:
Calories: 325 | Fat: 19g | Carbs: 37g | Protein: 3g | Fiber: 2g

EASY BREAKFAST BRAN MUFFINS

Prep Time: 10 minutes | **Cook Time:** 20 minutes
Servings: 10
Ingredients:
- 2 cups refined cereal
- 1 cup boiling water
- 1/2 cup brown sugar
- 1/2 cup butter
- 2 eggs
- 1/2-quart buttermilk
- 2 1/2 cups refined white flour

- 2 1/2 tsp baking soda
- 1/2 tsp salt

Directions:
1. Preheat the oven to 400°F. Soak 1 cup of cereal in 1 cup of boiling water and set aside.
2. In a mixer, merge the brown sugar and butter until it is fully mixed. Add each egg separately and beat until fluffy. Then, stir in the buttermilk and the soaked cereal mixture.
3. In another bowl, combine salt, flour and baking soda. Add the flour mixture into the batter and ensure not to over mix.
4. Add in the remaining cup of cereal. Set the batter evenly into 10 greased or paper-lined muffin tins. Bake for 15-20 minutes. Allow cooling before serving.

Nutrition:
Calories: 440 | Fat: 20g | Carbs: 57g | Protein: 9g | Fiber: 3g

APPLE OATMEAL

Prep Time: 10 minutes | **Cook Time:** 1-2 minutes
Servings: 1
Ingredients:
- 1/2 cup instant oatmeal
- 3/4 cup milk or water
- 1/2 cup apples, peeled and cooked pureed
- 1 tsp brown sugar

Directions:
1. In a microwave-safe bowl, mix oats, milk or water and apples. Cook in a microwave on high.
2. Stir and cook for another 30 seconds. Sprinkle with brown sugar and add a splash of milk.

Nutrition:
Calories: 295 | Fat: 5g | Carbs: 47g | Protein: 13g | Fiber: 5g

BREAKFAST BURRITO WRAP

Prep Time: 15 minutes | **Cook Time:** 15 minutes
Servings: 1
Ingredients:
- 1 tbsp extra-virgin olive oil
- 2 slices of turkey bacon
- 1/4 cup green bell peppers, seeded and chopped
- 2 eggs, beaten
- 2 tbsp milk
- 1/4 tsp salt
- 2 tbsp low-fat Monterrey Jack cheese, grated
- 1 white tortilla

Directions:
1. In a small non-stick pan, warm olive oil on medium heat and cook the turkey for about 2 minutes until slightly crispy.
2. Add bell peppers and continue to cook until warmed through. In a small bowl beat the eggs with milk and salt.
3. Gently, stir in your eggs until almost cooked through. Turn the heat down then add the cheese.
4. Cover and continue cooking until the cheese has completely melted. Place the mixture on the tortilla and roll it into a burrito.

Nutrition:
Calories: 355 | Fat: 2g | Carbs: 14g | Protein: 23g | Fiber: 4g

ZUCCHINI OMELET

Prep Time: 15 minutes | **Cook Time:** 15 minutes
Servings: 4
Ingredients:
- 2 tbsp extra-virgin olive oil
- 1 medium zucchini, seeded and cubed
- 1/2 medium tomato, seeded and chopped
- 4 large eggs
- 1/4 cup milk
- 1 tsp salt
- 4 whole-wheat English muffins

Directions:
1. In a large non-stick pan, warm olive oil over moderate heat. Add the zucchini and tomato.
2. Cook vegetables for 5-10 minutes or until they are soft.
3. In a separate bowl, merge the eggs, milk and salt.
4. Add the egg mixture to the pan and stir to cook through. Set with white English muffins.

Nutrition:
Calories: 160 | Fat: 10g | Carbs: 14g | Protein: 6g | Fiber: 2g

COCONUT CHIA SEED PUDDING

Prep Time: 15 minutes | **Cook Time:** 0 minutes
Servings: 2
Ingredients:
- 6 tbsp Chia seeds
- 2 cups coconut milk, unsweetened)
- Blueberries for topping

Directions:
1. Merge the chia seeds and milk; mix well. Refrigerate overnight.
2. Stir in the berries and serve.

Nutrition:
Calories: 223 | Fat: 12g | Carbs: 18g | Protein: 10g | Fiber: 2g

SPICED OATMEAL

Prep Time: 2 minutes | **Cook Time:** 2 minutes
Servings: 2
Ingredients:
- 1/3 cup quick oats
- 1/4 tsp ground ginger
- 1/8 tsp ground cinnamon
- A dash of ground nutmeg
- A dash of ground clove
- 1 tbsp almond butter
- 1 cup Water

Directions:
1. Combine the oats and water. Microwave for 45 seconds, then stir and cook for another 30-45 seconds.
2. Add in the spices and drizzle on the almond butter before serving.

Nutrition:
Calories: 467 | Fat: 11g | Carbs: 33g | Protein: 5g | Fiber: 4g

BREAKFAST CEREAL

Prep Time: 5 minutes | **Cook Time:** 5 minutes
Servings: 4
Ingredients:
- 3 cups cooked old fashioned oatmeal
- 3 cups cooked quinoa
- 4 cups bananas, peeled and chopped

Directions:
1. Combine the oatmeal and quinoa; mix well.
2. Evenly, divide into 4 bowls and top with the bananas before serving.

Nutrition:
Calories: 228 | Fat: 3g | Carbs: 43g | Protein: 12g | Fiber: 6g

CAJUN OMELET

Prep Time: 5 minutes | **Cook Time:** 8 minutes
Servings: 2
Ingredients:
- 1/4-pound spicy sausage
- 1/3 cup sliced mushrooms
- 1/2 diced onion
- 4 large eggs
- 1/2 medium bell pepper, chopped
- 2 tbsp water
- A pinch of cayenne pepper (optional)
- Sea salt and fresh pepper to taste
- 1 tbsp Mustard

Directions:
1. Brown the sausage in a saucepan until cooked through. Add the mushrooms, onion and bell pepper. Cook for another 3-5 minutes, or until tender.
2. Meanwhile, whisk together the eggs, water, mustard and spices. Season with salt and pepper.
3. Top with your eggs over then reduce to low heat. Cook until the top is nearly set and then fold the omelet in half and cover.
4. Cook for another minute before serving hot.

Nutrition:
Calories: 467 | Fat: 14g | Carbs: 11g | Fiber: 2g

STRAWBERRY CASHEW CHIA PUDDING

Prep Time: 10 minutes | **Cook Time:** 0 minutes
Servings: 2
Ingredients:
- 6 tbsp chia seeds
- 2 cups cashew milk, unsweetened
- Strawberries, for topping

Directions:
1. Merge the chia seeds and milk; mix well. Refrigerate overnight.
2. Stir in the berries and serve.

Nutrition:
Calories: 223 | Fat: 12g | Carbs: 18g | Protein: 10g | Fiber: 2g

PEANUT BUTTER BANANA OATMEAL

Prep Time: 5 minutes | **Cook Time:** 0 minutes
Servings: 1
Ingredients:
- 1/3 cup quick oats
- 1/4 tsp cinnamon (optional)
- 1/2 sliced banana
- 1 tbsp peanut butter, unsweetened

Directions:
1. Merge all ingredients in a bowl with a lid. Refrigerate.

Nutrition:
Calories: 645 | Fat: 32g | Carbs: 65g | Protein: 36g | Fiber: 5g

OVERNIGHT PEACH OATMEAL

Prep Time: 10 minutes | **Cook Time:** 0 minutes
Servings: 2
Ingredients:
- 1/2 cup old fashioned oats
- 2/3 cup skim milk
- 1/2 cup plain Greek yogurt
- 1 tbsp chia seeds
- 1/2 tsp Vanilla

- 1/2 cup peach, peeled and diced
- 1 medium banana, peeled and chopped

Directions:
1. Combine the oats, milk, yogurt, chia seeds and vanilla in a bowl with a lid.
2. Refrigerate for 12 hours.
3. Top with the fruits before serving.

Nutrition:
Calories: 282 | Fat: 6g | Carbs: 48g | Protein: 10g | Fiber: 2g

COCONUT PANCAKES

Prep Time: 10 minutes | **Cook Time:** 10 minutes
Servings: 2
Ingredients:
- 1/2 cup coconut milk, plus additional as needed
- 1/2 tbsp maple syrup
- 1/4 cup coconut flour
- 1/2 tsp salt
- 2 eggs
- 1/2 tbsp coconut oil or almond butter, plus additional for greasing the pan
- 1/2 tsp vanilla extract
- 1/2 tsp baking soda

Directions:
1. Using an electric mixer, combine the coconut milk, maple syrup, eggs, coconut oil, and vanilla in a medium mixing cup.
2. Combine the baking soda, coconut flour, and salt in a shallow mixing bowl.
3. Set the dry ingredients with the wet ingredients in a mixing bowl and beat until smooth and lump-free.
4. If the batter is too dense, add more liquid to thin it down to a typical pancake batter consistency.
5. Using coconut oil, lightly grease a big skillet or pan. Preheat the oven to medium-high.
6. Cook until golden brown on the rim for another 2 minutes.
7. Continue cooking the leftover batter while stacking the pancake on a tray.

Nutrition:
Calories: 193 | Fat: 11g | Carbs: 15g | Protein: 9g | Fiber: 6g

LEMON BAKED EGGS

Prep Time: 5 minutes | **Cook Time:** 10 minutes
Servings: 1
Ingredients:
- 2 eggs
- 2 slices of cheddar cheese, low-fat
- Salt, to taste
- 1 tsp lemon, julienned
- 2 tbsp parsley, chopped
- 1 crusty white roll

Directions:
1. Preheat the oven to 180°C.
2. Spray the dish with olive oil.
3. Slice the cheddar cheese into three strips.
4. Line the edges of the dish with cheese. Break the eggs in the middle.
5. Place julienned lemon over the egg and sprinkle with fresh parsley.
6. Place dish into the oven and cook for 8 to 10 minutes.
7. Serve with crusty bread rolls.

Nutrition:
Calories: 233 | Fat: 16.8g | Carbs: 0.6g | Protein: 21.3g | Fiber: 2 g

BANANA PANCAKES

Prep Time: 10 minutes | **Cook Time:** 5-10 minutes
Servings: 4
Ingredients:
- 349 g firm silken tofu
- 400 ml dairy-free milk
- 4 tbsp grapeseed oil
- 1 tbsp vanilla extract
- 250 g flour, gluten-free
- 2 tsp cinnamon powder
- 1 tbsp baking powder
- 4 tbsp sugar
- 4 tbsp smooth peanut butter
- 2 bananas, peeled, sliced
- Maple syrup, to serve

Directions:
1. Add tofu, vanilla, cinnamon, and half of the dairy-free milk into the blender and blend until smooth.
2. Add remaining dairy-free milk to the mixture.
3. Pour baking powder and flour into another bowl. Make a hole in the center of the dry mixture and pour the wet mixture in it and blend until smooth.
4. Add 2 tsp of oil into the pan and place it over medium flame.
5. Pour batter into the pan and cook for two minutes. Flip and cook for two minutes more.
6. Spread peanut butter onto the pancakes.
7. Garnish with sliced banana.
8. Drizzle with maple syrup.

Nutrition:
Calories: 193 | Fat: 6.6g | Carbs: 29.2g | Protein: 5g | Fiber: 2g

DEVILED EGG

Prep Time: 10 minutes | **Cook Time:** 0 minutes
Servings: 12
Ingredients:
- 3 tbsp whole egg mayonnaise
- 6 eggs
- 1 pinch of turmeric powder
- 1 pinch of mustard powder
- Salt and pepper, to taste

- 1 pinch paprika
- 1 packet water cracker

Directions:
1. Add eggs into the saucepan and cover with water. Place it over medium flame. Bring to a boil. When boiled, cook the eggs for four and a half minutes.
2. Remove from the flame. Add eggs into the cold water for one minute.
3. Then, peel and slice them in half, lengthwise.
4. Scoop out the yolks and add them to the bowl. Let mash with pepper, salt, mustard, mayonnaise, and turmeric.
5. Slice a little piece of the rounded bottom of the egg white halves. Place onto the cracker or plate. Place the yolk mixture into the white egg halves. Sprinkle with paprika.

Nutrition:
Calories: 125.3 | Fat: 10.5g | Carbs: 0.7g | Protein: 6.4g | Fiber: 2g

CRUNCHY MAPLE SWEET POTATOES

Prep Time: 5 minutes | **Cook Time:** 30 minutes
Servings: 4
Ingredients:
- 1 pinch allspice
- 2 tbsp pure maple syrup
- 1/4 cup cashew nuts, crushed

Potatoes:
- Extra-virgin olive oil spray
- 500 g white potatoes, peeled
- 1 sweet potato, peeled
- 1/4 cup plain white flour
- 1/2 cup apple juice
- 1 tbsp butter
- 1 tsp sweet soy sauce
- 1 tbsp maple syrup
- 1 pinch cinnamon
- Salt and pepper, to taste

Directions:
1. Preheat the oven to 180°C.
2. Mix all ingredients into the dish, place it into the oven, and bake until golden and crunchy.
3. Keep it aside.

Potatoes:
4. Let boil the potatoes for 15 minutes.
5. Spray the baking dish with extra virgin olive oil.
6. Slice potatoes into chunks and place them onto the dish.
7. Add all other ingredients into the bowl and combine them well.
8. Pour mixture over the potatoes and cover with a lid and bake for ten minutes.
9. Sprinkle with nuts.

Nutrition:
Calories: 92 | Fat: 2g | Carbs: 18g | Protein: 1.3g | Fiber: 1g

BANANA CAKE

Prep Time: 20 minutes | **Cook Time:** 1 hour 15 minutes
Servings: 15
Ingredients:
- 1 1/3 cup bananas, mashed
- 2 1/2 tbsp lemon juice
- 1 1/2 cups milk
- 3 cups flour
- 1 1/2 tsp baking soda
- 1/4 tsp salt
- 2/3 cup butter, softened
- 1 cup white sugar
- 1/2 cup brown sugar
- 3 eggs
- 1 tsp vanilla

Frosting:
- 8 oz cream cheese
- 1/3 cup butter, softened
- 3 1/2 cups powdered sugar
- 1 tsp lemon juice
- 1 1/2 tsp lemon zest from one lemon

Directions:
1. Preheat the oven to 350°F. Grease and flour the pan.
2. In a bowl, stir 1 1/2 tbsp lemon juice and one and a half cups of milk. Keep it aside.
3. Combine one tbsp lemon juice and mashed banana and keep it aside.
4. Add white sugar, brown sugar, and butter into the bowl and beat it well.
5. Add eggs and vanilla and combine at high speed until fluffy.
6. Mix the salt, baking soda, and flour into the bowl.
7. Add flour mixture and milk to the egg mixture and stir well.
8. Then, fold it into the bananas. Place mixture into the pan.
9. Bake it for one hour and ten minutes.
10. When done, place it into the freezer for forty-five minutes.

To prepare the frosting:
11. Cream the cream cheese and butter into the bowl. Add lemon juice and lemon zest and combine well.
12. Add powdered sugar and stir well. Top frosting over the cake.

Nutrition:
Calories: 470 | Fat: 19g | Carbs: 70g | Protein: 5g | Fiber: 1.1g

APPLE PUDDING

Prep Time: 10 minutes | **Cook Time:** 30 minutes
Servings: 6
Ingredients:
- 1/2 cup butter, melted
- 1 cup white sugar
- 1 cup all-purpose flour

- 2 tsp baking powder
- 1/4 tsp salt
- 1 cup milk
- 2 cups apple, chopped and peeled
- 1 tsp ground cinnamon

Directions:
1. Preheat the oven to 375°F.
2. Mix the milk, salt, baking powder, flour, sugar, and butter into the baking dish.
3. Mix the cinnamon and apples into the bowl and microwave it for two to five minutes. Place the apple into the middle of the batter.
4. Place it into the oven and bake for a half-hour.
5. Serve and enjoy!

Nutrition:
Calories: 384 | Fat: 16g | Carbs: 57.5g | Protein: 3.8g | Fiber: 1.2g

SUPER-FOOD SCRAMBLE

Prep Time: 10 minutes | **Cook Time:** 7 minutes
Servings: 3
Ingredients:
- 2 cups fresh spinach, chopped finely
- 1 tbsp olive oil
- Salt and freshly ground black pepper, to taste
- 1/2 cup cooked salmon, chopped finely
- 4 eggs, beaten

Directions:
1. In a skillet, heat the oil over high heat and cook the spinach with black pepper for about 2 minutes.
2. Stir in the salmon and reduce the heat to medium.
3. Add the eggs and cook for about 3-4 minutes, stirring frequently.
4. Serve immediately.

Nutrition:
Calories: 179 | Fat: 12.9g | Carbs: 1.2g | Protein: 15.3g | Fiber: 0.4g

FAMILY FAVORITE SCRAMBLE

Prep Time: 10 minutes | **Cook Time:** 5 minutes
Servings: 2
Ingredients:
- 4 eggs
- 1/4 tsp red pepper flakes, crushed
- Salt and freshly ground black pepper, to taste
- 1/4 cup fresh basil, chopped
- 1/2 cup tomatoes, peeled, seeded and chopped
- 1 tbsp olive oil

Directions:
1. In a large bowl, add eggs, red pepper flakes, salt and black pepper and beat well.
2. Add the basil and tomatoes and stir to combine.
3. In a large non-stick skillet, heat the oil over medium-high heat.
4. Add the egg mixture and cook for about 3-5 minutes, stirring continuously.
5. Serve immediately.

Nutrition:
Calories: 195 | Fat: 15.9g | Carbs: 2.6g | Protein: 11.6g | Fiber: 0.7g

TASTY VEGGIE OMELET

Prep Time: 15 minutes | **Cook Time:** 25 minutes
Servings: 4
Ingredients:
- 6 large eggs
- Sea salt and freshly ground black pepper, to taste
- 1/2 cup low-fat milk
- 1/3 cup fresh mushrooms, cut into slices
- 1/3 cup red bell pepper, seeded and chopped
- 1 tbsp chives, minced

Directions:
1. Preheat the oven to 350°F. Lightly, grease a pie dish.
2. In a bowl, add the eggs, salt, black pepper and coconut oil and beat until well combined.
3. In another bowl, mix the onion, bell pepper and mushrooms.
4. Transfer the egg mixture into the prepared pie dish evenly.
5. Top with the vegetable mixture evenly and sprinkle with chives evenly.
6. Bake for about 20-25 minutes.
7. Remove from the oven and set aside for about 5 minutes.
8. With a knife, cut into equal-sized wedges

Nutrition:
Calories: 125 | Fat: 7.8g | Carbs: 3.1g | Protein: 10.8g | Fiber: 0.2g

FLUFFY PUMPKIN PANCAKES

Prep Time: 10 minutes | **Cook Time:** 40 minutes
Servings: 10
Ingredients:
- 2 eggs
- 1 cup buckwheat flour
- 1 tbsp baking powder
- 1 tsp pumpkin pie spice
- 1/2 tsp salt
- 1 cup pumpkin puree
- 3/4 cup plus 2 tbsp low-fat milk
- 3 tbsp pure maple syrup
- 2 tbsp olive oil
- 1 tsp vanilla extract

Directions:
1. In a blender, add all ingredients and pulse until well combined.
2. Transfer the mixture into a bowl and set aside for about 10 minutes.
3. Heat a greased non-stick skillet over medium heat.
4. Place about 1/4 cup of the mixture and spread in an even circle.

5. Cook for about 2 minutes per side.
6. Repeat with the remaining mixture.
7. Serve warm.

SPER-TASTY CHICKEN MUFFINS

Prep Time: 15 minutes | **Cook Time:** 45 minutes
Servings: 8
Ingredients:
- 8 eggs
- Salt and freshly ground black pepper, as required
- 2 tbsp filtered water
- 7 oz cooked chicken, chopped finely
- 1 1/2 cup fresh spinach, chopped
- 1 cup green bell pepper, seeded and chopped finely
- 2 tbsp fresh parsley, chopped finely

Directions:
1. Preheat the oven to 350°F. Grease 8 cups of a muffin tin.
2. In a bowl, add eggs, salt, black pepper and water and beat until well combined.
3. Add the chicken, spinach, bell pepper and parsley and stir to combine.
4. Transfer the mixture into the prepared muffin cups evenly.
5. Bake for about 18-20 minutes or until golden brown.
6. Remove the muffin tin from the oven and place it onto a wire rack to cool for about 10 minutes.
7. Carefully invert the muffins onto a platter and serve warm.

Nutrition:
Calories: 107 | Fat: 5.2g | Carbs: 1.7g | Protein: 13.1g | Fiber: 0.4g

CLASSIC ZUCCHINI BREAD

Prep Time: 45 minutes | **Cook Time:** 15 minutes
Servings: 24
Ingredients:
- 3 cups all-purpose flour
- 2 tsp baking soda
- 1 tsp ground cinnamon
- 1 tsp ground nutmeg
- 2 cups Splenda
- 1 cup olive oil
- 3 eggs, beaten
- 2 tsp vanilla extract
- 2 cups zucchini, peeled, seeded and grated

Directions:
1. Preheat the oven to 325°F. Arrange a rack in the center of the oven. Grease 2 loaf pans.
2. In a medium bowl, mix the flour, baking soda and spices.
3. In another large bowl, add the Splenda and oil and beat until well combined.
4. Add the eggs and vanilla extract and beat until well combined.
5. Add the flour mixture and mix until just combined.
6. Gently, fold in the zucchini.
7. Place the mixture into the bread loaf pans evenly.
8. Bake for about 45-50 minutes or until a toothpick inserted in the center of the bread comes out clean.
9. Remove the bread pans from the oven and place them onto a wire rack to cool for about 15 minutes.
10. Carefully, invert the bread onto the wire rack to cool completely before slicing.
11. With a sharp knife, cut each bread loaf into desired-sized slices and serve.

Nutrition:
Calories: 219 | Fat: 9.2g | Carbs: 28.4g | Protein: 16.3g

Note: Nutrition info at top of page: Calories: 113 | Fat: 4.4g | Carbs: 16.5g | Protein: 3.6g | Fiber: 4.4g

LUNCH

BARBECUE BEEF STIR-FRY

Prep Time: 5 minutes | **Cook Time:** 25 minutes
Servings: 4
Ingredients:
- 1/4 cup Barbecue Sauce
- 3 tbsp beef broth, low-sodium
- 1 lb. beef sirloin steak, boneless, cut into strips
- 1 onion, sliced
- 1 carrot, thinly sliced
- 1 tbsp oil
- 2 cups hot cooked long-grain white rice

Directions:
1. Combine the broth and BBQ sauce into the bowl.
2. Rub 1 tbsp of meat and let stand for five minutes.
3. Add vegetables, meat, and oil into the skillet and cook over medium-high flame for four minutes.
4. Add remaining BBQ sauce mixture and combine well. Let simmer over medium-low flame for two minutes.
5. Serve and enjoy!

Nutrition:
Calories: 310 | Fat: 9g | Carbs: 34g | Protein: 23g | Fiber: 1.1g

CHICKEN SAFFRON RICE PILAF

Prep Time: 15 minutes | **Cook Time:** 30 minutes
Servings: 6
Ingredients:
- One pinch Saffron
- 1 tbsp ghee or olive oil
- 1 carrot, peeled, chopped
- 1 celery stalk, outside parts peeled, chopped
- 1 1/2 cups Basmati rice or jasmine rice
- 3 cups chicken broth, low-sodium
- 1 1/4 cups chicken breast, roasted, shredded
- 1 lemon
- Fresh parsley, chopped, to garnish

Directions:
1. Add saffron and water into the bowl and soak it.
2. Add ghee into the skillet and heat it. Then, add celery and carrots and sauté for three to four minutes until softened. Add rice and sauté until toasted.
3. Add saffron and chicken broth to the skillet, bring to a boil, lower the heat, and cook for twenty-five to thirty minutes.
4. Add shredded chicken to the rice and toss to combine.
5. Let sit for five minutes.
6. When ready to serve, add lemon juice over the rice.
7. Garnish with chopped parsley leaves.

Nutrition:
Calories: 259 | Fat: 5g | Carbs: 41g | Protein: 13g | Fiber: 7.1g

GREEN BEAN TUNA SALAD

Prep Time: 5 mins | **Cook Time:** 10 mins
Servings: 4
Ingredients:
- 3 pounds of green beans
- 1/2 cup mayonnaise
- 1/3 cup tarragon vinegar
- 1 tsp Dijon mustard
- Thinly sliced small shallots
- 12 oz drained tuna fish
- Finely chopped small sprigs of tarragon

Directions:
1. Put green beans in a big pot of simmering water,
2. Lower the heat, cover & boil for around five to ten minutes till the beans are tender.
3. To stop the cooking process, Drain & put the beans in chilled water. Drain & put aside.
4. Combine vinegar, mustard & mayonnaise in a big bowl. Put shallots, tuna fish & green beans; mix to coat with the dressing.
5. Cover & chill for one hour before serving. Serve with fresh tarragon as a garnish.

Nutrition:
Calories: 180 | Fat: 1g | Carbs: 4g | Protein: 3g | Fiber: 0.4g

SWEET POTATO HASH WITH SAUSAGE AND SPINACH

Prep Time: 5 minutes | **Cook Time:** 15 minutes
Servings: 4
Ingredients:
- 4 small chopped sweet potatoes
- 2 apples, cored and chopped
- 1 garlic clove, minced
- 1 pound ground sausage
- 10 oz chopped spinach
- Salt and pepper

Directions:
1. Brown the sausage until no pink remains. Add the remaining ingredients.
2. Cook until the spinach and apples are tender. Season to taste and serve hot.

Nutrition:
Calories: 544 | Fat: 2g | Carbs: 65g | Protein: 11g | Fiber: 2 g

GRILLED SHRIMP AND BEAN SALAD

Prep Time: 10 minutes | **Cook Time:** 15 minutes
Servings: 6
Ingredients:
- 1 1/2 pound peeled, cleaned, & deveined shrimp,
- 1/2 cup olive oil
- 2 Minced garlic cloves
- 1/2 tsp salt
- 2 small shallots, sliced thinly
- 1 tbsp chopped fresh Italian parsley
- 1 1/2 tbsp chopped fresh basil
- 1 tbsp red wine vinegar
- 28 oz drained and rinsed white cannellini beans

Directions:
1. Combine the olive oil 1/4 cup with the salt 1/4 tsp & garlic in a shallow glass dish. Put the shrimp & combine well. Put aside. Mix the shallots with leftover 1/4 cup oil & parsley, 1/4 tsp salt, vinegar & basil in the bowl. Nicely whisk in the beans.
2. On med-high heat, grill your shrimp, flipping once, till done, around three to five minutes. With the bean salad, enjoy the shrimp.

Nutrition:
Calories: 230 | Fat: 4g | Carbs: 7g | Protein: 4g | Fiber: 2.7g

GRILLED STEAK AND MIXED GREENS SALAD

Prep Time: 10 minutes | **Cook Time:** 5 minutes
Servings: 4
Ingredients:
- 1 pound boneless sirloin steak (1/2 inch thick)
- 1 cup Italian salad dressing
- 8 oz mixed salad greens
- 2 med seeded and chopped tomatoes
- 1 cup rinsed and drained cooked white beans
- 1 medium shredded carrot, 1 medium
- 1 thinly sliced celery
- 1 med shredded zucchini/summer squash

Directions:
1. In a bowl, marinate your steak with a half cup of the dressing & cover. Refrigerate it for thirty minutes.
2. Grill the steak for five to ten min on high heat or till the desired doneness is reached. Let the steak rest for 10 minutes.
3. In the meantime, Toss the greens with beans, tomatoes, celery, carrot, squash, as well as the leftover half a cup of dressing.
4. Thinly slice the steak across the grain. Vegetables should be placed on a serving plate. Serve with steak pieces on top.

Nutrition:
Calories: 220 | Fat: 2g | Carbs: 4g | Protein: 4g | Fiber: 4g

LENTIL TOMATO SALAD

Prep Time: 5 minutes | **Cook Time:** 10 minutes
Servings: 4
Ingredients:
- 15 oz can lentils
- 3/2 cups cherry tomatoes
- 1/4 cup white wine vinegar
- 1/8 cup chives

Directions:
1. The lentils should be drained and rinsed. Cherry tomatoes should be cut in half. Optional chives, sliced
2. in a mixing bowl, put all of the ingredients together. Season with salt and vinegar to taste.
3. Serve it or put it in the refrigerator in an airtight container to allow flavors to get more delicious.

Nutrition:
Calories: 190 | Fat: 1g | Carbs: 3g | Protein: 1g | Fiber: 1g

LIGHT SHRIMP AND BARLEY SALAD

Prep Time: 10 mins | **Cook Time:** 1 hour 15 minutes
Servings: 4
Ingredients:
- 1 cup barley
- 2 cups chicken broth
- 1/2 cup deveined, cooked & peeled shrimp
- 1 seeded & chopped green pepper
- 1 tsp Dijon mustard
- 1/2 cup mayonnaise
- 1/2 cup chopped fresh basil

Directions:
1. Carry chicken broth & barley to a simmer in a med saucepan. Lower the heat & boil for around 35 minutes.
2. Drain thoroughly & fluff with the fork.
3. Combine the shrimp, barley, mustard, green pepper, basil & mayonnaise in the big serving bowl, & let it cool for around 30 minutes.
4. Top it with fresh basil. Now enjoy it.

Nutrition:
Calories: 185 | Fat: 10g | Carbs: 8g | Protein: 5g | Fiber: 8.4g

MANGO BLACK BEAN SALAD

Prep Time: 5 minutes | **Cook Time:** 10 minutes
Servings: 6
Ingredients:
- 28 oz drained and rinsed black beans
- 4 peeled and diced mangoes

- 1 cup chopped fresh Italian parsley
- 2 finely chopped scallions
- 2 seeded & diced red peppers
- 2 tbsp olive oil
- 1/2 cup balsamic vinegar
- 1/4 tsp salt

Directions:
1. Mix beans with parsley, mangoes, red bell peppers & scallions in the big salad bowl.
2. Stir together the vinegar, salt & oil in the different small bowls. Put on the veggies and combine well. Enjoy.

Nutrition:
Calories: 210 | Fat: 1g | Carbs: 4g | Protein: 1g | Fiber: 0.4g

MEDITERRANEAN SALMON AND POTATO SALAD

Prep Time: 15 minutes | **Cook Time:** 18 minutes
Servings: 4
Ingredients:
- 1-pound red potatoes, peeled and cut into wedges
- 1/2 cup plus 2 tbsp more extra-virgin olive oil
- 2 tbsp balsamic vinegar
- 1 tbsp fresh rosemary, minced
- 2 cups peas, cooked and drained
- 4 (4 oz each) salmon fillets
- 2 tbsp lemon juice
- 1/4 tsp salt
- 2 cups English cucumber, sliced and seedless

Directions:
1. In a saucepan, set water to a boil and cook potatoes until tender, about 10 minutes.
2. Drain and set potatoes back into the pan. To make the dressing, in a bowl, set together 1/2 cup of olive oil, vinegar and rosemary.
3. Combine potatoes and peas with the dressing. Set aside. In a separate medium pan, warm the remaining 2 tbsp of olive oil over medium heat.
4. Add salmon fillets and set with lemon juice and salt.
5. Cook on both sides or until fish flakes easily. To serve, place cucumber slices on a serving plate top with potato salad and fish fillets.

Nutrition:
Calories: 463 | Fat: 4g | Carbs: 75g | Protein: 34g | Fiber: 8g

CELERY SOUP

Prep Time: 8 minutes | **Cook Time:** 10 minutes
Servings: 2
Ingredients:
- 1 tbsp olive oil
- 3 garlic cloves, minced
- 2 pounds fresh celery, chopped into 1-inch pieces
- 6 cups vegetable stock
- 1 tsp salt

Directions:
1. Reserve celery tops for later use. Warm up the oil over medium heat in a soup pot.
2. Cook the garlic until softened, about 3-5 minutes. Add celery stalks, salt and vegetable stock then bring to a boil.
3. Cover and reduce the heat to low and simmer until the celery softens. Let the soup cool for a bit then puree with a hand blender.
4. Add and cook the celery tops on medium heat for 5 minutes.

Nutrition:
Calories: 51 | Fat: 3g | Carbs: 4g | Protein: 2g | Fiber: 2g

PEA TUNA SALAD

Prep Time: 15 minutes | **Cook Time:** 0 minutes
Servings: 4
Ingredients:
- 3 pounds of cooked peas
- 1/2 cup low-fat mayonnaise
- 1/3 cup tarragon vinegar
- 1 tbsp honey Dijon mustard
- 2 small shallots, thinly sliced
- 2 (6 oz) cans of tuna fish, drained
- 2 small sprigs of fresh tarragon, finely chopped

Directions:
1. In a large bowl, merge mayonnaise, vinegar and mustard. Add tuna fish, shallots and peas; toss to coat with dressing.
2. Secure and refrigerate for 1 hour before serving. Set with fresh tarragon and serve.

Nutrition:
Calories: 246 | Fat: 13g | Carbs: 11g | Protein: 22g | Fiber: 1g

VEGETABLE SOUP

Prep Time: 15 minutes | **Cook Time:** 1 hour 20 minutes
Servings: 2
Ingredients:
- 2 tbsp extra-virgin olive oil
- 4 garlic cloves, finely chopped
- 2 celery stalks, finely sliced
- 2 carrots, finely sliced
- 6 cups water or chicken broth
- 1/4 tsp thyme
- 1/4 tsp rosemary
- 1 bay leaf
- 1 can (14 oz) of peas
- 1/2 tsp salt

Directions:
1. Warm up the oil over medium heat in a soup pot. Add garlic, celery, and carrots and continue to cook for 5 minutes, stirring occasionally.

2. Add water or chicken broth, thyme, rosemary and bay leaf. Cook until it comes to a boil.
3. Set the heat and simmer gently for about 45-60 minutes. Add peas and season with salt.
4. Let soup cool slightly, remove the bay leaf and puree with a hand blender, until creamy.

5. Serve in warmed soup bowls.

Nutrition:
Calories: 242 | Fat: 8g | Carbs: 34g | Protein: 12g | Fiber: 3g

CARROT AND TURKEY SOUP

Prep Time: 15 minutes | **Cook Time:** 40 minutes
Servings: 4
Ingredients:
- 1/2-pound lean ground turkey
- 1/2 bag frozen carrot
- 1/4 cup green peas
- 1 can (32 oz) chicken broth
- 2 medium tomatoes, seeded and roughly chopped
- 1 tsp garlic powder
- 1 tsp paprika
- 1 tsp oregano
- 1 bay leaf

Directions:
1. Over medium heat, set the ground turkey in a soup pot. Add peas, frozen carrot, paprika, tomatoes, garlic powder, bay leaf, oregano, and broth.
2. Set the pot to a boil, lower heat, cover, and simmer for 30 minutes.

Nutrition:
Calories: 436 | Fat: 12g | Carbs: 20g | Protein: 59g | Fiber: 6g

CREAMY PUMPKIN SOUP

Prep Time: 15 minutes | **Cook Time:** 1 hour 10 minutes
Servings: 4
Ingredients:
- 1 pumpkin, cut lengthwise, seeds removed and peeled
- 1 sweet potato, cut lengthwise and peeled
- 2 tbsp olive oil
- 4 garlic cloves, unpeeled
- 4 cups vegetable stock
- 1/4 cup light cream
- Salt to taste
- 1 tbsp chopped Shallots

Directions:
1. Preheat the oven to 375°F. Cut all the sides of the pumpkin, shallots and sweet potato with oil.
2. Transfer your vegetables with the garlic to a roasting pan. Set to roast for about 40 minutes or until tender.
3. Let the vegetables cool for a time and scoop out the flesh of the sweet potato and pumpkin.
4. In a soup pot, place the flesh of roasted vegetables, shallots and peeled garlic. Add the broth and set to a boil.
5. Set the heat, and let it simmer, covered for 30 minutes, stirring occasionally. Let the soup cool.
6. Set the soup with a hand blender, until smooth. Add the cream.
7. Season to taste and simmer until warmed through, about 5 minutes. Serve in warm soup bowls.

Nutrition:
Calories: 332 | Fat: 18g | Carbs: 32g | Protein: 12g | Fiber: 9g

MIXED BEAN SALAD

Prep Time: 10 minutes | **Cook Time:** 30 minutes
Servings: 6
Ingredients:
- 15 oz drained and rinsed green beans
- 15 oz drained and rinsed wax beans
- 15 oz drained and rinsed kidney beans
- 15 oz drained and rinsed garbanzo beans
- 1/4 cup chopped red onion
- 8 oz chopped & marinated artichokes
- 1/4 cup fresh orange juice
- 1/2 cup cider vinegar
- 1/2 cup olive oil

Directions:
1. Combine all the onion, artichokes & beans in the big serving bowl.
2. Combine the vinegar, olive oil & juice in a separate small bowl.
3. Put the dressing on a bean combination. Whisk to coat. Let it marinate for thirty minutes in the refrigerator before serving.

Nutrition:
Calories: 230 | Fat: 18g | Carbs: 12g | Protein: 8g | Fiber: 4.3g

QUICK SPINACH AND BLACK BEAN SALAD

Prep Time: 5 minutes | **Cook Time:** 10 minutes
Servings: 4
Ingredients:
- 2 cups cooked, drained, & rinsed black beans
- 1/4 cup finely chopped green onions
- 10 oz fresh spinach
- Seeded & minced red pepper
- Seeded & chopped yellow pepper
- 1/2 cup crumbled feta
- 1 cup Italian dressing

Directions:
1. Combine onions, beans, peppers, cheese & spinach in a med bowl. On top, Put the dressing & combine till combined

Nutrition:
Calories: 245 | Fat: 14g | Carbs: 13g | Protein: 6g | Fiber: 4.4g

SHRIMP, PASTA AND SPINACH SALAD

Prep Time: 10 minutes | **Cook Time:** 20 minutes
Servings: 2
Ingredients:
- 1/2 pound whole-wheat pasta
- 3/4 pound cooked med shrimp
- 2 cups fresh spinach
- Seeded & chopped Roma tomatoes
- 1/2 cup salad dressing,
- 1 tbsp chopped fresh basil
- 1/4 cups grated Parmesan cheese

Directions:
1. Carry the salted water big pot to a simmer. Cook the pasta as per the instructions till al dente. Drain.
2. As your pasta is cooking, combine spinach, shrimp, salad dressing, cooked pasta & tomatoes in the big bowl,
3. Put it in the refrigerator for around twenty minutes. Toss with cheese & basil. Enjoy.

Nutrition:
Calories: 252 | Fat: 17g | Carbs: 12g | Protein: 10g | Fiber: 1.1g

STIR-FRY GROUND CHICKEN AND GREEN BEANS

Prep Time: 5 minutes | **Cook Time:** 5-10 minutes
Servings: 2
Ingredients:
- 2 cups green beans
- 1 tbsp oil
- 1 slice ginger
- 1/2 lb. ground chicken
- 1 tbsp soy sauce
- 1 tsp rice wine
- 1 tsp sesame oil
- 1 tsp sugar

Directions:
1. Add green beans into the boiled water and cook until tender.
2. Drain it and put it into the bowl of ice water.
3. Add oil into the skillet and heat it. Then, add a ginger slice and fry for one to two minutes.
4. Add ground chicken and cook until no longer pink.
5. Add sugar, sesame oil, rice wine, and soy sauce and toss to combine.
6. Add drained green beans and cook them.
7. Serve and enjoy!

Nutrition:
Calories: 162 | Fat: 18g | Carbs: 10g | Protein: 22g | Fiber: 2g

STEWED LAMB

Prep Time: 5 minutes | **Cook Time:** 8 hours
Servings: 6
Ingredients:
- 1 1/2 kg lamb leg, boneless
- 2 tbsp extra-virgin olive oil
- 400 ml beef or vegetable broth
- 300 ml red wine
- 80 g wholemeal flour
- 400 g button mushrooms, sliced in half
- 1 tsp fresh rosemary leaves
- 1 kg potatoes, cut into quarters, red-skinned
- 2 celery sticks, chopped
- 2 carrots, cut into large chunks
- 1 cup Parsley, chopped

Directions:
1. Add olive oil into the saucepan and place it over medium flame.
2. Cook until browned. Add stock to the slow cooker, place the lamb with all ingredients into the slow cooker. Cook on low flame for 8 hours.
3. After eight hours, turn off the slow cooker and add cooled stock to the bowl to make a paste with wholemeal flour. Stir well.
4. Add flour paste and sprinkle with pepper and salt.
5. Sprinkle with fresh parsley leaves.

Nutrition:
Calories: 481 | Fat: 27g | Carbs: 22g | Protein: 28g | Fiber: 4g

PULLED CHICKEN SALAD

Prep Time: 5 minutes | **Cook Time:** 5 minutes
Servings: 4
Ingredients:
- 200 g pulled BBQ chicken, cooked
- 1/3 cup apricots, drained, thinly sliced
- 100 g orzo pasta
- 150 g spinach, stalks removed
- 70 g cheddar cheese, cut into small cubes
- 30 g parmesan cheese
- 1/4 cup parsley, chopped
- 1/3 cup noodles
- 5 tbsp olive oil
- 3 tbsp red wine vinegar
- Salt and pepper, to taste

Directions:
1. Shred cooked and cooled chicken with a fork.
2. Add cooked and cooled orzo pasta into the microwave dish. Top with parmesan cheese and microwave for one to two minutes.

3. Add apricots, chicken, parsley, and spinach into the bowl and mix it well. Then, add red wine vinegar and olive oil, sprinkle with pepper and salt, and pour over the salad. Combine it well.

LEMONGRASS BEEF

Prep Time: 5 minutes | **Cook Time:** 5-10 minutes
Servings: 4
Ingredients:
- 2 tbsp sesame oil
- 1 tbsp fish sauce
- 2 tbsp sweet chili sauce
- 2 packets basmati rice, microwave
- 2 tsp coconut, shredded
- 1 tbsp lemongrass paste
- 500 g beef, minced, grass-fed
- 1 tbsp Thai seasoning
- 100 g cucumber, peeled and cut into chunks
- 2 carrots, peeled and julienned
- 1/4 cup basil, chopped
- 1 lime, cut into four wedges

Directions:
1. Add sesame oil, lemongrass paste, fish sauce, and Thai seasoning into the wok and heat it. Add the minced beef and stir well and cook for three to four minutes until browned.
2. Cook the rice according to the instructions.
3. Add 1 tsp shredded coconut and stir well.
4. Add carrots, cucumber, rice, and minced beef into the bowl.
5. Sprinkle with Thai basil.
6. Pour sweet chili sauce and lime wedges over it.

Nutrition:
Calories: 450 | Fat: 19g | Carbs: 50g | Protein: 21g | Fiber: 3g

BEETROOT CARROT SALAD

Prep Time: 5 minutes | **Cook Time:** 40 minutes
Servings: 6
Ingredients:
- 3 beetroot, peeled
- 3 carrots, peeled
- 500 g halloumi, thickly sliced
- 1 tsp fresh oregano leaves
- 100 ml maple syrup
- 50 ml fresh lemon juice
- 50 g spinach leaves
- 200 g tahini, hulled
- 100 g noodles
- 2 tbsp extra virgin olive oil

Directions:
1. Preheat the oven to 180°C.
2. Wrap the beetroot and carrots into the foil and put it into the oven for forty minutes.
3. Let it cool and then cut into the wedges.
4. Add olive oil into the saucepan and place it over medium flame.
5. Turn off the flame and add oregano, lemon juice, and maple syrup and stir well.
6. Add 1 tbsp of hulled tahini onto the plate.
7. Top with beetroot and carrot wedges, halloumi and spinach leaves.
8. Sprinkle with crispy noodles.

Nutrition:
Calories: 206 | Fat: 6.6g | Carbs: 34.9g | Protein: 4.5 g | Fiber: 4g

VEGGIE BOWL

Prep Time: 10 minutes | **Cook Time:** 0 minutes
Servings: 2
Ingredients:
- 100 g white basmati rice
- 6 green beans
- Red pepper, peeled, diced, and roasted
- 1/4 ripe avocado, sliced lengthways
- 1/2 cup cucumber, sliced
- 6 asparagus stems
- 1 tuna slice
- 1/2 cup pumpkin chunks, peeled and roasted
- 1/2 lemon, cut into quarters
- 2 tsp ginger, pickled

Dressing:
- 1/2 cup orange juice, freshly squeezed
- 4 tbsp sesame oil
- Salt and pepper, 1 pinch

Directions:
1. Cook the rice and drain it well.
2. Blanche green beans.
3. Grill red pepper and remove skin and then dice it.
4. Thinly slice the avocado lengthways.
5. Cut the cucumber thinly.
6. Drain six stems of asparagus.
7. Drain tuna slices of oil.
8. Boil the pumpkin chunks.
9. Place the red pepper in a mound in the middle of the plates.
10. Arrange all ingredients on the plates.
11. Pour sesame oil over it. Sprinkle with pepper and salt.
12. Pour dressing over the bowl.

Nutrition:
Calories: 519 | Fat: 28.4g | Carbs: 59.2g | Protein: 13.2g | Fiber: 5g

POMEGRANATE SALAD

Prep Time: 5 minutes | **Cook Time:** 10 minutes
Servings: 4

4. Add crispy noodles before serving.

Nutrition:
Calories: 352 | Fat: 19g | Carbs: 14g | Protein: 29g | Fiber: 3g

Ingredients:
- 1 tsp chives, chopped
- 300 g zucchini
- 100 g baby spinach
- 1 Red pepper, skinned
- Extra-virgin olive oil spray

Dressing:
- 3 tbsp walnut oil
- 1&4 cup pomegranate juice
- 2 tsp Dijon mustard
- Salt, to taste

Directions:
1. Add all ingredients into the bowl and beat until combined for dressing.
2. Slice zucchini into chunks. Let chop the chives.
3. Spray the zucchini and chives with olive oil.
4. Place a frypan over medium flame.
5. Add chives and zucchini and fry until golden brown.
6. Then, add baby spinach leaves and stir well.
7. Turn off the flame. Pour dressing over the salad.

Nutrition:
Calories: 273 | Fat: 21.4g | Carbs: 14.9g | Protein: 9.5g | Fiber: 2g

DIJON ORANGE SUMMER SALAD

Prep Time: 10 minutes | **Cook Time:** 0 minutes
Servings: 2
Ingredients:
- 150 g baby spinach leaves
- 2 oranges, peeled, deseeded and sliced thinly
- 60 g crushed macadamia nuts
- 100 g feta cheese

Dressing:
- 1 tbsp thyme leaves
- 4 tbsp extra-virgin olive oil
- 1 tbsp Dijon mustard
- 4 tbsp lemon juice
- 2 crusty sourdough white bread rolls

Directions:
1. Add salad ingredients into the bowl.
2. Add dressing ingredients into the jar and shake it well.
3. Pour dressing over the salad. Combine it well.
4. Serve with a sourdough white bread roll.

Nutrition:
Calories: 27 | Carbs: 6.7g | Protein: 0.2g | Fiber: 3g

PULAO RICE PRAWNS

Prep Time: 5 minutes | **Cook Time:** 10 minutes
Servings: 4
Ingredients:
- 20 prawns, deveined, shelled
- 3 tbsp extra virgin olive oil
- 500 ml water
- 200 ml coconut milk
- 3 cardamoms
- 2 bay leaves
- 1 pinch of red chili powder
- 1/2 tsp turmeric powder
- 1/4 cup fresh coriander, chopped
- Black pepper, to taste
- 1 pinch Garam masala powder
- 1 pinch of asafoetida powder

Directions:
1. Add olive oil to the pan. Heat it. Then, add black pepper, cardamoms, bay leaves, and spices clove and cook for one to two minutes until fragrant, about one to two minutes.
2. Add cardamom, bay leaves, and cloves into the tea leaf ball.
3. Add asafoetida powder, turmeric, garam masala, chili powder, salt, and prawns and combine well. Drain and add rice to the pan and cover with 500 ml water and 200 ml coconut milk.
4. Lower the heat and simmer until cooked thoroughly.
5. Garnish with fresh coriander leaves.

Nutrition:
Calories: 424 | Fat: 11g | Carbs: 62g | Protein: 19g | Fiber: 2g

WHITE RADISH CRUNCH SALAD

Prep Time: 5 minutes | **Cook Time:** 0 minutes
Servings: 2
Ingredients:
- 200 g radish, julienned
- 200 g cucumber, shredded
- 50 g noodles
- 1 tsp ginger, grated, steamed
- 1/4 Nori sheet, thinly sliced

Dressing:
- 1 tsp soy sauce
- 1 tsp rice vinegar
- 1 tsp maple syrup
- 1 tbsp orange juice
- 1 tbsp sesame oil

Directions:
1. Combine cucumber, ginger, and radish into the bowl. Pour dressing ingredients over it. Top with nori and noodles. Stir well.
2. Serve!

Nutrition:
Calories: 82 | Fat: 7g | Carbs: 5g | Protein: 1g | Fiber: 2g

APPLE AND MUSHROOM SOUP

Prep Time: 5 minutes | **Cook Time:** 5 minutes
Servings: 2
Ingredients:
- 400 ml water

- 1/2 green apple, peeled, cored and grated
- 100 g pre-cooked rice noodles
- 1/4 cup green chives, chopped
- 2 mushrooms, sliced
- 100 g silken tofu, crumbled
- 1 slice of roasted seaweed

Directions:
1. Rinse the rice noodles in hot water and then strain them.
2. Add all ingredients and stir for one to two minutes.
3. Then, add crushed seaweed flakes.
4. Serve!

Nutrition:
Calories: 366 | Fat: 19g | Carbs: 41.1g | Protein: 11g | Fiber: 3g

SPRING WATERCRESS SOUP

Prep Time: 5 minutes | **Cook Time:** 20-25 minutes
Servings: 4
Ingredients:
- 1 bunch watercress, rinsed
- 1 tbsp olive oil
- 1 green onion, diced, green part only
- 4 cups chicken stock
- 4 cups baby arugula
- Sea salt, to taste
- 1 tbsp chives, snipped
- 2 tbsp greek yogurt

Directions:
1. Separate the thick and tough stems from the watercress leaves.
2. Dice the stems. Reserve the leaves.
3. Add oil to the pot or Dutch oven and place it over a medium-high flame.
4. Then, add the green onion (green part only) and diced watercress stems into the pot, lower the heat to medium, and sprinkle with salt.
5. Cook for five minutes.
6. Add stock and bring to a boil over medium-high flame.
7. When boiled, lower the heat to medium-low and simmer for fifteen minutes.
8. Add reserved watercress leaves and arugula and cook until wilted.
9. Turn off the flame.
10. Add soup into the immersion blender and blend until smooth.
11. Place soup back in the pan/pot and warm through.
12. Garnish with chopped chives.

Nutrition:
Calories: 174 | Fat: 7g | Carbs: 19g | Protein: 10g | Fiber: 0.1g

OYSTER SAUCE TOFU

Prep Time: 10 minutes | **Cook Time:** 15 minutes
Servings: 4
Ingredients:
- 700 g Tofu
- 2 tsp oil
- 1 ginger slice, peeled, minced
- 1 scallion, trimmed, chopped
- 1 1/2 cups chicken broth or vegetable broth, low sodium
- 3 tbsp oyster sauce
- 2 tsp rice wine
- 2 tsp cornstarch
- 1 tsp water
- 1 tsp sesame oil

Directions:
1. Slice tofu into bite-sized squares and keep it aside.
2. Add oil into the skillet and heat it.
3. Then, add ginger and green part of chopped scallions and cook for one to two minutes.
4. Add tofu, rice wine, broth, and oyster sauce and bring to a boil.
5. Lower the heat to medium-low and simmer for five minutes.
6. Add water and cornstarch into the bowl and stir to make a slurry.
7. Add tofu into the gravy and drizzle with sesame oil, and sprinkle with green parts of scallions.

Nutrition:
Calories: 58 | Fat: 3g | Carbs: 4g | Protein: 2g | Fiber: 1.1g

POTATO AND ROSEMARY RISOTTO

Prep Time: 10 minutes | **Cook Time:** 30 minutes
Servings: 3
Ingredients:
- 2 tbsp olive oil
- 1 rosemary sprig, chopped
- 1 green onion, diced, green part only
- 2/3 cup arborio rice
- 1 Yukon gold potato, rinsed, peeled scrubbed, diced
- 3 1/2 cups chicken stock, low-sodium
- 1 tbsp parmesan cheese, grated
- 1 tsp butter
- Salt and pepper, to taste

Directions:
1. Add olive oil into the Dutch oven and heat it over a medium-high flame.
2. Add rosemary and cook for one minute. Then, add green onion and cook for two minutes until translucent.
3. Turn the heat down to medium and sprinkle with salt. Let sweat for eight minutes.
4. Remove the lid and elevate the heat to medium-high and then add rice to it. Combine it well.
5. Add potato and cook for one minute more.
6. Add chicken stock and bring to a boil.
7. Lower the heat to low and simmer for twenty minutes until al dente.

8. Add butter and parmesan cheese and turn off the flame. Let sit for five minutes.
9. Add more stock if needed.

Nutrition:
Calories: 377 | Fat: 13g | Carbs: 55g | Protein: 12g | Fiber: 8.5g

CHEESY BAKED TORTILLAS

Prep Time: 10 minutes | **Cook Time:** 40 minutes
Servings: 4
Ingredients:
- 255 g pizza sauce
- 20 ml extra-virgin olive oil
- Extra-virgin olive oil spray
- Plain Greek yogurt, as needed
- Juice of 1 whole lime
- 1 tsp onion powder
- 1/2 tsp sweet paprika
- 250 g cheddar cheese, low-fat
- 250 g chicken, cooked, shredded
- 400 g white potato, peeled
- 400 g basmati rice, cooked and drained
- Salt, to taste
- 6 flour tortillas

Directions:
1. Preheat the oven to 210°C.
2. Spray the potatoes with olive oil spray.
3. Sprinkle with paprika powder and place it into the oven and bake for 20 minutes.
4. Add onion powder and olive oil into the pan and heat it for one minute.
5. Add tofu or chicken, 180 g of pizza sauce, pepper, salt, and lemon juice, and combine well.
6. Layout tortillas onto the clean surface and top with chicken or tofu mixture, rice, and baked potatoes and top with cheese.
7. Roll the burritos and place them onto the dish.
8. Top with remaining cheese and bake for 15 to 20 minutes.

Nutrition:
Calories: 389 | Fat: 20g | Carbs: 31g | Protein: 22g | Fiber: 4g

SMOKY RICE

Prep Time: 10 minutes | **Cook Time:** 20 minutes
Servings: 4
Ingredients:
- 400 g white basmati rice
- 200 ml pasta
- 1/2 green onion, peeled and chopped, green part only
- 1/4 red capsicum, chopped
- 4 tbsp extra-virgin olive oil
- 70 g tomato puree
- 3 bay leaves
- 1 tsp paprika
- 1 tsp cumin
- Black pepper, one pinch
- Chili, one pinch
- 4 tbsp coconut oil
- Banana, peeled and chopped
- Salt, to taste

Directions:
Rice:
1. Rinse rice and soak for twenty minutes.
2. Let it boil for five minutes. Then, drain it.
3. Add black pepper, paprika, cumin, chili, half green onion (green part only), pasta, and red capsicum into the blender and blend until smooth.
4. Add oil into the saucepan and place it over medium flame.
5. Add capsicum mixture to the pan and sprinkle with salt and cook for a few minutes until fragrant. Then, add tomato puree and bay leaves and cook for five minutes.
6. Add drained rice and one cup of water and simmer for eight minutes until the rice is soft. Discard bay leaves. Keep it aside.
7. Banana: Add coconut oil and banana into the pan and cook until golden.
8. Add banana over the rice. Serve!

Nutrition:
Calories: 447 | Fat: 11g | Carbs: 69g | Protein: 11g | Fiber: 3g

ZUCCHINI LASAGNA

Prep Time: 10 minutes | **Cook Time:** 40 minutes
Servings: 4
Ingredients:
- 800 g zucchini, grated
- 1 tsp green onion, green part only
- 1 tbsp chives, chopped
- 1 tbsp dried oregano
- 250 g ricotta, low-fat
- 50 g cheddar cheese, low-fat, shredded
- 350 ml passata
- 9 dried lasagna sheets, gluten-free
- Extra virgin oil, as needed
- Salt and pepper, to taste

Directions:
1. Preheat the oven to 210°C.
2. Add olive oil into the frying pan and heat it.
3. Add green onion and zucchini and cook for three minutes.
4. Lower the heat, add 25g of low-fat cheddar cheese and ricotta, and sprinkle with pepper and salt. Keep it aside.
5. Let boil the lasagna sheet in the salted water for five to six minutes.
6. Then, drain it. Add some olive oil to the pasta.
7. Place lasagna sheet onto the baking dish, add ricotta and zucchini mixture, and sprinkle with fresh chives and oregano. Then, add tomato

passata.
8. Lower the heat of the oven to 180°C.
9. Bake the lasagna for thirty minutes.
10. Serve with salad.

GREEK CHICKEN SKEWERS

Prep Time: 20 minutes | **Cook Time:** 20 minutes
Servings: 4
Ingredients:
- 1/4 cup lemon juice
- 1/4 cup Wok oil
- 1/8 cup Red wine vinegar
- 1 tbsp onion flakes
- 1 tbsp garlic, minced
- 1 lemon, zested
- 1 tsp greek seasoning
- 1 tsp poultry seasoning
- 1 tsp dried oregano
- 1 tsp ground black pepper
- 1/2 tsp dried thyme
- 3 chicken breasts, cut into 1-inch pieces, skinless and boneless

Directions:
1. Whisk the thyme, pepper, oregano, poultry seasoning, Greek seasoning, lemon zest, garlic, onion flakes, vinegar, oil, and lemon juice into the bowl. Place it in the re-sealable plastic bag.
2. Add chicken and coat with marinade and seal the bag. Place it in the refrigerator for two hours.
3. Preheat the oven to 350°F.
4. Discard marinade and thread chicken onto the skewers.
5. Place skewers onto the baking sheet.
6. Cook for twenty minutes until golden brown.

Nutrition:
Calories: 248 | Fat: 17g | Carbs: 4.1g | Protein: 18.1g | Fiber: 0.6g

ROAST BEEF

Prep Time: 5 minutes | **Cook Time:** 1 hour
Servings: 6
Ingredients:
- 3 pounds beef eye of round roast
- 1/2 tsp kosher salt
- 1/2 tsp garlic powder
- 1/4 tsp Freshly ground black pepper

Directions:
1. Preheat the oven to 375°F.
2. Place roast into the pan and sprinkle with pepper, garlic powder, and salt. Cook it in the oven for one hour.
3. Let cool it for fifteen to twenty minutes.
4. Serve and enjoy!

Nutrition:
Calories: 48 | Fat: 32.4g | Carbs: 0.2g | Protein: 44.8g | Fiber: 6g

GRILLED FISH STEAKS

Prep Time: 10 minutes | **Cook Time:** 10 minutes
Servings: 2
Ingredients:
- 1 garlic clove, minced
- 6 tbsp olive oil
- 1 tbsp dried basil
- 1 tsp salt
- 1 tsp ground black pepper
- 1 tsp lemon juice
- 1 tsp fresh parsley, chopped
- 6 oz halibut fillets

Directions:
1. Mix the parsley, lemon juice, pepper, salt, basil, olive oil, and garlic into the bowl.
2. Add halibut fillets into the glass dish and place marinade over it.
3. Place it in the refrigerator for one hour.
4. Oil the grate and preheat the grill on high heat.
5. Discard marinade and place halibut fillets onto the grill, and cook for five minutes per side.
6. When done, serve and enjoy!

Nutrition:
Calories: 554 | Fat: 43.7g | Carbs: 2.2g | Protein: 36.3g | Fiber: 0.6g

LAMB CHOPS

Prep Time: 30 minutes | **Cook Time:** 30 minutes
Servings: 2
Ingredients:
- 2 lb lamb chops, cut 3/4" thick, 4 pieces
- Kosher salt and Black pepper, for seasoning
- 1 tbsp garlic, minced
- 2 tsp rosemary, chopped
- 2 tsp thyme, chopped
- 1/2 tsp parsley, chopped
- 1/4 cup extra-virgin olive oil

Directions:
1. Rub the lamb chops with pepper and salt.
2. Mix the two tbsp olive oil, parsley, thyme, rosemary, and garlic into the bowl.
3. Rub this paste on each side of the lamb chops and let it marinate for a half-hour.
4. Place two tbsp olive oil into the frying pan over medium-high flame.
5. Add lamb chops and cook for two to three minutes.
6. Flip and cook for three to four minutes more.
7. Let it cool for ten minutes.
8. Serve and enjoy!

Nutrition:
Calories: 465 | Fat: 38g | Carbs: 12g | Protein: 14g | Fiber: 0.5g

EGGPLANT CROQUETTES

Prep Time: 15 minutes | **Cook Time:** 20 minutes
Servings: 6
Ingredients:
- 2 eggplants, peeled and cubed
- 1 cup cheddar cheese, shredded
- 1 cup Italian seasoned bread crumbs
- 2 eggs, beaten
- 2 tbsp dried parsley
- 2 tbsp onion, chopped
- 1 garlic clove, minced
- 1 cup vegetable oil, for frying
- 1 tsp salt
- 1/2 ground black pepper

Directions:
1. Microwave the eggplant over medium-high heat for three minutes.
2. Flip and cook for two minutes more.
3. If the eggplant did not tender, cook for two minutes more.
4. Then, drain it and mash the eggplants.
5. Mix the salt, garlic, onion, parsley, eggs, cheese, breadcrumbs, and mashed eggplant.
6. Make the patties from the eggplant mixture.
7. Add oil into the skillet and heat it. Place eggplant patties into the skillet and fry until golden brown for five minutes.
8. Serve and enjoy!

Nutrition:
Calories: 266 | Fat: 14.4g | Carbs: 23.6g | Protein: 12g | Fiber: 3g

CUCUMBER EGG SALAD

Prep Time: 10 minutes | **Cook Time:** 15 minutes
Servings: 4
Ingredients:
- 4 eggs
- 4 cucumbers, seedless
- 4 dill pickles
- 3 tbsp mayonnaise

Directions:
1. Add eggs to the saucepan and cover it with cold water. Let boil it.
2. Remove from the flame. Let stand eggs in hot water for ten to twelve minutes.
3. Remove from the hot water and cool it.
4. Peel eggs and chop them. Add it to the salad bowl.
5. Cube the pickles, and the cucumber and add to the eggs.
6. Add mayonnaise and combine it well.
7. Place it into the fridge until chill.

Nutrition:
Calories: 176 | Fat: 13.4g | Carbs: 8g | Protein: 7.6g | Fiber: 1.5g

GARDEN VEGGIES QUICHE

Prep Time: 15 minutes | **Cook Time:** 20 minutes
Servings: 4
Ingredients:
- 6 eggs
- 1/2 cup low-fat milk
- Salt and freshly ground black pepper, to taste
- 2 cups fresh baby spinach, chopped
- 1/2 cup green bell pepper, seeded and chopped
- 1 scallion, chopped
- 1/4 cup fresh parsley, chopped
- 1 tbsp fresh chives, minced

Directions:
1. Preheat the oven to 400°F. Lightly grease a pie dish.
2. In a bowl, add eggs, almond milk, salt and black pepper and beat until well combined. Set aside.
3. In another bowl, add the vegetables and herbs and mix well.
4. In the bottom of the prepared pie dish, place the veggie mixture evenly and top with the egg mixture.
5. Bake for about 20 minutes or until a wooden skewer inserted in the center comes out clean.
6. Remove the pie dish from the oven and set aside for about 5 minutes before slicing.
7. Cut into desired-sized wedges and serve warm.

Nutrition:
Calories: 118 | Fat: 7g | Carbs: 4.3g | Protein: 10.1g | Fiber: 0.8g

GREEK INSPIRED CUCUMBER SALAD

Prep Time: 10 minutes | **Cook Time:** 0 minutes
Servings: 4
Ingredients:
- 4 medium cucumbers, peeled, seeded and chopped
- 1/2 cup low-fat Greek yogurt
- 1 1/2 tbsp fresh dill, chopped
- 1 tbsp fresh lemon juice
- Salt and freshly ground black pepper, as required

Directions:
1. In a large bowl, add all the ingredients and mix well.
2. Serve immediately.

Nutrition:
Calories: 71 | Carbs: 12g | Protein: 4g | Fiber: 1.7g

LIGHT VEGGIE SALAD

Prep Time: 10 minutes | **Cook Time:** 0 minutes
Servings: 5
Ingredients:
- 2 cups cucumbers, seeded and chopped
- 2 cups red tomatoes, seeded and chopped
- 2 tbsp extra-virgin olive oil
- 2 tbsp fresh lime juice
- Salt, to taste

Directions:
1. In a large serving bowl, add all the ingredients and toss to coat well.
2. Serve immediately.

Nutrition:
Calories: 68 | Fat: 5.8g | Carbs: 4.4g | Protein: 0.9g | Fiber: 1.1g

EASTERN EUROPEAN SOUP

Cook Time: 5 minutes | **Prep Time:** 10 minutes
Servings: 3
Ingredients:
- 2 cups fat-free yogurt
- 4 tsp fresh lemon juice
- 2 cups beets, trimmed, peeled and chopped
- 2 tbsp fresh dill
- Salt, as required
- 1 tbsp fresh chives, minced

Directions:
1. In a high-speed blender, add all ingredients except for chives and pulse until smooth.
2. Transfer the soup into a pan over medium heat and cook for about 3-5 minutes or until heated through.
3. Serve immediately with the garnishing of chives.

Nutrition:
Calories: 149 | Fat: 0.6g | Carbs: 25.2g | Protein: 11.8g | Fiber: 2.5g

CITRUS GLAZED CARROTS

Prep Time: 15 minutes | **Cook Time:** 15 minutes
Servings: 6
Ingredients:
- 1 1/2 lb. carrots, peeled and chopped
- 1/2 cup water
- 2 tbsp olive oil
- Salt, to taste
- 3 tbsp fresh orange juice

Directions:
1. In a large skillet, add the carrots, water, boil and salt over medium heat and bring to a boil.
2. Reduce heat to low and simmer; covered for about 6 minutes.
3. Add the orange juice and stir to combine.
4. Increase the heat to high and cook, uncovered for about 5-8 minutes, tossing frequently.
5. Serve immediately.

BRAISED ASPARAGUS

Prep Time: 10 minutes | **Cook Time:** 8 minutes
Servings: 2
Ingredients:
- 1/2 cup chicken bone broth
- 1 tbsp olive oil
- 1 (1/2-inch) lemon peel
- 1 cup asparagus, trimmed

Directions:
1. In a small pan add the broth, oil and lemon peel over medium heat and bring to a boil.
2. Add the asparagus and cook, covered for about 3-4 minutes. Discard the lemon peel and serve.

Nutrition:
Calories: 82 | Fat: 7.1g | Carbs: 2.6g | Protein: 3.7g | Fiber: 1.4g

SPRING FLAVORED PASTA

Prep Time: 10 minutes | **Cook Time:** 10 minutes
Servings: 4
Ingredients:
- 2 tbsp olive oil
- 1 lb. asparagus, trimmed
- Salt and freshly ground black pepper, to taste
- 1/2 lb. cooked hot pasta, drained

Directions:
1. In a skillet, heat the oil over medium heat and cook the asparagus, salt and black pepper for about 8-10 minutes, stirring occasionally.
2. Place the hot pasta and toss to coat well.
3. Serve immediately.

Nutrition:
Calories: 246 | Fat: 2.4g | Carbs: 35.2g | Protein: 8.9g | Fiber: 2.4g

VERSATILE MAC 'N CHEESE

Prep Time: 15 minutes | **Cook Time:** 12 minutes
Servings: 1
Ingredients:
- 2 cups elbow macaroni
- 1 1/2 s butternut squash, peeled and cubed
- 1 cup low-fat Swiss cheese, shredded
- 1/3 cup low-fat milk
- 1 tbsp olive oil

- Salt and freshly ground black pepper, to taste

Directions:
1. In a large pot of boiling salted water, cook and drain the macaroni.
2. In a skillet over medium-low heat, cook the pumpkin cubes until tender.
3. Add the cheese and milk and cook for about 3 minutes, stirring continuously.
4. Add the macaroni, oil, salt and black pepper and stir to combine. Serve hot.

Nutrition:
Calories: 321 | Fat: 11.9g | Carbs: 40g | Protein: 14g | Fiber: 2.4g

GLUTEN-FREE CURRY

Prep Time: 15 minutes | **Cook Time:** 20 minutes
Servings: 6
Ingredients:
- 2 cups tomatoes, peeled, seeded and chopped
- 1 1/2 cups water
- 2 tbsp olive oil
- 1 tsp fresh ginger, chopped
- 1/4 tsp ground turmeric
- 2 cups fresh shiitake mushrooms, sliced
- 5 cups fresh button mushrooms, sliced
- 1/4 cup fat-free yogurt, whipped
- Salt and freshly ground black pepper, to taste

Directions:
1. In a food processor, add the tomatoes and 1/4 cup of water and pulse until smooth paste forms.
2. In a pan, heat the oil over medium heat and sauté the ginger and turmeric for about 1 minute.
3. Add the tomato paste and cook for about 5 minutes.
4. Stir in the mushrooms, yogurt, and remaining water and bring to a boil. Cook for about 10-12 minutes, stirring occasionally.
5. Season with salt and black pepper and remove from the heat. Serve hot.

Nutrition:
Calories: 70 | Fat: 5g | Carbs: 5.3g | Protein: 3g | Fiber: 1.4g

NEW YEAR'S LUNCHEON MEAL

Prep Time: 10 minutes | **Cook Time:** 0 minutes
Servings: 2
Ingredients:
- 1 large avocado, halved and pitted
- 1 (5-oz) can of water-packed tuna, drained and flaked
- 3 tbsp fat-free yogurt
- 2 tbsp fresh lemon juice
- 1 tsp fresh parsley, chopped finely
- Salt and freshly ground black pepper, to taste

Directions:
1. Carefully, remove abut about 2-3 tbsp of flesh from each avocado half.
2. Arrange the avocado halves onto a platter and drizzle each with 1 tsp of lemon juice.
3. Chop the avocado flesh and transfer it into a bowl.
4. In the bowl of avocado flesh, add tuna, yogurt, parsley, remaining lemon juice, salt, and black pepper, and stir to combine.
5. Divide the tuna mixture into both avocado halves evenly. Serve immediately.

Nutrition:
Calories: 215 | Fat: 11.8g | Carbs: 7g | Protein: 20.6g | Fiber: 3.2g

ENTERTAINING WRAPS

Prep Time: 15 minutes | **Cook Time:** 10 minutes
Servings: 5
Ingredients:
For Chicken:
- 2 tbsp olive oil
- 1 tsp fresh ginger, minced
- 1 1/4 lb. ground chicken
- Salt and freshly ground black pepper, to taste

For Wraps:
- 10 romaine lettuce leaves
- 1 1/2 cups carrot, peeled and julienned
- 2 tbsp fresh parsley, chopped finely
- 2 tbsp fresh lime juice

Directions:
1. In a skillet, heat the oil over medium heat and sauté the ginger for about 1 minute.
2. Add the ground chicken, salt, and black pepper and cook for about 7-9 minutes, breaking up the meat into smaller pieces with a wooden spoon.
3. Remove from the heat and set aside to cool.
4. Arrange the lettuce leaves onto serving plates.
5. Place the cooked chicken over each lettuce leaf and top with carrot and cilantro.
6. Drizzle with lime juice and serve immediately.

Nutrition:
Calories: 280 | Fat: 14g | Carbs: 3.8g | Protein: 33.2g | Fiber: 0.9g

AMAZING CHICKEN PLATTER

Prep Time: 15 minutes | **Cook Time:** 18 minutes
Servings: 6
Ingredients:
- 2 tbsp olive oil, divided
- 4 (4-oz) boneless, skinless chicken breasts, cut into small pieces
- Salt and freshly ground black pepper, to taste
- 1 tsp fresh ginger, grated
- 4 cups fresh mushrooms, sliced
- 1 cup chicken bone broth

Directions:
1. In a large skillet, heat 1 tbsp of oil over medium-high heat and stir fry the chicken pieces, salt, and black pepper for about 4-5 minutes or until golden brown.
2. With a slotted spoon, transfer the chicken pieces onto a plate.
3. In the same skillet, heat the remaining oil over medium heat and sauté the onion, and ginger for about 1 minute.
4. Add the mushrooms and cook for about 6-7 minutes, stirring frequently.
5. Add the cooked chicken and coconut milk and stir fry for about 3-4 minutes
6. Add in the salt and black pepper and remove from the heat.
7. Serve hot.

Nutrition:
Calories: 200 | Fat: 10.4g | Carbs: 1.6g | Protein: 24.8g | Fiber: 0.5g

COLORFUL CHICKEN DINNER

Prep Time: 15 minutes | **Cook Time:** 20 minutes
Servings: 6
Ingredients:
- 3 tbsp olive oil, divided
- 1 large yellow bell pepper, seeded and sliced
- 1 large red bell pepper, seeded and sliced
- 1 large green bell pepper, seeded and sliced
- 1 lb. boneless, skinless chicken breasts, sliced
- 1 tsp dried oregano, crushed
- 1/4 tsp garlic powder
- 1/4 tsp ground cumin
- Salt and freshly ground black pepper, to taste
- 1/4 cup chicken bone broth

Directions:
1. In a skillet, heat 1 tbsp of oil over medium-high heat and cook the bell peppers for about 4-5 minutes.
2. With a slotted spoon, transfer the peppers mixture onto a plate.
3. In the same skillet, heat the remaining over medium-high heat and cook the chicken for about 8 minutes, stirring frequently.
4. Stir in the thyme, spices, salt, black pepper, and broth, and bring to a boil.
5. Add the peppers mixture and stir to combine.
6. Reduce the heat to medium and cook for about 3-5 minutes or until all the liquid is absorbed, stirring occasionally. Serve immediately.

Nutrition:
Calories: 226 | Fat: 12.8g | Carbs: 4.8g | Protein: 22.9g | Fiber: 0.9g

EASIEST TUNA SALAD

Prep Time: 15 minutes | **Cook Time:** 0 minutes
Servings: 4
Ingredients:
For Dressing:
- 2 tbsp fresh dill, minced
- 2 tbsp olive oil
- 1 tbsp fresh lime juice
- Salt and freshly ground black pepper, to taste

For Salad:
- 2 (6-oz) cans of water-packed tuna, drained and flaked
- 6 hard-boiled eggs, peeled and sliced
- 1 cup tomato, peeled, seeded and chopped
- 1 large cucumber, peeled, seeded and sliced

Directions:
1. For the dressing: In a small bowl, add all the ingredients and beat until well combined.
2. For the salad: In another large serving bowl, add all the ingredients and mix well.
3. Divide the tuna mixture onto serving plates.
4. Drizzle with dressing and serve.

Nutrition:
Calories: 277 | Fat: 14.5g | Carbs: 5.9g | Protein: 31.2g | Fiber: 1.1g

LEMONY SALMON

Prep Time: 10 minutes | **Cook Time:** 14 minutes
Servings: 4
Ingredients:
- 1 tbsp fresh lemon zest, grated
- 2 tbsp extra-virgin olive oil
- 2 tbsp fresh lemon juice
- Salt and freshly ground black pepper, to taste
- 4 (6-oz) boneless, skinless salmon fillets

Directions:
1. Preheat the grill to medium-high heat. Grease the grill grate.
2. In a bowl, place all ingredients except for salmon fillets and mix well.
3. Add the salmon fillets and coat with garlic mixture generously.
4. Place the salmon fillets onto the grill and cook for about 6-7 minutes per side. Serve hot.

Nutrition:
Calories: 290 | Fat: 21.5g | Carbs: 1g | Protein: 33.2g | Fiber: 0.2g

SPINACH AND APPLE SALAD

Prep Time: 10 minutes | **Cook Time:** 5 minutes
Servings: 2
Ingredients:
- 1/2 Pound fresh spinach
- 1/2 cup thinly sliced cabbage
- Unpeeled & thinly sliced pear
- 1/4 cup finely chopped green onions
- 1 tbsp chopped fresh basil

- 2 tsp balsamic vinegar
- 1/3 cup fresh orange juice
- 1/4 cup olive oil

Directions:
1. Combine the cabbage, pear & spinach in the big salad bowl. Stir together the basil, green onions, orange juice, olive oil & balsamic vinegar in the small bowl to make the dressing. Put the dressing on the salad. Enjoy.

Nutrition:
Calories: 187 | Fat: 12g | Carbs: 7g | Protein: 3g | Fiber: 0.8g

TUNA AND BEAN SALAD

Prep Time: 10 minutes | **Cook Time:** 15 minutes
Servings: 4
Ingredients:
- 28 oz cannellini beans
- 4 cups arugula
- 12 oz drained tuna fish
- 4 tbsp olive oil
- 2 tbsp lemon juice
- 1/4 tsp salt
- 1 tbsp chopped Italian parsley
- 1/2 cup finely chopped green onions

Directions:
1. Put the beans on the serving dish. Put the tuna equally on the beans. On the top of the tuna, Put the arugula.
2. Prepare the dressing in a separate med bowl by stirring the lemon juice, oil, parsley & salt.
3. Put the dressing on the beans & tuna. Drizzle the onions on the bean salad & combine well. Enjoy.

Nutrition:
Calories: 187 | Fat: 16g | Carbs: 8g | Protein: 12g | Fiber: 0.3g

VEGGIE AND RICE SALAD

Prep Time: 10 minutes | **Cook Time:** 10 minutes
Servings: 6
Ingredients:
- 1 1/2 tsp olive oil
- Seeded & chopped green bell peppers
- 1 cup chopped green beans
- Chopped onion
- Chopped carrots
- 1 cup sliced mushrooms
- Unpeeled, cooked & cubed potatoes
- 1/2 tsp cumin
- 1/2 tsp oregano
- 3 cups cooked & cooled brown rice
- 1 1/2 tbsp reduced-sodium soy sauce
- 1/4 chopped Italian parsley
- 2 tbsp lemon juice

Directions:
1. Heat olive oil on med-high heat in the big non-stick skillet.
2. Cook green beans, peppers, carrots & onions for around seven minutes. Put the potatoes & mushrooms then continue cooking
3. Put oregano, soy sauce & cumin.
4. Move the combination to the big salad bowl & let it cool at room temp.
5. Put rice, lemon juice & chopped parsley. Combine it. Now Serve.

Nutrition:
Calories: 222 | Fat: 4g | Carbs: 6g | Protein: 2g | Fiber: 2.1g

ZESTY BEAN AND TOMATO SALAD

Prep Time: 5 minutes | **Cook Time:** 10 minutes
Servings: 4
Ingredients:
- 28 oz drained & rinsed white beans
- 2 cups seeded and chopped tomatoes
- 2 cups (Cut into 1-inch pieces) Green beans,
- 1/4 cup chopped Italian parsley
- 2 cups arugula
- 1/2 cup olive oil
- 2 tbsp fresh lemon juice
- 1/4 tsp Salt
- 2 tbsp Chopped fresh basil
- 2 tbsp Grated Parmesan cheese

Directions:
1. Combine tomatoes, beans, arugula & parsley in a med salad bowl. Put aside.
2. Stir together lemon juice, oil, basil & salt to make the dressing.
3. Toss the veggies with dressing & put them in the refrigerator for one hour before serving. Garnish with grated cheese & enjoy.

Nutrition:
Calories: 115 | Fat: 5g | Carbs: 3g | Protein: 1g | Fiber: 1.2 g

DINNER

GROUND BEEF TOSTADA

Prep Time: 15 minutes | **Cook Time:** 50 minutes
Servings: 8
Ingredients:
- 1 1/2 lbs ground beef
- 1 tsp salt
- 1 tbsp chili powder
- 1 tsp oregano
- 1 tsp ground cumin
- 1 white onion, diced
- 2 Jalapeños, seeded and diced
- 1/4 cup tomato paste
- 16 oz tomatoes, diced, roasted
- 2 carrots, peeled and diced
- 1 Yukon gold potato, diced

Assemble:
- Tostadas
- 2 cups refried beans
- Cotija cheese
- Sour cream
- Red onions, pickled
- Cilantro chopped

Directions:
1. Add cumin, chili powder, oregano, salt, kosher salt, and ground beef into the stockpot and cook over medium-high flame. Let cook for six to seven minutes.
2. Then, add tomato paste, jalapenos, and onion and stir well. Cook for a few minutes more. Then, add tomatoes and their juices and lower the heat and cook for twenty minutes.
3. Add carrot and diced potatoes and cook for twenty minutes more. Stir well. Add water if it gets too thick.
4. Assemble: Place refried beans onto the tostada and top with ground beef mixture. Then, add chopped cilantro, pickled red onion, and sour cream.

Nutrition:
Calories: 235 | Fat: 12g | Carbs: 10g | Protein: 19g | Fiber: 4.4g

DELICIOUS COMBO DINNER

Prep Time: 15 minutes | **Cook Time:** 15 minutes
Servings: 5
Ingredients:
- 2 tbsp olive oil
- 1 lb. prawns, peeled and deveined
- 1 lb. asparagus, trimmed
- Salt and freshly ground black pepper, to taste
- 1 tsp fresh ginger, minced
- 2 tbsp fresh lemon juice

Directions:
1. In a skillet, heat 1 tbsp of oil over medium-high heat and cook the prawns with salt and black pepper for about 3-4 minutes.
2. With a slotted spoon, transfer the prawns into a bowl. Set aside.
3. In the same skillet, heat the remaining oil over medium-high heat and cook the asparagus, ginger, salt and black pepper for about 6-8 minutes, stirring frequently.
4. Stir in the prawns and cook for about 1 minute.
5. Stir in the lemon juice and remove from the heat.
6. Serve hot.

Nutrition:
Calories: 176 | Fat: 7.3g | Carbs: 5.1g | Protein: 22.7g | Fiber: 1.9g

BEEF BARLEY SOUP

Prep Time: 10 minutes | **Cooking Time:** 1 hour 10
Servings 6
Ingredients:
- 2 tbsp olive oil
- 1 lb ground beef
- 1 cup onion, chopped
- 1/2 tbsp garlic, minced
- 3 carrots, peeled and sliced
- 1/2 cup dry barley
- 2-3 bay leaves
- 2 cups tomato sauce
- 1 tbsp soy sauce
- 1 tbsp miso paste
- 2 cups water
- 1 tbsp fresh parsley, for garnish

Directions:
1. Add olive oil into the pot and cook over medium-high flame for two minutes. Add ground beef and cook for five to seven minutes until browned.
2. Then, add garlic and onion and cook for three to four minutes more.
3. Add bay leaves, barley, carrots, and stir well, and cook for two minutes.
4. Add water, miso paste, soy sauce, and tomato sauce and stir well.
5. Let simmer for one hour.
6. Garnish with fresh parsley leaves.

Nutrition:
Calories: 234 | Fat: 4.7g | Carbs: 28.6g | Protein: 21.2g | Fiber: 4.3g

GROUND BEEF AND RICE BOWLS

Prep Time: 5 minutes | **Cook Time:** 15 minutes
Servings: 4

Ingredients:
- 1 pound lean ground beef

- 3 garlic cloves, minced
- 1/4 cup brown sugar
- 1/4 cup soy sauce, low-sodium
- 2 tsp sesame oil
- 1/4 tsp ground ginger
- 1/4 tsp red pepper flakes, crushed
- 1/4 tsp pepper
- 2 cups hot cooked white or brown rice
- Sliced green onions and sesame seeds, for garnish

Directions:
1. Add ground beef into the skillet and cook over medium flame until no longer pink.
2. Whisk the pepper, red pepper flakes, sesame oil, soy sauce, and brown sugar into the bowl.
3. Place this mixture over the ground beef and simmer for one to two minutes.
4. Garnish with sesame seeds and green onions.

Nutrition:
Calories: 238 | Fat: 8g | Carbs: 16g | Protein: 25g | Fiber: 0.4g

FISH STICKS

Prep Time: 10 minutes | **Cook Time:** 15 minutes
Servings: 4
Ingredients:
- 1/3 cup all-purpose flour
- 1/2 tsp salt
- 1/8-1/4 tsp pepper
- 2 eggs
- 1 cup panko bread crumbs
- 1/3 cup parmesan cheese, grated
- 2 tbsp garlic-herb seasoning blend
- 1 lb tilapia fillets

Directions:
1. Preheat the oven to 450°F.
2. Combine the pepper, salt, and flour into the bowl.
3. Whisk the eggs in another bowl. Toss breadcrumbs with seasoning blend and cheese.
4. Slice fillets into the strips. Immerse fish in flour mixture and coat it well.
5. Immerse in eggs and coat it well.
6. Place onto the baking sheet and bake it for ten to twelve minutes.
7. Serve and enjoy!

Nutrition:
Calories: 281 | Fat: 11g | Carbs: 16g | Protein: 28g | Fiber: 0.6g

BEET SOUP

Prep Time: 20 minutes | **Cook Time:** 40 minutes
Servings: 4
Ingredients:
- 3 tbsp olive oil
- 1 onion, chopped
- 3 garlic cloves, chopped
- 6 beets, peeled and chopped
- 2 cups beef stock
- Salt and freshly ground pepper, to taste
- Heavy cream

Directions:
1. Add olive oil into the saucepan and heat it over medium flame.
2. Then, add garlic and onion and stir well. Let cook for five minutes until soft. Add beets and cook for one minute.
3. Add pepper, salt, and stock, and stir well. Let boil it for twenty to thirty minutes. Remove from the flame. Let's cool it.
4. Add soup into the food processor and blend until smooth.
5. Place soup back in the saucepan and heat it.
6. Then, place it into the bowls. Garnish with sour cream.

Nutrition:
Calories: 229 | Fat: 16.4g | Carbs: 17g | Protein: 4.8g | Fiber: 0.8g

CHICKEN BURGERS

Prep Time: 10 minutes | **Cook Time:** 10 minutes
Servings: 4
Ingredients:
- 1 pound extra-lean ground chicken
- 1/2 cup breadcrumbs
- 1/2 onion, grated
- 1 egg
- 2 garlic cloves, minced
- Salt and ground black pepper
- 2 tsp olive oil

Directions:
1. Combine the black pepper, salt, garlic, egg, onion, ground chicken, and 1/4 cup of breadcrumbs into the bowl.
2. Make patties from the mixture.
3. Place the remaining 1/4 cup of breadcrumbs into the dish and roll the patties into the breadcrumbs.
4. Add olive oil into the skillet and cook over medium-high flame.
5. Place patties in the oil and cook for five to six minutes.
6. Turnover and cook for three to four minutes.
7. Serve and enjoy!

Nutrition:
Calories: 238 | Fat: 7.8g | Carbs: 11.5g | Protein: 28.8g | Fiber: 0.7g

PUMPKIN WAFFLES

Prep Time: 10 minutes | **Cooking Time:** 20 minutes
Servings: 12
Ingredients:

Dry Ingredients:
- 2 cups all-purpose flour
- 1/4 cup brown sugar

- 1 tsp baking powder
- 1/2 tsp baking soda
- 1/4 tsp salt
- 1-2 tsp pumpkin spice
- 1 tsp cinnamon

Wet Ingredients:
- 3 eggs
- 1 1/3 cup milk
- 1/4 maple syrup
- 3 tbsp oil or melted butter
- 1 cup pumpkin

Directions:
1. Add dry ingredients into the bowl and stir well.
2. Whisk the melted butter, pumpkin, maple syrup, milk, and eggs into the jug.
3. Add wet ingredients to the dry ingredients and combine them well.
4. Place mixture into the waffle maker and bake for twenty minutes.
5. When done, serve and enjoy!

Nutrition:
Calories: 183 | Fat: 6g | Carbs: 28g | Protein: 5g | Fiber: 1.1g

BEAN SOUP

Prep Time: 5 minutes | **Cook Time:** 1 hour 15 minutes
Servings: 8
Ingredients:
- 16 oz beans
- 7 cups water
- 1 ham bone
- 2 cups ham, diced
- 1/4 cup onion, minced
- 1/2 tsp salt
- Ground black pepper, one pinch
- 1 bay leaf
- 1/2 cup carrots, sliced
- 1/2 cup celery, sliced

Directions:
1. Add rinsed beans into the pot and then add water and boil it for two minutes.
2. When done, remove from the flame. Cover with a lid and let sit for one hour.
3. Add bay leaves, pepper, salt, onion, cubed ham, and ham bone and boil it. Lower the heat and simmer for one hour and fifteen minutes.
4. Add celery and carrots and cook until tender.
5. Remove bone and ham bone and place them back in the soup.
6. Serve and enjoy!

Nutrition:
Calories: 247 | Fat: 3.8g | Carbs: 36.7g | Protein: 17.4g | Fiber: 0.5g

CARROT CUCUMBER SALAD

Prep Time: 20 minutes | **Chill time:** 4 hours
Servings: 4
Ingredients:
- 1/4 cup rice wine vinegar
- 2 tbsp fresh cilantro, snipped
- 1 tbsp sesame oil, toasted
- 1/4 tsp salt
- 1/8 tsp chili powder
- 1/8 tsp black pepper
- 1 cucumber, halved lengthwise and cut into slices
- 2 carrots, cut into matchstick-size pieces
- 1/2 red onion, thinly sliced

Directions:
1. Add black pepper, chili powder, salt, oil, cilantro, and vinegar into the bowl and whisk it well.
2. Add red onion, carrots, and cucumber and stir well. Toss to combine.
3. Let's chill for two to four hours.
4. Serve!

Nutrition:
Calories: 60 | Fat: 3.6g | Carbs: 8.2g | Protein: 0.9g | Fiber: 0.8g

LEMON CHICKEN AND RICE

Prep Time: 5 minutes | **Cook Time:** 20 minutes
Servings: 4
Ingredients:
- 2 tbsp butter
- 1 lb chicken breasts, cut into strips, boneless, skinless
- 1 onion, chopped
- 1 carrot, thinly sliced
- 2 garlic cloves, minced
- 1 tbsp cornstarch
- 14 oz chicken broth
- 2 tbsp lemon juice
- 1/4 tsp salt
- 1 cup frozen peas
- 1 1/2 cup uncooked instant rice

Directions:
1. Add butter into the skillet and cook over medium-high flame.
2. Then, add garlic, carrot, chicken, and onion and cook for five to seven minutes.
3. Combine the salt, lemon juice, broth, and cornstarch into the bowl, and then add to the skillet. Let cook and stir for one to two minutes.
4. Add peas and rice and stir well.
5. When done, remove from the flame.
6. Let stand for five minutes.
7. Serve and enjoy!

Nutrition:
Calories: 370 | Fat: 9g | Carbs: 41g | Protein: 29g | Fiber: 0.1g

PEACHY PORK WITH RICE

Prep Time: 5 minutes | **Cook Time:** 20 minutes
Servings: 4
Ingredients:
- 1 cup brown rice, cooked
- 1 lb pork tenderloin, cut into 1-inch cubes
- 2 tbsp olive oil
- 2 tbsp taco seasoning, low-sodium
- 1 cup salsa
- 3 tbsp peach preserves

Directions:
1. Add pork into the bowl and drizzle with oil. Sprinkle with taco seasoning and toss to combine.
2. Add pork into the skillet and cook for eight to ten minutes.
3. Add peach preserve and salsa and stir well.
4. Serve with cooked rice.

Nutrition:
Calories: 387 | Fat: 12g | Carbs: 42g | Protein: 25g | Fiber: 2.3g

SKILLET HAM AND RICE

Prep Time: 5 minutes | **Cook Time:** 20 minutes
Servings: 2
Ingredients:
- 1 tsp olive oil
- 1 onion, chopped
- 1 cup fresh mushrooms, sliced
- 1 cup ham, fully cooked, cubed
- 1/8 tsp pepper
- 1/2 cup chicken broth, low-sodium
- 1/4 cup water
- 1/4 cup uncooked instant rice
- 2 green onions, sliced
- 1/4 cup parmesan cheese, shredded

Directions:
1. Add oil into the skillet and cook over medium-high flame.
2. Add mushroom and onion and cook until tender.
3. Add water, pepper, broth, and ham and stir well.
4. Add rice and stir well. Lower the heat and simmer for five minutes.
5. Top with cheese and green onions.

Nutrition:
Calories: 322 | Fat: 8g | Carbs: 38g | Protein: 24g | Fiber: 2.2g

HONEY CHICKEN KABOBS

Prep Time: 15 minutes | **Cook Time:** 15 minutes
Servings: 12
Ingredients:
- 1/4 cup vegetable oil
- 1/3 cup honey
- 1/3 cup soy sauce
- 1/4 tsp ground black pepper
- 8 chicken breast halves, boneless, skinless, cut into 1-inch cubes
- 2 garlic cloves
- 5 onions, cut into 2-inch pieces
- 2 red bell peppers, cut into 2-inch pieces

Directions:
1. Add pepper, soy sauce, honey, and oil into the bowl and whisk it well.
2. Reserve a small amount of marinade for later use.
3. Add peppers, onions, garlic, and chicken into the bowl and marinate it in the refrigerator for two hours.
4. Preheat the grill over high heat.
5. Discard marinade from the vegetables and chicken and thread it onto the skewers.
6. Oil the grill grate. Place skewers onto the grill and cook for twelve to fifteen minutes.
7. Serve and enjoy!

Nutrition:
Calories: 179 | Fat: 6.6g | Carbs: 12.4g | Protein: 17.4g | Fiber: 0.8g

BAKED CHICKEN BREASTS

Prep Time: 15 minutes | **Cook Time:** 25 minutes
Servings: 4
Ingredients:
- 4 chicken breast halves, boneless, skinless
- 2 tbsp olive oil
- 1 tbsp coarse sea salt
- Creole seasoning
- 1 tbsp water

Directions:
1. Preheat the oven to 400°F.
2. Rub chicken breast with olive oil and season with creole seasoning and salt. Place onto the broiler pan.
3. Bake for ten minutes. Flip and cook for fifteen minutes more.
4. When done, remove the chicken from the pan.
5. Serve and enjoy!

Nutrition:
Calories: 191 | Fat: 9.6g | Carbs: 0.1g | Protein: 24.6g | Fiber: 2g

LOADED PUMPKIN CHOWDER

Prep Time: 10 minutes | **Cook Time:** 25 minutes
Servings: 2

Ingredients:
- 200 g pumpkin puree, mashed, peeled, boiled
- 200 ml water

- 200 g pumpkin, peeled, boiled and cut into chunks
- 1 carrot, peeled and julienned
- 2 tbsp extra-virgin olive oil
- 1 chicken breast, precooked
- 1/2 cup baby spinach, chopped
- 1 tsp celery powder
- 1 chicken stock cube, low-salted
- 1 bay leaf
- Salt and pepper to taste

Directions:
1. Add olive oil into the saucepan and heat it.
2. Add water, bay leaf, celery powder, and pureed pumpkin and simmer for ten minutes.
3. Add pumpkin chunks and shredded chicken to the pan and bring to simmer for five to seven minutes.
4. Add baby spinach and julienned carrot and cook for five minutes.
5. Discard bay leaf.
6. Serve!

Nutrition:
Calories: 127 | Fat: 2g | Carbs: 22g | Protein: 5g | Fiber: 4g

FISH STEW

Prep Time: 10 minutes | **Cook Time:** 20 minutes
Servings: 4
Ingredients:
- 6 extra virgin olive oil
- 1 onion, chopped
- 3 garlic cloves, minced
- 2/3 cup fresh parsley leaves, chopped
- 1 1/2 tomato, chopped
- 2 tsp tomato paste, optional
- 1 cup clam juice
- 1/2 cup dry white wine
- 1 1/2 lbs fish fillets, cut into pieces
- Pinch dried oregano
- Pinch dried thyme
- 1/8 tsp tabasco sauce
- 1/8 tsp freshly ground black pepper
- 1 tsp salt

Directions:
1. Add olive oil into the pot and cook over medium-high flame.
2. Add onion and cook for four minutes. Then, add garlic and cook for one minute more. Then, add parsley and cook for two minutes more.
3. Add tomato paste and tomato and cook for ten minutes more.
4. Add fish, dry white wine, and clam juice and simmer for three to five minutes. Then, place Tabasco, thyme, oregano, pepper, and salt.
5. Sprinkle with pepper and salt if needed. Place soup into the bowls.
6. Serve and enjoy!

Nutrition:
Calories: 389 | Fat: 23g | Carbs: 7g | Protein: 33g | Fiber: 2g

MUSHROOM SOUP

Prep Time: 10 minutes | **Cook Time:** 30 minutes
Servings: 4
Ingredients:
- 4 tbsp butter
- 1 tbsp oil
- 2 onions, diced
- 4 garlic cloves, minced
- 1 1/2 fresh brown mushrooms, sliced
- 4 tsp thyme, chopped
- 1/2 cup white wine
- 6 cups all-purpose flour
- 4 cups chicken broth or stock, low-sodium
- 1-2 tsp salt
- 1/2-1 tsp black cracked pepper
- 2 beef bouillon cubes, crumbled
- 1 cup heavy cream
- Fresh parsley and thyme, chopped, to serve

Directions:
1. Add oil and butter into the pot and cook over medium-high flame.
2. Then, add onion and cook for two to three minutes. Add garlic and cook for one minute more.
3. Add two tsp thyme and mushrooms and cook for five minutes.
4. Add wine and cook for three minutes.
5. Add flour over the mushrooms and cook for two minutes. Add stock and combine it well. Lower the heat and sprinkle with bouillon cubes, pepper, and salt.
6. Let simmer for ten to fifteen minutes.
7. Lower the heat and then add cream and stir well.
8. Sprinkle with pepper and salt if needed.
9. Sprinkle with fresh parsley and thyme.

Nutrition:
Calories: 271 | Fat: 13g | Carbs: 21g | Protein: 8g | Fiber: 4g

CHICKEN SOUP

Prep Time: 10 minutes | **Cook Time:** 30 minutes
Servings: 10
Ingredients:
- 3 pounds of whole chicken
- 4 carrots, halved
- 4 celery stalks, halved
- 1 onion, halved
- Water, to cover
- Salt and pepper, to taste
- 1 tsp chicken bouillon granules

Directions:
1. Add onion, celery, carrots, and chicken into the pot and then add cold water and simmer until chicken is tender.
2. Remove all content from the pot and then strain it through a strainer.

3. Chop the onion, celery, and carrots and remove the bones from the meat. Sprinkle with chicken bouillon, pepper, and salt.
4. Place onion, chicken, carrots, and celery back in the pot.
5. Stir and serve!

Nutrition:
Calories: 157 | Fat: 8.9g | Carbs: 4.2g | Protein: 13.1g | Fiber: 1.6g

PUMPKIN CASSEROLE

Prep Time: 5 minutes | **Cook Time:** 1 hour
Servings: 11
Ingredients:
- 2 cups pumpkin puree
- 1 cup evaporated milk
- 1 cup white sugar
- 1/2 cup self-rising flour
- 2 eggs
- 1 tsp vanilla extract
- 1/2 cup butter
- Ground cinnamon, two pinches

Directions:
1. Preheat the oven to 350°F.
2. Mix the ground cinnamon, melted butter, vanilla, eggs, flour, sugar, pumpkin, and evaporated milk. Place mixture into the casserole dish.
3. Place it into the oven and bake for one hour.
4. Serve and enjoy!

Nutrition:
Calories: 219 | Fat: 11g | Carbs: 27.2g | Protein: 3.7g | Fiber: 2.7g

FRESH TOMATO JUICE

Prep Time: 15 minutes | **Cook Time:** 40 minutes
Servings: 12
Ingredients:
- 10 lb tomatoes, washed, quartered, and cores removed
- Salt and black pepper, to taste
- 6 1/2 tbsp lemon juice
- Pepper, onion powder, paprika, cayenne, celery salt, chili powder or hot sauce, optional

Directions:
1. Prepare all ingredients.
2. Add tomatoes into the saucepan and simmer for thirty minutes until tender.
3. Place strainer over the bowl. Add tomatoes and separate the juice, seeds, skins, and chunks.
4. Place the remaining juice back in the pan and heat it.
5. Add pepper, lemon juice, and salt and boil it. Add optional seasoning if you want.
6. When done, transfer juice to the glass.

Nutrition:
Calories: 69 | Fat: 5.2g | Carbs: 15g | Protein: 3g | Fiber: 5.2g

CHICKEN CUTLETS

Prep Time: 10 minutes | **Cook Time:** 15 minutes
Servings: 4
Ingredients:
- 4 tsp red wine vinegar
- 2 tsp minced garlic cloves
- 2 tsp dried sage leaves
- 1 pound chicken breast cutlets
- Salt and pepper, to taste
- 1/4 cup refined white flour
- 2 tsp olive oil

Directions:
1. Set a good amount of plastic wrap on the kitchen counter; sprinkle with half the combined sage, garlic and vinegar.
2. Put the chicken breast on the plastic wrap; sprinkle with the rest of the vinegar mixture. Season lightly with pepper and salt.
3. Secure the chicken with the second sheet of plastic wrap. Use a kitchen mallet to pound the breast until it is flattened. Let stand for 5 minutes.
4. Set the chicken on both sides with flour. In a skillet, heat the oil over medium heat.
5. Add half of the chicken breast and cook for 1 1/2 minutes or until it is browned on the bottom.
6. Turn on the other side and let it cook for 3 minutes.
7. Remove the chicken breast and place it on an oven-proof serving plate so that you can keep it warm.
8. Reduce the liquid by half. Pour the mixture over the chicken breast; serve immediately.

Nutrition:
Calories: 549 | Fat: 6g | Carbs: 7g | Protein: 114g | Fiber: 4g

SLOW COOKER SALSA TURKEY

Prep Time: 8 minutes | **Cooking Time:** 7 hours
Servings: 4
Ingredients:
- 2 pounds of turkey breasts, boneless and skinless
- 1 cup salsa
- 1 cup small tomatoes, diced, canned choose low-sodium
- 2 tbsp taco seasoning
- 1/2 cup celery, finely diced
- 1/2 cup carrots, shredded
- 3 tbsp low-fat sour cream

Directions:
1. Add the turkey to your slow cooker. Season it with taco seasoning then top with salsa and vegetables.
2. Add in 1/2 cup of water. Set to cook on low for 7 hours (internal temperature should be 165°F when done).

3. Shred the turkey with 2 forks, add sour cream and stir. Enjoy.

Nutrition:
Calories: 178 | Fat: 4g | Carbs: 7g | Protein: 27g | Fiber: 6.1g

SRIRACHA LIME CHICKEN AND APPLE SALAD
Prep Time: 10 minutes | **Cook Time:** 15 minutes
Servings: 4
Ingredients:
Sriracha Lime Chicken:
- 2 organic chicken breasts
- 3 tbsp sriracha
- 1 lime, juiced
- 1/4 tsp fine sea salt
- 1/4 tsp freshly ground pepper

Fruit Salad:
- 4 apples, peeled, cored and diced
- 1 cup organic grape tomatoes
- 1/3 cup red onion, finely chopped

Lime Vinaigrette:
- 1/3 cup light olive oil
- 1/4 cup apple cider vinegar
- 2 limes, juiced
- A dash of fine sea salt

Directions:
1. Use salt and pepper to season the chicken on both sides. Spread on the sriracha and lime and let sit for 20 minutes.
2. Cook the chicken per side over medium heat, or until done. Grill the apple with the chicken.
3. Meanwhile, whisk together the dressing and season to taste.
4. Arrange the salad, topping it with red onion and tomatoes.
5. Serve as a side to the chicken and apple.

Nutrition:
Calories: 484 | Fat: 28g | Carbs: 32g | Protein: 30g | Fiber: 8g

PAN-SEARED SCALLOPS WITH LEMON-GINGER VINAIGRETTE
Prep Time: 10 minutes | **Cook Time:** 10 minutes
Servings: 2
Ingredients:
- 1 pound sea scallops
- 1 tbsp extra-virgin olive oil
- 1/4 tsp sea salt
- 2 tbsp lemon-ginger vinaigrette
- A pinch of freshly ground black pepper

Directions:
1. Heat the olive oil in a non-stick skillet or pan over medium-high heat until it starts shimmering.
2. Add the scallops to the skillet or pan after seasoning them with pepper and salt. Cook for 3 minutes per side or until the fish is only opaque.
3. Serve with a dollop of vinaigrette on top.

Nutrition:
Calories: 280 | Fat: 16g | Carbs: 5g | Protein: 29g | Fiber: 0g

ROASTED SALMON AND ASPARAGUS
Prep Time: 5 minutes | **Cook Time:** 15 minutes
Servings: 2
Ingredients:
- 1 tbsp extra-virgin olive oil
- 1 pound salmon, cut into two fillets
- 1/2 lemon zest and slices
- 1/2-pound asparagus spears, trimmed
- 1 tsp sea salt, divided
- 1/8 tsp freshly cracked black pepper

Directions:
1. Preheat the oven to 425°F.
2. Stir the asparagus with half of the salt and olive oil. At the base of a roasting tray, spread in a continuous sheet.
3. Season the salmon with salt and pepper. Place the asparagus on top of the skin-side down.
4. Lemon zest should be sprinkled over the asparagus, salmon, and lemon slices. Set them over the top.
5. Roast for around 15 minutes until the flesh of the fish is opaque, in the preheated oven.

Nutrition:
Calories: 308 | Fat: 18g | Carbs: 5g | Protein: 36g | Fiber: 2g

COD WITH GINGER AND BLACK BEANS
Prep Time: 10 minutes | **Cook Time:** 15 minutes
Servings: 2
Ingredients:
- 2 (6 oz) cod fillets
- 1/2 tsp sea salt, divided
- 3 minced garlic cloves
- 2 tbsp chopped fresh cilantro leaves
- 1 tbsp extra-virgin olive oil
- 1/2 tbsp grated fresh ginger
- 2 tbsp freshly ground black pepper
- 1/2 (14 oz) can of black beans, drained

Directions:
1. Heat the olive oil in a big non-stick skillet or pan over medium-high heat until it starts shimmering.
2. Half of the salt, ginger, and pepper are used to season the fish. Cook for around 4 minutes per side in the hot oil until the fish is opaque. Detach the cod from the pan and place it on a plate with aluminum foil tented over it.

3. Add the garlic to the skillet or pan and return it to the heat. Cook for 30 seconds while continuously stirring.
4. Mix the black beans and the remaining salt. Cook, stirring regularly, for 5 minutes.

5. Add the cilantro and serve the black beans on top of the cod.

Nutrition:
Calories: 419 | Fat: 2g | Carbs: 33g | Protein: 50g | Fiber: 8g

HALIBUT CURRY

Prep Time: 10 minutes | **Cook Time:** 10 minutes
Servings: 2
Ingredients:
- 1 tsp ground turmeric
- 1 pound halibut, skin, and bones removed, cut into 1-inch pieces
- 1/2 (14 oz) can of coconut milk
- 1/8 tsp ground black pepper
- 1 tbsp extra-virgin olive oil
- 1 tsp curry powder
- 2 cups of no-salt-added chicken broth
- 1/4 tsp sea salt

Directions:
1. Heat the olive oil in a non-stick skillet or pan over medium-high heat until it starts shimmering.
2. Add the curry powder and turmeric to a bowl. To bloom the spices, cook for 2 minutes, stirring continuously.
3. Stir in halibut, coconut milk, chicken broth, pepper, and salt. Lower the heat to medium-low and bring to a simmer. Cook, stirring regularly, for 6-7 minutes, or until the fish is opaque.

Nutrition:
Calories: 429 | Fat: 47g | Carbs: 5g | Protein: 27g | Fiber: 1g

CHICKEN CACCIATORE

Prep Time: 10 minutes | **Cook Time:** 20 minutes
Servings: 2
Ingredients:
- 1-pound skinless chicken, cut into bite-size pieces
- 1/4 cup black olives, chopped
- 1/2 tsp onion powder
- A pinch of freshly ground black pepper
- 1 tbsp extra-virgin olive oil
- 1 (28 oz) can of crushed tomatoes, drained
- 1/2 tsp garlic powder
- 1/4 tsp sea salt

Directions:
1. Heat the olive oil in a non-stick skillet or pan over medium-high heat until it starts shimmering.
2. Cook until the chicken is browned.
3. Add the tomatoes, garlic powder, olives, salt, onion powder, and pepper, then stir to combine. Cook, stirring regularly, for 10 minutes.

Nutrition:
Calories: 305 | Fat: 11g | Carbs: 34g | Protein: 19g | Fiber: 13g

CHICKEN AND BELL PEPPER SAUTÉ

Prep Time: 5 minutes | **Cook Time:** 15 minutes
Servings: 2
Ingredients:
- 1 chopped bell pepper
- 1-pound skinless chicken breasts, cut into bite-size pieces
- 1 1/2 tbsp extra-virgin olive oil
- 1/2 chopped onion
- 3 minced garlic cloves
- 1/8 tsp ground black pepper
- 1/4 tsp sea salt

Directions:
1. Heat the olive oil in a non-stick skillet or pan over medium-high heat until it starts shimmering.
2. Add the onion, red bell pepper, and chicken. Cook, stirring regularly, for 10 minutes.
3. Stir in the salt, garlic, and pepper in a mixing bowl. Cook for 30 seconds while continuously stirring.

Nutrition:
Calories: 179 | Fat: 13g | Carbs: 6g | Protein: 10g | Fiber: 1g

CHICKEN SALAD SANDWICHES

Prep Time: 15 minutes | **Cook Time:** 0 minutes
Servings: 2
Ingredients:
- 2 tbsp anti-inflammatory mayonnaise
- 1 tbsp chopped fresh tarragon leaves
- 1 cup chicken, chopped, cooked and skinless (from 1 rotisserie chicken)
- 1/2 minced red bell pepper
- 1 tsp Dijon mustard
- 4 slices of whole-wheat bread
- 1/4 tsp sea salt

Directions:
1. Combine the chicken, red bell pepper, mayonnaise, mustard, tarragon, and salt in a medium mixing bowl.
2. Spread on 2 pieces of bread and top with the remaining bread.

Nutrition:
Calories: 315 | Fat: 9g | Carbs: 30g | Protein: 28g | Fiber: 4g

ROSEMARY CHICKEN

Cook Time: 20 minutes | **Prep Time:** 15 minutes

Servings: 2

Ingredients:
- 1 tbsp extra-virgin olive oil
- 1 pound chicken breast tenders
- 1 tbsp chopped fresh rosemary leaves
- 1/8 tsp ground black pepper
- 1/4 tsp sea salt

Directions:
1. Preheat the oven to 425°F.
2. Set the chicken tenders on a baking sheet with a rim. Sprinkle with salt, rosemary, and pepper after brushing them with olive oil.
3. For 15-20 minutes, keep in the oven, just before the juices run clear.

Nutrition:
Calories: 389 | Fat: 20g | Carbs: 1g | Protein: 49g | Fiber: 1g

CRYSTALLIZED GINGER

Prep Time: 55 minutes | **Cook Time:** 45 minutes
Servings: 1

Ingredients:
- Ginger root
- 3 cups water
- 3 cups white sugar

Directions:
1. Peel the ginger and cut it into 1/8-inch-thick rounds.
2. You need 3 cups of water and 3 cups of sugar for each cup of prepared ginger.
3. Bring the water/sugar to a boil in a large saucepan and whisk to dissolve the sugar.
4. When the sugar has melted, add the ginger and cook for 45 minutes, virtually non-stop stirring.
5. You want the ginger to be soft and have a transparent appearance.
6. Drain the liquid from the ginger and set it aside.
7. Set it aside and dry it for about 30 minutes—it will be sticky—before coating it with sugar.
8. Put it to dry on waxed paper, which will take a few hours and a lot of slapping.
9. Keep the container airtight.
10. You can use the residual syrup in pancakes, waffles or ice cream by boiling it and reducing it to a syrup that tastes like a cross between maple syrup and honey.

Nutrition:
Calories: 421 | Fat: 15g | Carbs: 75g | Fiber: 2g

SCRAMBLED EGGS AND SMOKED SALMON CROISSANTS

Prep Time: 5 minutes | **Cook Time:** 45 minutes
Servings: 1

Ingredients:
- 4 large day-old all-butter croissants
- 12 large eggs
- 50 g cold unsalted butter, diced
- 4 tbsp double cream
- 1-2 tbsp snipped chives
- 300 g smoked salmon slices

Directions:
1. Trim the ends of the croissants before cutting them into 4 or 6 thick circles and season generously with salt and pepper.
2. Crack the eggs into a cold, heavy-bottomed nonstick skillet; do not season. Add a few knobs of butter to the skillet and bring to a simmer. Stir the eggs often but not continuously with a wooden spoon to mix the yolks and whites.
3. Remove the skillet from the heat when the eggs begin to scramble and scrape the egg off the sides and bottom of the skillet with a spatula. Return to the heat and continue to stir and scrape the pan until the eggs have the consistency of soft curds. This should take 5 to 6 minutes. Keep the mixture moist and soft by not overcooking it.
4. Meanwhile, toast the croissants in a dry skillet over medium heat for 1-2 minutes per side, until golden brown. Arrange the toasted pieces on separate plates.
5. Remove the pan from the heat when the eggs are almost done, add another knob of butter and season well. Return the pan to the heat and add the cream. Remove the pan from the heat when the butter has melted and mixed with the chives.
6. Place the scrambled eggs on the toasted croissants, top with pieces of smoked salmon and serve immediately.

Nutrition:
Calories: 428 | Fat: 21g | Carbs: 44g | Fiber: 3.1g

SANGO DE CHOCLO AND GREEN PLANTAINS WITH SHRIMP

Prep Time: 30 minutes | **Cook Time:** 35 minutes
Servings: 6

Ingredients:
- 2 lbs prawns
- 4 large corn of tender grain
- 2 large green plantains, raw, grated, or blended
- 1 tomato
- 1 pepper
- 1 medium onion
- 1 white onion branch
- 4 chopped parsley branches
- 6 tbsp oil
- 4 tbsp ground peanut
- 6 lemons

Directions:
1. Boil the shrimp in 6 cups of salted water, preferably with the shells on so that they release all the flavors, and peel them. This water is sieved and put in the sauce, which is already made with oil, tomato, peppers, onions, and spices.

2. When the water is boiling, the green corn is removed and grated or liquefied.
3. If they are large halves, add the shrimp, approximately 5 minutes before removing from the heat, mix and stir frequently for 25 minutes with a wooden spatula. If they are small and whole, additional water can be added according to the taste of the person doing the cooking. For me it is neither too soft nor too watery; it is a happy medium.
4. Add the chopped parsley just before serving. 1/2 cup of lemon to squeeze on each plate as requested by the diner. When serving, garnish with parsley.

Nutrition:
Calories: 328 | Fat: 32g | Carbs: 58g | Fiber: 5.2g

MINI PALEO SALMON CAKES AND LEMONY HERB AIOLI

Prep Time: 15 minutes | **Cook Time:** 40 minutes
Servings: 1
Ingredients:
- 12 oz cooked salmon
- 4 green onions
- 1 tbsp fresh parsley
- 1 tbsp Dijon mustard
- 1 tbsp lemon juice and zest
- 3 tbsp capers
- 1 egg
- Lemon wedges
- Lemon herb aioli
- 1 egg yolk
- 1 tbsp fresh lemon juice
- 1 large garlic clove
- 1 tbsp fresh parsley
- 1 tsp fresh dill
- 1/2 tsp ground black pepper
- 1/2 tsp Dijon mustard
- 1/2 cup olive oil
- 1/4 cup mashed sweet potato
- 3/4 tsp sea salt

Directions:
1. Preheat the oven to 350°F/180°C.
2. Combine all salmon cake ingredients in a large bowl. Using a fork, mix all ingredients. Place small patties in the baking pan, about 3 inches in diameter. Bake for 25-30 minutes, or until edges are firm and golden brown. Be sure to flip the patties halfway through the baking time.
3. Aioli with lemon and herbs
4. Make the aioli while the salmon cakes are baking. An immersion blender is the easiest method to create it, but it can also be made in a food processor, blender or electric mixer.
5. In a small bowl or blender/processor, combine the egg yolk, lemon juice and mustard. Begin whisking or combining all the ingredients until the mixture thickens. Next, slowly add the olive oil. Adding the oil is crucial, as too much at once can create a runny or watery aioli. Add more oil as the mixture thickens until you have a thick, creamy mayonnaise.
6. Combine the remaining lemon juice with the garlic, parsley and dill by hand. Season to taste with salt if necessary. Serve the aioli alongside the salmon cakes on a small plate. Refrigerate leftovers for up to one week in an airtight container.

Nutrition:
Calories: 528 | Fat: 25g | Carbs: 27g | Fiber: 3g

LOW FODMAP ONE PAN CHICKEN DINNER BAKE

Prep Time: 10 minutes | **Cook Time:** 45 minutes
Servings: 4
Ingredients:
- 1 1/2 lb skinless, boneless chicken thighs
- 1 lb scrubbed potatoes
- 1 cup of green beans
- 1 cup frozen carrots
- 1/4 cup unsalted butter
- 1 tsp kosher salt
- 1 tsp Italian herb seasoning
- 1/2 tsp ground black pepper
- 1/4 cup scallions

Directions:
1. Preheat the oven to 350°F. Using olive oil spray, coat a 13" x 9" baking pan.
2. Place the chicken thighs in the long center of the baking dish. Serve chicken with potatoes on one side and green beans and carrots on the other.
3. Mix the melted butter, salt, Italian herbs and pepper in a bowl. Over the chicken, potatoes and vegetables, drizzle the sauce. Finally, add the spring onions.
4. Cover the pan tightly with foil and bake for 1 hour and 15 minutes, or until the chicken is cooked through and the potatoes and vegetables are tender. Serve.

Nutrition:
Calories: 268 | Fat: 25g | Carbs: 22g | Fiber: 2.4g | Proteins: 15g

FRIENDLY CHICKEN FINGERS

Prep Time: 21 minutes | **Cook Time:** 40 minutes
Servings: 4
Ingredients:
- 1/2 cup low FODMAP breadcrumbs
- 1/4 cup freshly grated parmesan
- 1 tsp dried thyme
- Salt and pepper to taste
- 1 tsp dried parsley (crumbled)
- 1/4 cup rice flour
- 2 eggs
- 2-3 chicken breasts
- 2 tbsp olive oil

Directions:
1. Prepare a dish with bread crumbs, salt, parmesan, thyme and pepper and parsley.
2. In a small bowl, gently beat the eggs with a fork. Place the rice flour in a bowl and set aside with the other ingredients.
3. The chicken breasts should be cut into 1/4-1/2-inch slices. Dredge the chicken pieces in the rice flour, then in the egg to coat, and finally in the breadcrumb mixture, one at a time. Before removing the chicken strip from the mixture, pat it a few times so that the breadcrumbs adhere firmly.
4. Heat 1 tbsp of olive oil in the skillet after all the chicken strips have been coated. Add half of the chicken strips to the skillet when it is thoroughly heated. Cook, turning once, for 6 minutes. When needed, add the remaining oil.
5. Transfer the chicken strips to a rack to drain and cool after cooking is complete. Continue with the second batch.

Nutrition:
Calories: 274 | Fat: 13g | Carbs: 22g | Fiber: 1.4g

BEST LOW FODMAP CHOCOLATE CHIP COOKIES

Prep Time: 15 minutes | **Cook Time:** 50 minutes
Servings: 36
Ingredients:
- 1/2 cup butter softened
- 1/2 cup sugar
- 1/2 cup packed brown sugar
- 1 large egg
- 1/4 tsp salt
- 1 tsp vanilla
- 1/2 cup white rice flour
- 3 tbsp sweet/glutinous rice flour
- 3 tbsp tapioca starch
- 1/2 tsp xantham gum
- 1/4 cup almond flour
- 1/2 tsp baking soda
- 3/4 cup chocolate chips

Directions:
1. Preheat the oven to 325°F. Using parchment paper, line a baking sheet.
2. Allow 30 minutes for the butter to soften in a bowl at room temperature. Alternatively, you can heat the butter in the microwave on low until it softens, but does not melt.
3. In a large bowl, beat the butter and sugar with a fork until well blended. In a separate bowl, whisk together the egg, salt and vanilla extract.
4. Whisk together the flour, almond flour, xanthan gum and baking soda in a separate bowl. Gradually stir in the flour mixture until it is completely incorporated into the butter mixture. Add the chocolate chips and mix well.
5. Refrigerate or freeze the dough for at least 10 minutes.
6. Using a spoon, drop a spoonful of batter onto the baking sheet. Bake for about 10 minutes, or until the bottoms are lightly browned, and the tops are still soft (but not runny). Let them cool on the baking sheet for 5 minutes before transferring them to a cooling rack.

Nutrition:
Calories: 432 | Fat: 24g | Carbs: 54g | Fiber: 1.2g

LOW FODMAP MEDITERRANEAN GRILLED CHEESE

Prep Time: 15 minutes | **Cook Time:** 45 minutes
Servings: 1
Ingredients:
- 2 tsp butter
- 2 bread slices
- 2 Roma tomato slices
- 1/4 cup spinach leaves
- 2 tbsp pitted Kalamata olives
- 1 ounce sliced fresh mozzarella (28 grams)
- 1 tbsp feta cheese (10 grams)

Directions:
1. Spread both sides of each slice of low FODMAP bread with butter.
2. Combine tomato slices, olives, mozzarella, spinach, and feta cheese on one piece of bread. Place the second piece of bread on top of the first.
3. Heat the sandwich press. Grill (or cook in a skillet, rotating after 2-3 minutes per side) the sandwich until the bread is lightly browned and the cheese is melted.
4. Warm the dish before serving.

Nutrition:
Calories: 444 | Fat: 26g | Carbs: 34g | Fiber: 2.4g

LOW FODMAP BANANA NUT OATMEAL MUFFINS

Prep Time: 20 minutes | **Cook Time:** 35 minutes
Servings: 2
Ingredients:
- 2 large ripe bananas
- 2 1/2 cups quick oats
- 1 1/2 cups lactose-free milk
- 1/4 cup pure maple syrup
- 1 large egg, lightly beaten
- 2 tbsp canola oil
- 1 tsp baking powder
- 1 1/2 tsp ground cinnamon
- 1 tsp vanilla extract
- 1/4 tsp salt
- 1/2 cup chopped walnuts
- 1/4 cup enjoy life dairy-free mini chocolate chips

Directions:
1. Preheat the oven to 350°F and spray a 12-count nonstick muffin pan.
2. Mash the bananas with a fork in a large bowl.
3. Combine the oats and milk in a mixing bowl. Stir until everything is well blended. Let soak for 5 to

10 minutes, or until most of the liquid has been absorbed.
4. Add the maple syrup, egg, baking powder, canola oil, cinnamon, vanilla and salt to the oat mixture. Stir until well blended. Combine the nuts, chocolate, and chocolate chips in a mixing bowl.
5. Fill each muffin cup with one-third cup of batter. Bake for 30-35 minutes, or until the top is lightly browned and Boz back when touched gently in the center. Cool for 10 minutes in the pan before transferring to a cooling rack.
6. Refrigerate leftover muffins for up to two days or freeze in an airtight, resealable bag for up to 3 months.

Nutrition:
Calories: 428 | Fat: 2g | Carbs: 43g | Fiber: 3.2g

PUMPKIN OATMEAL MUFFINS WITH CHOCOLATE CHIPS

Prep Time: 15 minutes | **Cook Time:** 1 hour
Servings: 12
Ingredients:
- 2 1/2 cups quick oats
- 1 1/2 cups lactose-free milk
- 3/4 cup pumpkin puree
- 1/2 cup pure maple syrup
- 1 large egg, lightly beaten
- 2 tbsp canola oil
- 1 tsp baking powder
- 1 1/2 tsp ground cinnamon
- 3/4 tsp ground ginger
- 1/2 tsp ground nutmeg
- 1/4 tsp ground cloves
- 1/4 tsp salt
- 1/4 cup enjoy life dairy-free mini chocolate chips

Directions:
1. Preheat the oven to 350°F and spray a 12-count nonstick muffin pan.
2. Combine the oats, milk and pumpkin puree in a large bowl. Stir until no pumpkin lumps remain. Let stand for 5 to 10 minutes, or until most of the liquid has been absorbed.
3. Add the maple syrup, egg, cinnamon, ginger, canola oil, baking powder, nutmeg, cloves and salt to the oat mixture. Stir until everything is well blended. Add the chocolate or chocolate chips and stir to combine.
4. Fill each muffin cup with one-third cup of batter. Bake for 30-35 minutes, or until the top is lightly browned and Boz back when touched gently in the center. Cool for 10 minutes in the pan before transferring to a cooling rack.
5. Refrigerate leftover muffins for up to two days or freeze in an airtight, resealable bag for up to 3 months.

Nutrition:
Calories: 468 | Fat: 22g | Carbs: 32g | Fiber: 5.1g

FLAVORFUL SHRIMP KABOBS

Prep Time: 15 minutes | **Cook Time:** 8 minutes
Servings: 4
Ingredients:
- 1/4 cup olive oil
- 2 tbsp fresh lime juice
- 1 tsp honey
- 1/2 tsp paprika
- 1/4 tsp ground cumin
- Salt and freshly ground black pepper, to taste
- 1 lb. medium raw shrimp, peeled and deveined

Directions:
1. In a large bowl, add all the ingredients except for shrimp and mix well.
2. Add the shrimp and coat with the herb mixture generously.
3. Refrigerate to marinate for at least 30 minutes.
4. Preheat the grill to medium-high heat. Grease the grill grate.
5. Thread the shrimp onto pre-soaked wooden skewers.
6. Place the skewers onto the grill and cook for about 2-4 minutes per side.
7. Remove from the grill and place onto a platter for about 5 minutes before serving.

Nutrition:
Calories: 250 | Fat: 14.6g | Carbs: 3.4g | Fiber: 0.1g

PAN-SEARED SCALLOPS

Prep Time: 15 minutes | **Cook Time:** 7 minutes
Servings: 4
Ingredients:
- 1 1/4 lb. fresh sea scallops, side muscles removed
- Salt and freshly ground black pepper, to taste
- 2 tbsp olive oil
- 1 tbsp fresh parsley, minced

Directions:
1. Sprinkle the scallops with salt and black pepper.
2. In a large skillet, heat the oil over medium-high heat and cook the scallops for about 2-3 minutes per side.
3. Stir in the parsley and remove from the heat.
4. Serve hot.

Nutrition:
Calories: 185 | Fat: 8.1g | Carbs: 3.4g | Fiber: 0g

MEDITERRANEAN SHRIMP SALAD

Prep Time: 15 minutes | **Cook Time:** 3 minutes
Servings: 5
Ingredients:
- 1 lb. shrimp, peeled and deveined

- 1 lemon, quartered
- 2 tbsp olive oil
- 2 tsp fresh lemon juice
- Salt and freshly ground black pepper, to taste
- 3 tomatoes, peeled, seeded and sliced
- 1/4 cup olives, pitted
- 1/4 cup fresh cilantro, chopped finely

Directions:
1. In a pan of lightly salted water, add the quartered lemon and bring to a boil.
2. Add the shrimp and cook for about 2-3 minutes or until pink and opaque.
3. With a slotted spoon, transfer the shrimp into a bowl of ice water to stop the cooking process.
4. Drain the shrimp completely and then pat dry with paper towels.
5. In a small bowl, add the oil, lemon juice, salt, and black pepper, and beat until well combined.
6. Divide the shrimp, tomato, olives, and cilantro onto serving plates.
7. Drizzle with oil mixture and serve.

Nutrition:
Calories: 178 | Fat: 8g | Carbs: 5g | Fiber: 1.2g

HEALTH-CONSCIOUS PEOPLE'S SALAD

Prep Time: 15 minutes | **Cook Time:** 0 minutes
Servings: 2
Ingredients:
- 1/4 cup low-fat mozzarella cheese, cubed
- 1/4 cup tomato, peeled, seeded and chopped
- 1 tbsp fresh dill, chopped
- 1 tsp fresh lemon juice
- Salt, to taste
- 6 oz cooked salmon, chopped

Directions:
1. In a small bowl, add all the ingredients and stir to combine.
2. Serve immediately.

Nutrition:
Calories: 131 | Fat: 6g | Carbs: 1.9g | Fiber: 0.5g

ITALIAN PASTA SOUP

Cook Time: 25 minutes | **Prep Time:** 15 minutes
Servings: 5
Ingredients:
- 1 potato, peeled and chopped
- 1 carrot, peeled and chopped
- 5 1/4 cups chicken bone broth
- 1/2 cup tomato, peeled, seeded and chopped
- 3/4 lb. asparagus tips
- 1/2 cup cooked small pasta
- Salt and freshly ground black pepper, to taste

Directions:
1. In a pan, add the potato, carrot and broth over medium-high heat and bring to a boil.
2. Reduce the heat to low and cook, covered for about 15 minutes or until vegetables become tender.
3. Add the tomatoes and asparagus and cook for about 4-5 minutes.
4. Stir in the cooked pasta, salt and black pepper and cook for about 2-3 minutes.
5. Serve hot.

Nutrition:
Calories: 147 | Fat: 0.5g | Carbs: 23.2g | Fiber: 3g

PURE COMFORT SOUP

Cook Time: 20 minutes | **Prep Time:** 10 minutes
Servings: 4
Ingredients:
- 6 cups chicken bone broth
- 1/3 cup orzo
- 6 large egg yolks
- 1 1/2 cups cooked chicken, shredded
- 1/4 cup fresh lemon juice
- Salt and freshly ground black pepper, to taste

Directions:
1. In a large pan, add the broth over medium-high heat and bring to a boil.
2. Add the pasta and cook for about 8-9 minutes.
3. Slowly, add 1 cup of the hot broth, beating continuously.
4. Add the egg mixture to the pan, stirring continuously.
5. Reduce the heat to medium and cook for about 5-7 minutes, stirring, frequently.
6. Stir in the cooked chicken, salt and black pepper and cook for about 1-2 minutes.
7. Remove from the heat and serve hot.

Nutrition:
Calories: 269 | Fat: 8.7g | Carbs: 11.9g | Fiber: 0.6g

GOOF-FOR-YOU STEW

Cook Time: 18 minutes | **Prep Time:** 15 minutes
Servings: 8
Ingredients:
- 2 1/2 cups fresh tomatoes, peeled, seeded and chopped
- 4 cups fish bone broth
- 1 lb. salmon fillets, cubed
- 1 lb. shrimp, peeled and deveined
- 2 tbsp fresh lime juice
- Salt and freshly ground black pepper, to taste
- 3 tbsp fresh parsley, chopped

Directions:
1. In a large soup pan, add the tomatoes and broth and bring to a boil.
2. Reduce the heat to medium and simmer for about 5 minutes.
3. Add the salmon and simmer for about 3-4 minutes.
4. Stir in the shrimp and cook for about 4-5 minutes.

5. Stir in lemon juice, salt, and black pepper, and remove from heat.
6. Serve hot with the garnishing of parsley.

Nutrition:
Calories: 173 | Fat: 5.5g | Carbs: 3.2g | Fiber: 0.7g

ZERO-FIBER: CHICKEN DISH

Cook Time: 10 minutes | **Prep Time:** 16 minutes
Servings: 6
Ingredients:
- 4 (6-oz) boneless, skinless chicken breast halves
- Salt and freshly ground black pepper, to taste
- 2 tbsp olive oil

Directions:
1. Season each chicken breast half with salt and black pepper evenly.
2. Place chicken breast halves over a rack set in a rimmed baking sheet.
3. Refrigerate for at least 30 minutes.
4. Remove from refrigerator and pat dry with paper towels.
5. In a skillet, heat the oil over medium-low heat.
6. Place the chicken breast halves, smooth-side down, and cook for about 9-10 minutes, without moving.
7. Flip the chicken breasts and cook for about 6 minutes or until cooked through.
8. Remove from the heat and let the chicken stand in the pan for about 3 minutes.
9. Now, place the chicken breasts onto a cutting board.
10. Cut each chicken breast into slices and serve.

Nutrition:
Calories: 255 | Fat: 13.1g

CARROT GINGER SOUP

Prep Time: 20 minutes | **Cook Time:** 21 minutes
Servings: 4
Ingredients:
- 1 tbsp avocado oil
- 1 large yellow onion, peeled and chopped
- 1-pound carrots, peeled and chopped
- 1 tbsp fresh ginger, peeled and minced
- 1 1/2 tsp salt
- 3 cups vegetable broth

Directions:
1. Add the oil to the inner pot, allowing it to heat for 1 minute.
2. Add the onion, carrots, ginger, and salt then sauté for 5 minutes. Press the Cancel button.
3. Add the broth and secure the lid. Adjust the time to 15 minutes.
4. Blend the soup until smooth and then serve.

Nutrition:
Calories: 99 | Fat: 4g | Carbs: 16g | Fiber: 4g | Protein: 1g

ZUCCHINI, CASHEW, THYME SOUP

Prep Time: 10 minutes | **Cook Time:** 15 minutes
Servings: 4
Ingredients:
- 3 zucchini
- 1 green onion, green part only
- 1 cup raw cashews
- 3 thyme spears
- 1 tbsp fresh thyme leaves
- Salt and pepper, to taste

Directions:
1. Let soak the cashews in the boiled water.
2. Cut the green onion and zucchini into big chunks.
3. Add green onion and zucchini into the pot. Cover with water. Add thyme spears and bring to a boil for fifteen minutes.
4. Transfer it to the blender and blend until smooth.
5. Add pepper, salt, cashews, and one tbsp thyme leaves and blend until smooth.

Nutrition:
Calories: 181 | Fat: 7g | Carbs: 27g | Protein: 7g

HIGH-FIBER DIET: BREAKFAST

COCOA ALMOND FRENCH TOAST

Prep Time: 5 minutes | **Cook Time:** 5 minutes
Servings: 2
Ingredients:
- 1/2 cup unsweetened almond milk
- 1/3 cup thawed & frozen egg product
- 1/2 tsp ground cinnamon
- 1/2 tsp ground nutmeg
- 1/4 cup finely chopped dark chocolate-flavor almonds
- Cooking spray (Nonstick)
- 4 slices of light whole-wheat bread
- 2 tbsp chocolate-flavor syrup (sugar-free)
- 1/4 cup fresh raspberries

Directions:
1. Beat together eggs, almond milk, nutmeg & cinnamon in a shallow dish. For garnish, half a tbsp of the minced almonds should be set aside. In a separate shallow dish, put the leftover minced almonds.
2. Spray a skillet with non-stick cooking spray. Preheat the skillet to med heat. In the meantime, dip every piece of bread into an egg combination and flip to coat each side (around 10 seconds per side, soak the bread in egg mixture). In the almonds, Dip the soaked bread, making sure all sides are coated.
3. Fry slices of almond-coated bread for around four to six minutes on a warm skillet, or till its color changes to the golden brown, flipping once midway through. Using a sharp knife, cut the slices in half diagonally. Put the ingredients on two serving dishes.
4. Sprinkle the chocolate syrup on the slices of bread, garnish with raspberries. Drizzle with the remaining minced almonds.

Nutrition:
Calories: 250 | Fat: 11g | Carbs: 28g | Fiber: 8g | Protein: 15g

CHERRY SMOOTHIE

Prep Time: 5 minutes | **Cook Time:** 5 minutes
Servings: 1
Ingredients:
- 1/2 cup oat milk
- 1 tbsp almond butter
- 1 tsp cocoa powder
- 1/2 tsp vanilla extract
- 1 cup dark sweet cherries (frozen)
- 1 tbsp (Optional) brown sugar

Directions:
1. In the blender, put the almond butter, oat milk, vanilla, cocoa, sugar (if using) & cherries, then process it till smooth.

Nutrition:
Calories: 232 | Fat: 9g | Carbs: 31g | Fiber: 6g | Protein: 6g

HAM & EGG BREAKFAST BURRITO

Prep Time: 10 minutes | **Cook Time:** 10 minutes
Servings: 1
Ingredients:
- 2 tbsp mild salsa
- 1 ounce reduced-sodium & low-fat thinly sliced cooked ham
- 1 to 2 dashes of hot pepper sauce (bottled)
- 1/4 cup refrigerated egg product
- 1 warmed reduced-carb whole-wheat tortilla (high-Fiber)

Directions:
1. With cooking spray, lightly coat the non-stick pan. Put ham, hot pepper sauce & salsa; heat it for three minutes. Put the egg product; lower the heat to medium.
2. Cook it without whisking, till the mixture starts to set around the edge & on the bottom. Use the spatula/large spoon to lift & fold the somewhat cooked egg combination so that the uncooked part flows beneath.
3. Continue cooking till the egg combination is fully cooked however is still moist or glossy (cook for around two to three minutes).
4. Into the tortilla, Put the egg combination. Roll up the tortilla.

Nutrition:
Calories: 157 | Fat: 4g | Carbs: 22g | Fiber: 13g | Protein: 18g

PB & J OATS

Prep Time: 5 minutes | **Cook Time:** 10 minutes
Servings: 2
Ingredients:
- 1 1/3 cup water
- 2/3 cup 5-grain rolled cereal
- 1/4 tsp salt
- 1 tbsp creamy peanut butter
- 1 tbsp strawberry preserves (sugar-free)
- 2 sliced strawberries

Directions:
1. Combine oats, salt & water in a big microwave-safe bowl. Microwave it for three to five minutes.

Remove & wait for one to two minutes. Firmly whisk peanut butter with oats for around twenty seconds.
2. In a microwave-safe bowl, Put the strawberry preserves & microwave them for around ten seconds or till the preserves are fully warmed & thinned.
3. Split the oats between 2 bowls & sprinkle with the strawberry. Top every bowl with some strawberry slices.

Nutrition:
Calories: 179 | Fat: 5g | Carbs: 28g | Fiber: 6g | Protein: 7g

ARTICHOKE & EGG TARTINE

Prep Time: 5 minutes | **Cook Time:** 10 minutes
Servings: 1
Ingredients:
- 1 tsp extra-virgin olive oil
- 1/2 cup finely minced, thawed & frozen artichoke hearts
- 1 sliced scallion
- 1/4 tsp dried oregano
- 1/8 tsp ground pepper
- 1 slice of toasted whole-wheat bread
- 2 fried eggs

Directions:
1. In the small pan, heat the oil. Put scallion, artichoke hearts, pepper & oregano, and fry till hot. Scatter on the toast & garnish with eggs.

Nutrition:
Calories: 314 | Fat: 16g | Carbs: 23g | Fiber: 9.1g | Protein: 19g

STRAWBERRY-PINEAPPLE SMOOTHIE

Prep Time: 15 minutes | **Cook Time:** 5 minutes
Servings: 1
Ingredients:
- 1 cup frozen strawberries
- 1 cup minced fresh pineapple
- 3/4 cup cold unsweetened almond milk
- 1 tbsp almond butter

Directions:
1. Combine pineapple, strawberries, almond butter & almond milk in the mixer. Process till smooth. If required, put additional almond milk for preferred consistency. Serve instantly.

Nutrition:
Calories: 255 | Fat: 11g | Carbs: 39g | Fiber: 12.1g | Protein: 5g

PEACH-BLUEBERRY PARFAITS

Prep Time: 5 minutes | **Cook Time:** 5 minutes
Servings: 2
Ingredients:
- 6 oz fat-free blueberry yogurt
- 1 cup multi-grain clusters cereal
- 1 pitted & cut up peach
- 1/2 cup fresh blueberries
- 1/4 tsp ground cinnamon

Directions:
1. Split half yogurt between 2 dessert bowls/glasses; garnish with cereal half. Garnish with the blueberries/peach's half & the cinnamon. Repeat the layers with leftover cereal, yogurt, blueberries & peaches.

Nutrition:
Calories: 166 | Fat: 1g | Carbs: 34g | Fiber: 9.2g | Protein: 11g

SOUTHWEST BREAKFAST QUESADILLA

Prep Time: 5 minutes | **Cook Time:** 10 minutes
Servings: 1
Ingredients:
- Cooking spray
- 1/4 cup thawed & frozen egg product
- 1/8-1/4 tsp southwest chipotle seasoning mix (salt-free)
- 1 whole-wheat flour tortilla
- 2 tbsp chopped part-skim mozzarella cheese
- 2 tbsp rinsed & drained canned black beans (no salt)
- 2 tbsp frozen fresh Pico de gallo

Directions:
1. With the non-stick cooking spray, spray a med non-stick pan. Preheat the pan on med heat. Put the egg on a hot pan, and drizzle with seasoning mix. Cook on med heat, without whisking, till egg starts to set around the edge & on the bottom. Use the large spoon or spatula to lift & fold a somewhat cooked egg allowing the uncooked part to flow beneath. Carry on cooking on med heat for thirty to sixty seconds or till the egg is fully cooked.
2. Instantly put the cooked egg into the tortilla on one side. Garnish with beans, cheese, & Pico de Gallo (2 tbsp.) Fold the tortilla across the filling to cover, press nicely.
3. With a paper towel, Clean the same pan. Spray the pan with cooking spray. Pan Preheated on med heat. In the hot pan, cook the filled tortilla for around two minutes or till the tortilla color changes to brown & the filling is fully heated, flipping once. Garnish with extra Pico de Gallo.

Nutrition:
Calories: 175 | Fat: 5g | Carbs: 24g | Fiber: 13.6g | Protein: 19g

RASPBERRY YOGURT CEREAL BOWL

Prep Time: 5 minutes | **Cook Time:** 5 minutes
Servings: 1
Ingredients:
- 1 cup nonfat yogurt
- 1/2 cup mini sliced-wheat cereal
- 1/4 cup refreshing raspberries
- 2 tsp small chocolate chips
- 1 tsp pumpkin seeds
- 1/4 tsp ground cinnamon

Directions:
1. In the bowl, put the yogurt & top with chopped raspberries, wheat, pumpkin seeds, cinnamon & chocolate chips.

Nutrition:
Calories: 290 | Fat: 2g | Carbs: 47g | Fiber: 6.4g | Protein: 18g

BEAN & BACON BREAKFAST TACOS

Prep Time: 5 minutes | **Cook Time:** 10 minutes
Servings: 1
Ingredients:
- 1 tsp extra-virgin olive oil
- 1 cup finely minced kale
- 1/2 cup rinsed canned cannellini beans (reduced-sodium)
- 2 warmed corn tortillas
- 1 tbsp shredded Cheddar cheese
- 1 piece of crumbled cooked bacon

Directions:
1. In a med skillet, Heat the oil on med heat. Put kale & beans, then cook, whisking, till hot, around two minutes. Enjoy in corn tortillas garnished with bacon & cheese.

Nutrition:
Calories: 282 | Fat: 12g | Carbs: 33g | Fiber: 8.4g | Protein: 12g

PEANUT BUTTER & FIG CRISPBREADS

Prep Time: 5 minutes | **Cook Time:** 5 minutes
Servings: 1
Ingredients:
- 2 ryes crispbreads
- 2 tbsp natural peanut butter
- 4 sliced dried figs
- 2 tbsp pepitas
- 1 tsp coconut flakes

Directions:
1. Garnish every crispbread with half the fig slices, one tbsp peanut butter, half tsp coconut flakes & one tsp pepitas.

Nutrition:
Calories: 407 | Fat: 20g | Carbs: 45g | Fiber: 8.3g | Protein: 11g

STRAWBERRY-RICOTTA WAFFLE SANDWICH

Prep Time: 5 minutes | **Cook Time:** 5 minutes
Servings: 1
Ingredients:
- 1/4 cup whole-milk ricotta cheese
- 1 tsp minced fresh mint/basil
- 1/2 tsp vanilla extract
- 2 frozen & toasted whole-grain waffles
- 2 tsp pure maple syrup
- 1/2 cup sliced fresh strawberries

Directions:
1. In the small bowl, combine mint/basil, vanilla & ricotta. With 1 tsp syrup, sprinkle every waffle.
2. Garnish one waffle with the ricotta mixture & strawberries, then cover with the remaining waffle.

Nutrition:
Calories: 313 | Fat: 13g | Carbs: 43g | Fiber: 8.9g | Protein: 12g

MAKE-&-TAKE BREAKFAST SAUSAGE SANDWICH

Prep Time: 5 minutes | **Cook Time:** 5 minutes
Servings: 2
Ingredients:
- English muffins (light multi-grain), cover with the remaining waffle.
- 2 frozen turkey sausage patties (cooked)
- 1/2 ounce low-fat cheddar cheese
- 4 tsp mango chutney

Directions:
1. Divide & toast your English muffins. In the meantime, put the frozen sausage patties in the microwave as per the instructions.
2. As toasted muffins are hot, put the cheese slice at every English muffin's bottom. Garnish cheese with the sausage patty, English muffin tops & mango chutney.

Nutrition:
Calories: 229 | Fat: 8g | Carbs: 33g | Fiber: 9g | Protein: 15g

LOADED PITA POCKETS

Prep Time: 5 minutes | **Cook Time:** 5 minutes
Servings: 1
Ingredients:
- 1 whole halved wheat pita
- 1/2 cup reduced-fat cottage cheese
- 4 chopped walnut halves
- 1 sliced small banana

Directions:

1. Fill every pita half with walnuts, banana & cottage cheese.

Nutrition:
Calories: 307 | Fat: 2g | Carbs: 46g | Fiber: 12.6g | Protein: 21g

WEST COAST AVOCADO TOAST

Prep Time: 5 minutes | **Cook Time:** 5 minutes
Servings: 1
Ingredients:
- 1 cup mixed salad greens
- 1 tsp red wine vinegar
- 1 tsp additional-virgin olive oil
- Pinch of pepper
- Pinch of salt
- 2 slices of toasted whole-wheat bread (sprouted)
- 1/4 cup plain hummus
- 1/4 cup alfalfa sprouts
- 1/4 sliced avocado
- 2 tsp sunflower seeds (unsalted)

Directions:
1. Toss the greens with oil, vinegar, pepper & salt in the bowl. Scatter every toast slice with two tbsp of hummus. Garnish with avocado, sprouts & greens, then drizzle with the sunflower seeds.

Nutrition:
Calories: 429 | Fat: 3g | Carbs: 46g | Fiber: 16g | Protein: 16g

MANGO RASPBERRY SMOOTHIE

Prep Time: 5 minutes | **Cook Time:** 5 minutes
Servings: 1
Ingredients:
- 1/2 cup water
- 1/4 med avocado
- 1 tbsp lemon juice
- 3/4 cup frozen mango
- 1/4 cup frozen raspberries

Directions:
1. In the mixer, put water, lemon juice, avocado, raspberries, agave & mango. Combine till smooth.

Nutrition:
Calories: 188 | Fat: 7g | Carbs: 32g | Fiber: 9g | Protein: 1g

PEANUT BUTTER & CHIA BERRY JAM ENGLISH MUFFIN

Prep Time: 5 minutes | **Cook Time:** 5 minutes
Servings: 1
Ingredients:
- 1/2 cup frozen unsweetened combined berries
- 2 tsp chia seeds
- 2 tsp peanut butter
- 1 toasted wheat English muffin

Directions:
1. In a med microwave-safe bowl, microwave the berries for thirty seconds; whisk & microwave it for another thirty seconds. Whisk in chia seeds.
2. On the English muffin, Scatter the peanut butter. Garnish with the berry-chia combination.

Nutrition:
Calories: 262 | Fat: 9g | Carbs: 40g | Fiber: 10g | Protein: 10g

GREEN EGGS & HAM BAGEL BREAKFAST SANDWICH

Prep Time: 2 minutes | **Cook Time:** 3 minutes
Servings: 1
Ingredients:
- 3 oz halved wheat bagel
- 1 slice of reduced-sodium Swiss cheese
- 1 slice of Canadian bacon
- 1 tsp extra-virgin olive oil
- 1 egg
- 1/2 cup coarsely minced baby spinach
- Ground pepper pinch

Directions:
1. Toast your bagel. Put the Canadian bacon & cheese on the bottom half.
2. In a pan (non-stick), heat the oil on med-high heat. Put spinach, pepper & egg, then cook, whisking, till set, around one minute.
3. Put the egg combination on the bacon & cheese. Season with the leftover bagel half. Slice in half & serve.

Nutrition:
Calories: 446 | Fat: 17g | Carbs: 50g | Fiber: 8.3g | Protein: 26g

PUMPKIN PIE SMOOTHIE

Prep Time: 5 minutes | **Cook Time:** 5 minutes
Servings: 1
Ingredients:
- 1 frozen banana
- 1/2 cup unsweetened almond milk
- 1/2 cup whole-milk Greek yogurt
- 1/2 cup canned pumpkin puree
- 1/8 tsp pumpkin pie spice
- 1 to 2 tsp pure maple syrup

Directions:
1. Put the almond milk, yogurt, banana, pumpkin pie spice, maple syrup & pumpkin puree. Process it till smooth.

Nutrition:
Calories: 247 | Fat: 6g | Carbs: 41g | Fiber: 6g | Protein: 10g

PEANUT BUTTER-CHOCOLATE CHIP OVERNIGHT OATS WITH BANANA

Prep Time: 10 mins | **Cook Time:** 8 hours 20 mins
Servings: 4
Ingredients:
- 2 cups divided unsweetened almond milk
- 4 tbsp divided natural peanut butter
- 8 tsp divided pure maple syrup
- 2 cups divided rolled oats
- 4 pinches divided salt
- 4 tbsp divided mini chocolate chips
- 2 halved & divided bananas

Directions:
1. Mix 1 tbsp peanut butter, 2 tsp maple syrup & 1/2 cup milk in a bowl/mason jar; whisk till blended. Whisk in half cup oats, 1 tbsp chocolate chips & a pinch of salt.
2. Use the different bowls for every serving; go over with the leftover ingredients. Cover-up & refrigerate it overnight. Cut half the banana into every serving before serving.

Nutrition:
Calories: 409 | Fat: 15g | Carbs: 59g | Fiber: 8.1g | Protein: 10g

BAKED BANANA CUPS

Prep Time: 15 minutes | **Cook Time:** 50 minutes
Servings: 12
Ingredients:
- 3 cups rolled oats
- 1 1/2 cups low-fat milk
- 2 mashed ripe bananas
- 1/3 cup packed brown sugar
- 2 lightly beaten eggs
- 1 tsp baking powder
- 1 tsp ground cinnamon
- 1 tsp vanilla extract
- 1/2 tsp salt
- 1/2 cup toasted & chopped pecans

Directions:
1. Oven Preheated to 375°F. With cooking spray, coat the muffin tin.
2. Combine the milk, oats, brown sugar, bananas, baking powder, eggs, vanilla, salt & cinnamon in the bowl. Fold up the pecans.
3. Split the combination of around 1/3 cup each between the muffin cups. Bake till the toothpick injected in the middle gets out clean, around twenty-five minutes.
4. Let it cool in the skillet for ten minutes, then put it on the wire rack.

Nutrition:
Calories: 176 | Fat: 6g | Carbs: 26g | Fiber: 7.4g | Protein: 5g

PEANUT BUTTER-BANANA ENGLISH MUFFIN

Prep Time: 5 minutes | **Cook Time:** 5 minutes
Servings: 1
Ingredients:
- 1 toasted whole-wheat English muffin
- 1 tbsp peanut butter
- 1/2 sliced banana
- Ground cinnamon, pinch

Directions:
1. Garnish English muffin with banana, cinnamon & peanut butter.

Nutrition:
Calories: 330 | Fat: 10g | Carbs: 56g | Fiber: 9g | Protein: 10g

WHITE BEAN & AVOCADO TOAST

Prep Time: 5 minutes | **Cook Time:** 5 minutes
Servings: 1
Ingredients:
- 1 slice of toasted whole-wheat bread, 1 slice
- 1/4 mashed avocado
- 1/2 cup rinsed & drained canned white beans
- Ground pepper & Kosher salt, to taste
- 1 pinch of crushed red pepper

Directions:
1. Garnish toast with white beans & mashed avocado. Top with a pinch of pepper, crushed red pepper & salt.

Nutrition:
Calories: 230 | Fat: 2g | Carbs: 34g | Fiber: 11.5g | Protein: 11g

BERRY-ALMOND SMOOTHIE BOWL

Prep Time: 5 minutes | **Cook Time:** 10 minutes
Servings: 1
Ingredients:
- 2/3 cup frozen raspberries
- 1/2 cup frozen sliced banana
- 1/2 cup unsweetened almond milk
- 5 tbsp divided sliced almonds
- 1/4 tsp ground cinnamon
- 1/8 tsp ground cardamom
- 1/8 tsp vanilla extract
- 1/4 cup blueberries
- 1 tbsp unsweetened coconut flakes

Directions:
1. In the blender, put banana, raspberries, 3 tbsp almonds, almond milk, cardamom, vanilla & cinnamon & process it tills very smooth.
2. In the bowl, put the smoothie & garnish with 2 tbsp almonds, coconut & blueberries.

Nutrition:
Calories: 350 | Fat: 19g | Carbs: 45g | Fiber: 15.5g | Protein: 9g

AVOCADO TOAST WITH BURRATA

Prep Time: 5 minutes | **Cook Time:** 5 minutes
Servings: 1
Ingredients:
- 1 slice of whole-grain toast
- 1/2 thinly sliced ripe avocado
- 1 tsp lemon juice
- 1/8 tsp kosher salt
- 1/8 tsp ground pepper
- 1 1/2 oz fresh mozzarella cheese
- 1 tbsp thinly sliced fresh basil
- 1 tsp chopped fresh chives
- Aleppo pepper, pinch

Directions:
1. With avocado, Top the toast. Sprinkle with lemon juice & season with pepper & salt. Garnish with basil, burrata/mozzarella, Aleppo pepper & chives.

Nutrition:
Calories: 439 | Fat: 28g | Carbs: 36g | Fiber: 12g | Protein: 18g

BAKED OATMEAL

Prep Time: 10 minutes | **Cook Time:** 30 minutes
Servings: 6
Ingredients:
- 1/2 cup (125 g) applesauce
- 3/4 cup (170 g) brown sugar
- 2 eggs
- 1 cup (235 ml) skim milk
- 3 cups (240 g) quick-cooking oats
- 2 tsp baking powder
- 1/2 tsp cinnamon
- 1 cup (80 g) chopped walnuts

Directions:
1. Combine the applesauce, sugar, eggs, and milk; mix well.
2. Merge remaining ingredients and then combine with the first mixture.
3. Bake in a 9 x 13-inch (23 x 33 cm) pan coated with non-stick vegetable oil spray for 30 minutes at 350°F (180°C, gas mark 4). Serve with hot milk.

Nutrition:
Calories: 329 | Fat: 17g | Carbs: 9g | Fiber: 5.1g | Protein: 37g

HOMESTYLE PANCAKE MIX

Cook Time: 30 minutes | **Prep Time:** 10 minutes
Servings: 16
Ingredients:
- 6 cups whole-wheat pastry flour
- 1 1/2 cups (210 g) cornmeal
- 1/2 cup (100 g) sugar
- 1 1/2 cups (102 g) non-fat dry milk
- 2 tbsp (28 g) baking powder

Directions:
1. Merge all ingredients and store them in a tightly covered jar. To cook, add 1 cup of water to 1 cup of the mix; use less water if you want a thicker pancake. Stir only until lumps disappear.
2. Coat a non-stick skillet or griddle with non-stick vegetable oil spray and preheat until drops of cold-water bounce and sputter.
3. Drop the batter to the desired size and cook until bubbles form and edges begin to dry. Turn only once.

Nutrition:
Calories: 75 | Fat: 1.7g | Carbs: 0.1g | Fiber: 14g | Protein: 13.4g

MULTIGRAIN PANCAKES

Prep Time: 10 minutes | **Cook Time:** 30 minutes
Servings: 6
Ingredients:
- 1 1/2 cup whole-wheat pastry flour
- 1/4 cup cornmeal
- 1/4 cup rolled oats
- 2 egg whites
- 2 tbsp oat bran
- 2 tbsp wheat germ
- 2 tbsp toasted wheat cereal, such as Wheaten
- 1 tsp baking soda
- 1/2 tsp baking powder
- 1 tsp vanilla extract
- 1 1/2 cups (355 ml) skim milk

Directions:
1. Create a thick batter by mixing the dry ingredients with milk. Let stand for 30 minutes.
2. At the same time, beat the egg whites until they form peaks and, after resting, incorporate them into the batter.
3. Pour onto the griddle and cook the pancakes on both sides.

Nutrition:
Calories: 303 | Fat: 14g | Carbs: 15g | Fiber: 10g | Protein: 30g

CINNAMON-OAT BRAN PANCAKES

Prep Time: 10 minutes | **Cook Time:** 30 minutes
Servings: 6

Ingredients:
- 3/4 cup oat bran (75 g)
- 3/4 cup whole-wheat pastry flour
- 1 tbsp sugar
- 1/2 tsp baking powder
- 1/2 tsp cinnamon
- 1/4 tsp baking soda
- 1 1/4 cup buttermilk (295 ml)
- 1 tbsp canola oil (15 ml)
- 1/2 cup finely chopped pecans (55 g)

Directions:
1. In a medium mixing bowl, combine all dry ingredients. Set aside.
2. In another mixing bowl, combine the buttermilk and oil. Add to dry ingredients, stirring until just combined. Stir in the pecans.
3. Cook on the hot griddle. Set 1/4 cup of the batter for each pancake.

Nutrition:
Calories: 297 | Fat: 11g | Carbs: 18g | Fiber: 11g | Protein: 34g

WHOLE-WHEAT BUTTERMILK PANCAKES

Prep Time: 10 minutes | **Cook Time:** 30 minutes
Servings: 6
Ingredients:
- 1 cup whole-wheat flour
- 1/2 tsp baking soda
- 1/4 tsp cinnamon
- 1 1/4 cup buttermilk
- 2 eggs
- 3 tbsp canola oil

Directions:
1. Blend all dry ingredients. Merge the wet ingredients except for oil. Mix both mixtures. It will be slightly lumpy. Heat oil in a cast-iron skillet.
2. Pour 1/4 of the batter into the pan. When the pancake bubbles, turn and cook for 1-2 minutes more.

Nutrition:
Calories: 207 | Fat: 16g | Carbs: 5g | Fiber: 7g | Protein: 12g

CORNMEAL PANCAKES

Prep Time: 10 minutes | **Cook Time:** 30 minutes
Servings: 6
Ingredients:
- 1 cup (235 ml) boiling water
- 3/4 cup (105 g) cornmeal
- 1 1/4 cup (295 ml) buttermilk
- 2 eggs
- 1 cup whole-wheat pastry flour
- 1 tbsp baking powder
- 1/4 tsp baking soda
- 1/4 cup (60 ml) canola oil

Directions:
Mix water and cornmeal until a thick mixture is created. Beat eggs and add buttermilk, baking powder, and baking soda. Add to cornmeal mixture. Add canola oil.
Bake the pancakes on a hot griddle.

Nutrition:
Calories: 280 | Fat: 16g | Carbs: 5g | Fiber: 5g | Protein: 29g

OVEN-BAKED PANCAKE

Prep Time: 10 minutes | **Cook Time:** 30 minutes
Servings: 6
Ingredients:
- 3 eggs
- 1/2 cup whole-wheat pastry flour
- 1/2 cup (120 ml) skim milk
- 1/4 cup (55 g) unsalted butter, divided
- 2 tbsp (26 g) sugar
- 2 tbsp (18 g) slivered almonds, toasted
- 2 tbsp (30 ml) lemon juice

Directions:
1. Set the eggs with an electric mixer at medium speed until well blended. Gradually add flour, beating until smooth. Add milk and 2 tbsp (28 g) melted butter; beat until the batter is smooth.
2. Pour the batter into a 10-inch (25 cm) skillet coated with non-stick vegetable oil spray. Bake at 400°F for 15 minutes until the pancake is puffed and golden brown.
3. Sprinkle with sugar and toasted almonds. Combine the remaining butter and lemon juice; heat until butter melts. Serve over the hot pancake.

Nutrition:
Calories: 429 | Fat: 47g | Carbs: 5g | Fiber: 10g | Protein: 27g

BAKED PANCAKE

Prep Time: 10 minutes | **Cook Time:** 30 minutes
Servings: 4
Ingredients:
- 1 1/2 cup whole-wheat pastry flour
- 1 1/2 cup (355 ml) skim milk
- 4 eggs, slightly beaten
- 1/4 cup (55 g) unsalted butter
- 1 cup (170 g) sliced strawberries

Directions:
1. Gradually, add flour and milk to the eggs. Melt the butter in 9 x 13-inch (23 x 33 cm) pan.
2. Pour the batter over melted butter. Bake at 400°F for about 30 minutes.
3. Serve with fresh sliced strawberries.

Nutrition:
Calories: 270 | Fat: 11g | Carbs: 4g | Fiber: 4.3g | Protein: 39g

WHEAT WAFFLES

Prep Time: 10 minutes | **Cook Time:** 30 minutes
Servings: 8
Ingredients:
- 2 cups whole-wheat pastry flour
- 4 tsp (18 g) baking powder
- 2 tbsp (40 g) honey
- 1 3/4 cup (410 ml) skim milk
- 4 tbsp (60 ml) canola oil
- 2 eggs

Directions:
1. Mix all dry ingredients. Stir in the remaining ingredients. For lighter waffles, separate the eggs. Beat the egg whites and carefully fold in.
2. Set into a waffle iron coated with non-stick vegetable oil spray.

Nutrition:
Calories: 389 | Fat: 20g | Carbs: 1g | Fiber: 5g | Protein: 49g

OATMEAL WAFFLES

Prep Time: 10 minutes | **Cook Time:** 30 minutes
Servings: 5
Ingredients:
- 1 1/2 cup whole-wheat pastry flour
- 1 cup (80 g) quick-cooking oats
- 1 tbsp baking powder
- 1 tsp cinnamon
- 2 tbsp (30 g) brown sugar
- 3 tbsp (42 g) unsalted butter
- 1 1/2 cup (355 ml) skim milk
- 2 eggs, slightly beaten

Directions:
1. In a bowl, merge all dry ingredients and set aside. Melt the butter, and add milk and eggs. Mix well and then add to the flour mixture. Stir until well blended.
2. Set into a waffle iron coated with non-stick vegetable oil spray.

Nutrition:
Calories: 224 | Fat: 14g | Carbs: 15g | Fiber: 2g | Protein: 12g

BRAN APPLESAUCE MUFFINS

Prep Time: 10 minutes | **Cook Time:** 30 minutes
Servings: 12
Ingredients:
- 3/4 cup (30 g) bran flakes cereal, crushed
- 1/2 cup (100 g) sugar
- 1 tsp baking soda
- 1 tsp cinnamon
- 1/2 tsp nutmeg
- 1 cup (245 g) applesauce
- 1/2 cup (120 ml) canola oil
- 1 tsp vanilla extract
- 2 eggs
- 1/2 cup (75 g) raisins
- 1 tbsp sugar
- 1/2 tsp cinnamon

Directions:
1. Heat the oven to 400°F (200°C, gas mark 6). Set 12 muffin cups with baking paper or sprinkle with non-stick vegetable oil spray.
2. In a bowl, combine all ingredients except the sugar and cinnamon; mix well. Set the batter into the prepared muffin cups, filling 2/3 full. In a bowl, combine the sugar and cinnamon; sprinkle over the top of each muffin. Bake at 400°F for 20 minutes or until a toothpick inserted in the center comes out clean. Immediately remove from pan. Serve warm.

Nutrition:
Calories: 270 | Fat: 11g | Carbs: 4g | Fiber: 4.6g | Protein: 39g

OAT BRAN MUFFINS

Prep Time: 10 minutes | **Cook Time:** 17 minutes
Servings: 12
Ingredients:
- 2 1/4 cup (225 g) oat bran
- 1 tbsp baking powder
- 1/4 cup (35 g) raisins
- 1/4 cup (28 g) chopped pecans
- 2 eggs
- 2 tbsp (28 ml) olive oil
- 1/4 cup (85 g) honey
- 1 1/4 cup (295 ml) water

Directions:
1. Heat the oven to 425 F.
2. Place raisins, pecans, and all dry ingredients in a bowl.
3. Lightly beat in the eggs, olive oil, honey, and water. Mix this mixture with the dry ingredients.
4. Line muffin tins with paper liners and spread the mixture. Bake for 17 minutes.
5. Serve.

Nutrition:
Calories: 270 | Fat: 11g | Carbs: 4g | Fiber: 4.8g | Protein: 39g

ORANGE BRAN MUFFINS

Prep Time: 10 minutes | **Cook Time:** 25 minutes
Servings: 12
Ingredients:
- 2 1/2 cups (300 g) whole-wheat pastry flour
- 1 tbsp baking soda
- 3 cups (177 g) raisin bran cereal
- 1/2 cup (100 g) sugar
- 1 tsp cinnamon
- 1 1/2 tbsp orange peel
- 2 cups (460 g) plain fat-free yogurt
- 2 eggs, beaten
- 1/2 cup (120 ml) cooking oil

Directions:
1. In a bowl, merge flour and baking soda. Add the cereal, sugar, cinnamon, and orange peel, mixing well.
2. Briefly, but thoroughly mix in the yogurt, beaten eggs, and cooking oil. Set into muffin tins lined with paper liners or sprayed with non-stick vegetable oil spray.
3. Bake for 20 minutes in a 375°F (190°C, gas mark 5) oven.

Nutrition:
Calories: 270 | Fat: 11g | Carbs: 4g | Fiber: 5.8g | Protein: 39g

PASTA FRITTERS

Prep Time: 10 minutes | **Cook Time:** 30 minutes
Servings: 6
Ingredients:
- 2 cups (280 g) leftover spaghetti
- 1/4 cup (25 g) chopped scallions
- 1/2 cup (56 g) shredded zucchini
- 78 ml canola oil
- 1 egg
- 1 cup whole-wheat pastry flour
- 1 tsp black pepper
- 1 cup (235 ml) water

Directions:
1. About 35 minutes before serving, coarsely chop the cooked spaghetti, onions, and shred zucchini; set aside. In a 12-inch (30 cm) skillet, over high heat, heat canola oil until very hot.
2. Meanwhile, prepare the batter. In a bowl, with a wire whisker or fork, mix the egg, flour, pepper, and water.
3. Stir in the spaghetti mixture. Drop it into hot oil in the skillet by 1/4 cup into 4 mounds about 2 inches (5 cm) apart. With a spatula, flatten each to make 3-inch (7.5 cm) pancake.
4. Set the fritters until golden brown on both sides; drain them on paper towels. Keep warm. Repeat with the remaining mixture, adding more oil to the skillet if needed.

Nutrition:
Calories: 178 | Fat: 4g | Carbs: 7g | Fiber: 10g | Protein: 27g

CINNAMON HONEY SCONES

Prep Time: 10 minutes | **Cook Time:** 20 minutes
Servings: 5
Ingredients:
- 1 3/4 cup (220 g) whole-wheat pastry flour
- 1 1/2 tsp baking powder
- 1/4 tsp cinnamon
- 6 tbsp (85 g) unsalted butter, softened
- 1 tbsp (20 g) honey
- 1/2 cup (120 ml) skim milk
- 1 egg

Directions:
1. Preheat the oven to 450°F (230°C, gas mark 8). Line a baking sheet with aluminum foil.
2. In a bowl, merge the flour, baking powder, and cinnamon with a wooden spoon. Work the butter into the mixture by hand until it is yellow.
3. Add honey and milk, then the egg. Stir with a wooden spoon until thoroughly mixed.
4. Scoop a spoonful of dough and drop it onto the baking sheet. Leave 1 inch (2.5 cm) between each. Bake for 15 minutes or until golden brown. Cool for 5 minutes.

Nutrition:
Calories: 179 | Fat: 13g | Carbs: 6g | Fiber: 13g | Protein: 10g

OATMEAL RAISIN SCONES

Prep Time: 10 minutes | **Cook Time:** 20-25 minutes
Servings: 5
Ingredients:
- 2 cups whole-wheat pastry flour
- 3 tbsp (45 g) brown sugar
- 1 tsp baking powder
- 1/2 tsp baking soda
- 1/2 cup unsalted butter, chilled
- 1 1/2 cup (120 g) rolled oats
- 1/2 cup (75 g) raisins
- 1 cup (235 ml) buttermilk
- 2 tbsp cinnamon
- 2 tbsp (26 g) sugar

Directions:
1. Heat the oven to 375°F (190°C, gas mark 5). Merge flour, brown sugar, baking powder, and baking soda. Divide in the butter until the mixture resembles coarse crumbs.
2. Stir in oats and raisins. Add the buttermilk and mix with a fork until the dough forms a ball. Set out on a lightly floured board and knead for 6-8 minutes. Pat the dough into 1/2-inch (1 cm) thickness. Divide 8-10 rounds or wedges and place them on

an ungreased baking sheet. Sprinkle with sugar and cinnamon.
3. Bake for 20-25 minutes.

Nutrition:
Calories: 329 | Fat: 17g | Carbs: 9g | Fiber: 10g | Protein: 37g

WHOLE GRAIN SCONES

Prep Time: 10 minutes | **Cook Time:** 30 minutes
Servings: 5
Ingredients:
- 1 egg
- 1/2 cup (100 g) sugar
- 5 tbsp (75 ml) canola oil
- 1 tsp lemon peel
- 1/2 cup (40 g) rolled oats
- 1/4 cup (25 g) wheat bran
- 1 1/2 cup whole-wheat pastry flour
- 2 tbsp poppy seeds
- 1 tbsp baking powder
- 1/2 tsp cinnamon
- 1/2 cup (120 ml) skim milk

Lemon Topping:
- 3 tbsp (45 ml) lemon juice
- 1/4 cup (25 g) confectioners' sugar

Directions:
1. Preheat the oven to 375 F.
2. In a bowl, combine the oil, eggs, and sugar. In a separate bowl, mix all dry ingredients and lemon zest.
3. Mix the two preparations to create a thick dough. Add the milk and mix well. Divide the dough onto a baking sheet greased with vegetable oil, creating ten scones.
4. Bake until the crust is just golden brown and let cool for 10 minutes.
5. Mix the lemon topping ingredients and spread over each scone.

Nutrition:
Calories: 280 | Fat: 16g | Carbs: 5g | Fiber: 9g | Protein: 29g

GRANOLA

Prep Time: 10 minutes | **Cook Time:** 30 minutes
Servings: 30
Ingredients:
- 6 cups (480 g) rolled oats
- 6 cups rolled wheat
- 2 cups (290 g) sunflower seeds
- 4 oz (113 g) sesame seeds
- 2 cups (190 g) peanuts
- 3 cups (255 g) coconut
- 1 cup (112 g) wheat germ
- 1 1/2 cup (355 ml) canola oil
- 1 cup (340 g) honey
- 1/2 cup (170 g) molasses
- 1 tbsp (15 ml) vanilla extract
- 1 cup (145 g) raisins

Directions:
1. Merge all dry ingredients in a large bowl. Put aside.
2. Heat the oil, honey, molasses, and vanilla together and mix with the dry ingredients. Spread the mixture on baking sheets.
3. Bake at 350°F until light brown. Stir frequently to brown evenly. Detach from the oven and add the raisins or any other dried fruit.

Nutrition:
Calories: 270 | Fat: 11g | Carbs: 4g | Fiber: 7g

TOASTY NUT GRANOLA

Prep Time: 10 minutes | **Cook Time:** 35 minutes
Servings: 30
Ingredients:
- 6 cups (480 g) rolled oats
- 1 cup (110 g) chopped pecans
- 3/4 cup (84 g) wheat germ
- 1/2 cup (115 g) firmly packed brown sugar
- 1/2 cup (40 g) shredded coconut
- 1/2 cup (72 g) sesame seeds
- 1/2 cup (120 ml) canola oil
- 1/2 cup (170 g) honey
- 1 1/2 tsp vanilla extract

Directions:
1. Toast the oats in a 9 x 13-inch (23 x 33 cm) pan at 350°F (180°C, gas mark 4) for 10 minutes.
2. Merge the remaining ingredients in a large bowl and add the toasted oats.
3. Bake on 2 baking sheets at 350°F (180°C, gas mark 4) for 20-25 minutes. Stir when cool and store in the refrigerator.

Nutrition:
Calories: 270 | Fat: 11g | Carbs: 4g | Fiber: 6.2g | Protein: 39g

BREAKFAST BARS

Prep Time: 10 minutes | **Cook Time:** 30 minutes
Servings: 30
Ingredients:
- 1 cup (80 g) quick-cooking oats
- 1/2 cup whole-wheat flour
- 1/2 cup (58 g) crunchy wheat-barley cereal, such as Grape-Nuts
- 1/2 tsp cinnamon
- 1 egg
- 1/4 cup (60 g) applesauce
- 1/4 cup (85 g) honey
- 3 tbsp (45 g) brown sugar
- 2 tbsp (28 ml) canola oil
- 1/4 cup (36 g) sunflower seeds, unsalted
- 1/4 cup (30 g) chopped walnuts
- 7 oz (198 g) dried fruit

Directions:
1. Heat the oven to 325 F.
2. Line a baking sheet with aluminum foil and spray with nonstick vegetable oil.
3. Mix the flour, cereal, oats, and cinnamon in a bowl. Add and mix well together brown sugar, applesauce, egg, honey, and oil. Also, add nuts, sunflower seeds, and dried fruit. Spread the mixture evenly in the prepared baking dish.
4. Place in the oven and bake for 30 minutes. Allow cooling.
5. Cut into small bars and store in the refrigerator.

Nutrition:
Calories: 280 | Fat: 16g | Carbs: 5g | Fiber: 9.1g | Protein: 29g

WHOLE-WHEAT COFFEE CAKE

Prep Time: 10 minutes | **Cook Time:** 30-45 minutes
Servings: 12
Ingredients:
For the cake:
- 1 3/4 cup (210 g) whole-wheat pastry flour
- 1 tsp baking powder
- 1 tsp baking soda
- 1/2 cup (112 g) unsalted butter, softened
- 1 cup (133 g) sugar
- 2 eggs
- 1 tsp vanilla extract
- 1 cup (230 g) sour cream

For the Bran Nut Filling:
- 1 cup (75 g) packed brown sugar
- 1/2 cup bran flakes (20 g) cereal
- 1/2 cup (60 g) chopped walnuts
- 1 tsp cinnamon

Directions:
For the cake:
1. Merge flour, baking powder, and baking soda; set aside.
2. In a large bowl, beat the butter, sugar, eggs, and vanilla until light and fluffy. On low speed, mix and add the sour cream alternately with the flour mixture until properly blended.

For the Bran Nut Filling:
3. Combine all filling ingredients in a small bowl. To assemble the cake, spread 1/3 of the sour cream mixture in a 9-inch (23 cm) square pan coated with non-stick vegetable oil spray.
4. Sprinkle on about 1/2 cup of the filling. Repeat layering twice. Bake in a preheated oven at 350°F (180°C, gas mark 4) for 30-45 minutes. Cool slightly.

Nutrition:
Calories: 224 | Fat: 14g | Carbs: 15g | Fiber: 6.3g | Protein: 12g

BLACK BEANS AND AVOCADO TOASTS

Prep Time: 5 minutes | **Cook Time:** 15 minutes
Servings: 2
Ingredients:
- 2 slices of bread of your choice
- 1/2 avocado
- 4 tbsp boiled black beans
- 2 tbsp chopped green onions
- 1/2 lime
- 1/4 tsp sea salt

Directions:
1. Mash the avocado and spread it on the bread pieces.
2. Serve with black beans and green onion on top.
3. Sprinkle salt and lemon juice on top of each.
4. Serve as fast as possible!

Nutrition:
Calories: 64 | Carbs: 0g | Protein: 5g | Fat: 17g | Fiber: 13.6g

APPLES N' OATS BREAKFAST SMOOTHIE

Prep Time: 10 minutes | **Cook Time:** 10 minutes
Servings: 4
Ingredients:
- 2 cup milk of choice (non-dairy or dairy)
- 2 large or 2 small apples, any variety
- 1/3 cup old fashioned rolled oats
- 2 tbsp hemp hearts (can substitute chia or flaxseed)
- 3 tbsp almond butter
- 1/2 tsp ground cinnamon
- 1/2 cup ice (optional, to make it cold)

Directions:
1. In a blender, combine the milk and oats. Allow the oats to soften for a few minutes.
2. Peel and core the apple. If desired, peel.
3. Fill the blender halfway with the remaining ingredients. Puree until completely smooth. Can be made a day ahead of time and refrigerated, and covered.

Note: If adding flax or chia seeds, add 1/4 to 1/2 cup extra liquid to prevent the smoothie from becoming too thick.

Nutrition:
Calories: 358 | Carbs: 3g | Protein: 33 g | Fat: 12g | Fiber: 3.5g

CRUNCHY BREAKFAST TOPPING

Prep Time: 10 minutes | **Cook Time:** 30 minutes
Servings: 12

Ingredients:
- 1/4 cup (55 g) unsalted butter

- 1 1/4 cup (140 g) wheat germ
- 1/2 cup packed brown sugar
- 1/2 cup (47 g) ground almonds
- 1 tbsp grated orange peel
- 1/2 tsp cinnamon

Directions:
1. Melt the butter in a 9 x 13-inch (23 x 33 cm) baking pan in the oven for about 4 minutes.
2. Add the remaining ingredients and mix well. Bake until deep golden brown. Stir.
3. Cool and store in the refrigerator for up to 3 months.

Nutrition:
Calories: 178 | Fat: 4g | Carbs: 7g | Fiber: 9g | Protein: 27g

VEGETABLES AND FRUITS BREAKFAST

Prep Time: 10 minutes | **Cook Time:** 55 minutes
Servings: 6
Ingredients:
- 1/4 cup (60 ml) olive oil
- 2 baking potatoes, peeled and thinly sliced
- 1 cup (160 g) thinly sliced onion
- 2 cups (226 g) thinly sliced zucchini
- 1 cup red bell pepper, cut into 1/2-inch (1 cm) cubes
- 1 cup green bell pepper, cut into 1/2-inch (1 cm) cubes
- 12 eggs
- 2 tbsp chopped fresh parsley
- Salt and pepper

Directions:
1. Heat the oven to 450 F.
2. Pour oil into a square baking dish. Arrange potatoes and onion and bake for 20 minutes.
3. Arrange the zucchini slices, onion, and peppers on top of the potatoes. Arrange the eggs over the vegetables and season with salt, pepper, and chopped parsley. Bake for about 25 minutes until the top is golden brown.

Nutrition:
Calories: 270 | Fat: 11g | Carbs: 4g | Fiber: 11g | Protein: 39g

BLUEBERRY COCONUT SMOOTHIE BOWL

Prep Time: 5 minutes | **Cook Time:** 5 minutes
Servings: 1
Ingredients:
- 3 tbsp (15 g) unsweetened shredded coconut
- 3/4 cup unsweetened almond milk
- serving vegan vanilla protein powder
- 2 cup (125 g) frozen zucchini chunks
- 1/2 cup (50 g) frozen cauliflower
- 1/2 cup (75 g) frozen blueberries
- 1 tbsp Ceylon cinnamon (optional)
- Pinch of Himalayan crystal salt or another unrefined sea salt (optional, do not use table salt)

Directions:
1. In a high-speed blender, combine the coconut and liquid and mix for about a minute on high.
2. Add the other ingredients and process until thick and creamy. To keep it from thinning out, don't over-mix or leave it in the blender for too long, since the heat from the blender can melt it.
3. Scoop the mixture into a bowl, top with your preferred toppings, and serve with a spoon!

Nutrition:
Calories: 206 | Carbs: 36g | Protein: 21g | Fat: 19g | Fiber: 10g

NO-BAKE APRICOT OAT PROTEIN BARS

Prep Time: 30 minutes | **Cook Time:** 30 minutes
Servings: 10
Ingredients:
- 1/2 cup pumpkin seeds
- 4 cup gluten-free rolled oats
- 1/2 cup flax
- 3 cup dried Turkish Apricots (+ extra chopped for topping)
- Pinch of sea salt
- Hot water
- 1/2 tbsp cinnamon
- 1/4 cup of maple syrup (or honey if not vegan)
- 1/2 cup of vanilla protein powder (vegan)
- optional toppings
- 1/4 cup (optional) melting dark Chocolate (vegan/gluten-free)

Directions:
1. Combine the pumpkin, gluten-free oats, and flax. Blend until a "mealy" batter is produced (in a blender or food processor).
2. Pour the batter into a mixing basin.
3. Next, blend/pulse the apricots until they are finely chopped/diced. Blend in with the oats. Combine the protein powder, salt, and cinnamon in a mixing bowl.
4. Combine your maple syrup or honey, 1/3 cup boiling water, and vanilla essence in a separate small mixing dish. Stir everything together and add it to the dry ingredients (the apricot/oat/protein mixture).
5. Mix with hands, then press into a baking dish. Top with additional chopped apricots and oats. Add vegan chocolate (dark chocolate) here if desired.
6. Allow bars to chill in the refrigerator to set. Approximately 30 minutes.
7. When the batter has been set, cut it into 10 squares.
8. Store in the refrigerator.

Nutrition:
Calories: 232 | Carbs: 25g | Protein: 13g | Fat: 1.7g | Fiber: 13.5g

CINNAMON APPLE OMELET

Prep Time: 10 minutes | **Cook Time:** 30 minutes
Servings: 2
Ingredients:
- 4 tsp unsalted butter, divided
- 1 apple, peeled and thinly sliced
- 1/2 tsp cinnamon
- 1 tbsp (15 g) brown sugar
- 3 eggs
- 1 tbsp cream
- 1 tbsp sour cream

Directions:
1. Melt half the butter in a frying pan. Add the apple, brown sugar, and cinnamon and sauté until tender. Transfer to a bowl and set aside.
2. Beat eggs and cream until frothy and set aside. Add the second half of melted butter to this mixture.
3. Cook as for an omelet. Add the sour cream to the center of the eggs and top with the apple mixture. Fold over and serve.

Nutrition:
Calories: 389 | Carbs: 1g | Protein: 49g | Fat: 20 g | Fiber: 6g

MANGO GINGER SMOOTHIE

Prep Time: 5 minutes | **Cook Time:** 0 minutes
Servings: 1
Ingredients:
- 1/2 cup red lentils, cooked cooled
- 1 cup mango chunks, frozen
- 3/4 cup carrot juice
- 1 cup fresh ginger, chopped
- 1 tsp honey
- Ground cardamom, one pinch
- 3 ice cubes

Directions:
1. Add all ingredients into the blender and blend on high, about two to three minutes.
2. Garnish with cardamom.

Nutrition:
Calories: 352 | Carbs: 78.9g | Protein: 12.3g | Fat: 1.1g | Fiber: 46g

CINNAMON AND VANILLA CANTALOUPE SMOOTHIE

Prep Time: 5 minutes | **Cook Time:** 0 minutes
Servings: 2
Ingredients:
- 1 cantaloupe, peeled, deseeded and roughly chopped
- 1/2 tsp cinnamon
- 1 cup ice
- Seeds from 1/2 vanilla pod
- 1-2 tbsp raw honey

Directions:
1. Place all ingredients and ice in a blender and blend until smooth.

Nutrition:
Calories: 230 | Carbs: 19g | Protein: 20g | Fat: 13g | Fiber: 5.1g

WILD BLUEBERRY AND CHERRY SMOOTHIE

Prep Time: 5 minutes | **Cook Time:** 0 minutes
Servings: 2
Ingredients:
- 2 bananas fresh or frozen
- 1 cup fresh or frozen cherries pitted
- 1 tbsp wild blueberry powder
- 1/2 cup squeezed orange juice, fresh
- Water, enough to blend

Directions:
1. Place all ingredients in a blender and blend till very smooth. Pour it into glasses and serve.

Nutrition:
Calories: 220 | Carbs: 15g | Protein: 20g | Fat: 12g | Fiber: 4.1g

PEANUT BUTTER CHIA OVERNIGHT OATS

Prep Time: 10 minutes | **Cook Time:** 30 minutes
Servings: 1
Ingredients:
Scale:
- 3/4 cup rolled oats
- 2 tbsp chia seeds
- 1/2 tsp cinnamon
- Pinch of sea salt
- 2 cups unsweetened vanilla almond milk (or any plant milk)
- 1/2 cup filtered water
- 3 tsp vanilla extract (optional)
- 2 ripe bananas, mashed (but leave a few banana coins for topping!)
- 3 tbsp of PB Fit powder + 1 1/2 tbsp of water (or any nut butter, to taste)
- 1-2 tbsp maple syrup or agave for extra sweetness

Extras/Toppings:
- Crushed almonds
- Sliced banana coins
- Extra sprinkles of cinnamon!
- Cacao nibs (optional)
- Coconut flakes

Directions:
1. In a mason jar, combine the oats, chia seeds, cinnamon, and sea salt. Mix in the almond milk, water, vanilla extract, and mashed banana. Stir everything together until it's smooth.

2. In a small mixing dish, combine the PB powder and water until smooth. You may double the ingredients to get even more peanut butter taste! Pour the "peanut butter" mixture into the mason jar. Toppings can be added now or in the morning!

PUMPKIN PIE CHIA PUDDING

Prep Time: 10 minutes | **Cook Time:** 180 minutes
Servings: 2
Ingredients:
- 1/2 cup raw pecans
- 1/2 cup pumpkin puree (canned or fresh)
- 1/2 cups almond milk
- 2 tsp cinnamon
- 1/2 tsp ground ginger
- 1/2 tsp nutmeg
- Pinch of sea salt
- 1/4 cup chia seeds
- Optional toppings: fresh fruit, nut butter, whipped cream, cinnamon

Directions:
1. Toasted pecans Allow a small skillet to heat up over medium-low heat for about 30 seconds.

2 MINUTE FLOURLESS ENGLISH MUFFIN

Prep Time: 1 minute | **Cook Time:** 2 minutes
Servings: 1
Ingredients:
- 1/3 cup rolled oats (gluten-free, if necessary)
- 2 tbsp chia
- 1/2 tsp baking powder
- 2 tbsp unsweetened applesauce
- 3 tbsp milk of choice
- Optional: a pinch of salt

Directions:
1. Combine the oats, chia seeds, baking powder, and salt in a blender. Blend on high until the mixture is finely ground.

BLUEBERRY MUFFINS

Prep Time: 45 minutes | **Cook Time:** 15 minutes
Servings: 12
Ingredients:
- 1 ¾ cups almond flour
- ¼ cup coconut flour
- 1 tablespoon baking powder
- ¼ teaspoon baking soda
- ¼ teaspoon salt
- 1 cup blueberries
- 3 large eggs
- ½ cup reduced-fat milk
- ⅓ cup plus 2 tablespoons light brown sugar
- ¼ cup avocado oil
- 1 ½ teaspoons vanilla extract

3. Refrigerate for at least four hours or overnight. Using a spoon, dig in and enjoy!

Nutrition:
Calories: 55 | Carbs: 10g | Protein: 13g | Fat: 1g | Fiber: 6.5g

Toast the nuts for 4-5 minutes, stirring continuously, until golden brown.
2. In a high-powered blender or food processor, combine pecans, pumpkin, almond milk, cinnamon, ginger, nutmeg, and salt. About 1-2 minutes, process until smooth and all ingredients are mixed.
3. Transfer to a resealable medium-sized bowl. Stir in the chia seeds until well combined. Cover and place in the refrigerator for 3 hours or overnight.
4. Serve plain or with preferred toppings. Enjoy!

Nutrition:
Calories: 410 | Carbs: 27g | Protein: 38g | Fat: 18g | Fiber: 4.5g

2. Transfer to a mixing dish and stir in the applesauce and non-dairy milk to make a sticky dough.
3. Place the dough in a ramekin and press it down.
4. Microwave on high for 2 minutes.
5. Allow it to cool for 5 minutes before taking it from the ramekin.
6. Cut in half, toast, and serve with desired toppings.

Nutrition:
Calories: 174 | Carbs: 22g | Protein: 7g | Fat: 6g | Fiber: 3.1g

Directions:
1. Heat oven to 350 F and coat a muffin pan with cooking spray.
2. Combine almond flour, coconut flour, blueberries, baking powder, baking soda, and salt in a large bowl.
3. Beat milk, eggs, oil, brown sugar, and vanilla in another bowl.
4. Now add the dry ingredients from the first bowl and mix until combined.
5. Divide the batter among the muffin cups.
6. Bake the muffins for about 25 minutes.
7. Let them cool in the pan for 20 minutes.

Nutrition:
Calories: 203 | Carbs: 12g | Protein: 6.8g | Fat: 10g | Fiber: 5.1g

LUNCH

PACKED BURRITO

Prep Time: 10 minutes | **Cook Time:** 10 minutes
Servings: 4
Ingredients:
- 1/2 of medium red onion (chopped)
- 2 garlic cloves (minced)
- 12 oz of extra firm tofu
- 2 Tbsp olive oil
- 1/4 tbsp turmeric
- 1/4 tbsp cumin
- Sea salt & to taste
- 1/2 cup of black beans
- 1/2 of avocado (chopped into small pieces)
- 1/3 cup of salsa any of choice (For example: Pico de Gallo)
- 3 large whole-wheat tortillas

Directions:
1. Heat the oil in a medium-sized pan over medium heat. Once cooked, add your onions and season with salt and pepper. Cook until the mixture has been cooked down and color gently (about 4-5 minutes). Cook for another minute, frequently stirring, after adding your garlic.
2. Tofu should be added at this point. Stir in the turmeric, cumin, and another sprinkle of sea salt. Stir until completely mixed. Turn off the heat.
3. To construct your burritos, arrange all of your ingredients.
4. You may freeze them by placing them in a tight plastic bag.

Nutrition:
Calories: 519 | Carbs: 17g | Protein: 27g | Fat: 18g | Fiber: 15g

BLOOD ORANGE CHIA PUDDING

Prep Time: 5 minutes | **Cook Time:** 5 minutes
Servings: 2
Ingredients:
- 3 blood oranges, peeled (400 grams)
- 3/4 cup lite coconut milk
- 1/2 tsp cinnamon
- 1/3 cup chia seeds

Directions:
1. In a Vita-mix, high-powered blender, or food processor, combine the oranges, coconut milk, and cinnamon. About 1 minute, process until smooth and all ingredients are mixed.
2. Transfer to a resealable medium-sized bowl. Stir in the chia seeds until well blended. Cover and place in the refrigerator for 3 hours or overnight.
3. Serve plain or with preferred toppings.
4. Enjoy!

Nutrition:
Calories: 127 | Carbs: 14g | Protein: 8g | Fat: 12g | Fiber: 17g

AVOCADO & CAPER FLAGEL

Prep Time: 5 minutes | **Cook Time:** 5 minutes
Servings: 1
Ingredients:
- 1/2 toasted bagel/Flagel
- 2 tbsp low-fat cream cheese
- 1/4 sliced avocado
- 2 tbsp microgreens
- 1 tbsp rinsed capers

Directions:
1. With cream cheese, Spread Flagel/bagel. Garnish with microgreens, capers & avocado.

Nutrition:
Calories: 312 | Carbs: 37g | Protein: 10g | Fat: 15g | Fiber: 6.6g

SPRINGTIME TOFU SCRAMBLE

Prep Time: 15 minutes | **Cook Time:** 17 minutes
Servings: 4
Ingredients:
- 2 tbsp olive oil or virgin coconut oil
- 3 garlic cloves minced
- 3 leeks were thoroughly washed, halved, and thinly sliced (white and light green parts only)
- 2 cups baby spinach
- 4 small yellow squash quartered and sliced (about 1 1/2 cups)
- 6 oz baby Bella mushrooms washed, destemmed, and sliced
- 14 oz firm sprouted tofu
- 1/2 tsp turmeric
- 1 tbsp nutritional yeast
- 1/2 tsp truffle salt or Kala namak (i.e., black salt)
- 1/4 tsp sea salt
- 2 tbsp fresh chives

Directions:
1. Heat the oil in a large skillet over medium-low heat. Add the garlic, leek, spinach, squash, and mushrooms after that. Cook, occasionally stirring, for 10-12 minutes, or until the vegetables are soft.
2. Crumble the tofu and add the turmeric, nutritional yeast, truffle salt, salt, and black pepper to the pan. Cook for an additional 5 minutes.
3. Remove from the heat and toss in the chives.
4. If preferred, serve with avocado toast.

Nutrition:
Calories: 182 | Carbs: 11g | Protein: 10g | Fat: 72g | Fiber: 19g

DATE-SWEETENED BANANA BREAD

Prep Time: 20 minutes | **Cook Time:** 50 minutes
Servings: 8
Ingredients:
- 2 flax eggs (2 tbsp flax meal + 6 tbsp water)
- 2 cups gluten-free oat flour
- 2 tsp cinnamon
- 2 tsp baking powder
- 1/2 tsp baking soda
- 1/2 tsp salt
- 1 large ripe & spotty banana, mashed (about 1 1/2 cups)
- + 1 banana to top, sliced it in half lengthwise (optional)
- 1 cup pitted Medjool dates, packed
- 1/2 cup unsweetened non-dairy milk
- 1 1/2-2 tsp of pure vanilla extract (I used 2)
- One tsp of apple cider vinegar

Directions:
1. Preheat the oven to 350°F and line or lightly grease a 9-inch bread pan with parchment paper. Stir together the flax meal and the water. Set aside for about 15 minutes to thicken.
2. Combine the oat flour, baking soda, baking powder, salt, and cinnamon, in a large mixing basin. Set aside after thoroughly mixing.
3. Combine the dates, almond milk, vanilla essence, and apple cider vinegar in a food processor. Process until smooth, then use a spoon to incorporate the mashed banana and flax egg. Stir the date and banana mixture into the dry ingredients until a batter forms.
4. Pour the batter into the prepared loaf pan and top with the optional banana, sliced side up, if preferred.
5. Bake for 50-60 minutes, or until a toothpick inserted into the center comes out clean. Remove from the oven and set aside to cool fully before slicing.

Nutrition:
Calories: 429 | Carbs: 19g | Protein: 13g | Fat: 27g | Fiber: 6g

BLUEBERRY CHIA JAM

Prep Time: 20 minutes | **Cook Time:** 20 minutes
Servings: 4
Ingredients:
- 3 cups fresh blueberry
- 3-4 tbsp maple syrup
- 2 tbsp chia seeds
- 1/2 tsp vanilla extract (optional)

Directions:
1. In a medium nonstick saucepan over medium heat, combine blueberries and 3 tbsp maple syrup and bring to a low boil. Reduce the heat slightly and continue to cook for approximately 5 minutes, stirring often, or until all of the berries have darkened and become glossy, like small marbles. Mash the berries with a potato masher, keeping some whole for texture.
2. Reduce the heat to low and stir in the chia seeds. Allow it to boil for about 15 minutes, stirring regularly, or until thickened—it will thicken further in the fridge.
3. Take the pan off the heat and whisk in the vanilla extract.

Nutrition:
Calories: 134 | Carbs: 29g | Protein: 2g | Fat: 2g | Fiber: 6.5g

PUMPKIN PIE BUTTER

Prep Time: 10 minutes | **Cook Time:** 50 minutes
Servings: 2
Ingredients:
- 2 1/2 cups packed freshly roasted pumpkin (see below for instructions—can also use canned if you like)
- 1/2 tsp cinnamon
- 1/2 tsp ginger
- 1/2 tsp nutmeg
- 1/2 tsp ground cloves
- 1/4 tsp salt
- 2 tbsp maple syrup (optional—leave out for Whole30)

Directions:
1. Cut fresh pumpkin into large pieces, add oil roast it for 45 minutes-one hour at 375°F.
2. Melt the butter in a frying pan. Toast the pumpkin seeds for 3-6 minutes, stirring regularly, until they start to brown. Set them aside.
3. Allow the pumpkin to cool and remove the skin. Blend 3 minutes of the pulp with the spices, maple syrup (optional), and salt.
4. Store in an airtight glass jar in the refrigerator for two weeks, and enjoy!

Nutrition:
Calories: 76 | Carbs: 27g | Protein: 11g | Fat: 28g | Fiber: 4g

SPICED PUMPKIN GRANOLA

Prep Time: 5 minutes | **Cook Time:** 25 minutes
Servings: 4

Ingredients:
- 2 cups raw pumpkin seeds

- 2/3 cup raw sunflower seeds
- 4 tbsp flax seeds
- 1/2 tsp cinnamon
- 4 tsp pumpkin spice
- 1/4 tsp sea salt or coarse kosher salt
- 1/4 cup maple syrup
- 1/3 to 1/2 cup unsweetened coconut

Directions:
1. Preheat the oven to 325°F.
2. Set aside a baking sheet lined with parchment paper.
3. In a mixing bowl, combine all ingredients (except the coconut) in the order given. To mix, stir everything together.
4. Spread the mixture evenly on a baking sheet lined with parchment paper and bake for 20 minutes.
5. Bake for 20 minutes at 325°F.
6. Add the coconut to the pan and stir it in evenly with a spoon. Return the baking pan to the oven for an additional 5-7 minutes to roast the coconut.
7. Then, take the pan out of the oven and let the granola cool on the pan.
8. The granola should be ready to break into smaller pieces once it has cooled in the pan.
9. Enjoy with any optional mix-ins of your choice!

Nutrition:
Calories: 273 | Carbs: 15g | Protein: 7g | Fat: 1g | Fiber: 9g

COCONUT ALMOND PROTEIN BARS

Prep Time: 15 minutes | **Cook Time:** 15 minutes
Servings: 8

Ingredients:
- 2 1/2 cups of raw almonds
- 1/2 cup of unsweetened coconut flakes
- 1/4 cup of dried mango (about 4-5 pieces). It should be noted that dried apricots and pineapple may be used instead.
- 1/4 cup or 2 scoops of (60 grams) protein powder of choice
- Three tsp of cinnamon (optional)
- Pinch of sea salt
- 1/3 to 1/2 cup honey or maple syrup
- 1/3 to 1/2 cup hot water (purified)
- Four tsp pure vanilla extract

Directions:
1. To begin, place the almonds and coconut in a high-powered blender or food processor and pulse until an almond meal-like texture is created.
2. Set aside in a large mixing basin.
3. The dried mango is then ground up. They might be difficult to digest at times. If you don't have a high-powered blender or food processor, chop the mango into smaller pieces using a sharp knife.
4. Remove the dried mango from the food processor and combine it with the almond coconut mixture. Combine the protein powder, cinnamon, and salt in a mixing bowl. Set aside.
5. Separately, in a small mixing dish. Combine honey or maple syrup, boiling water, and vanilla extract in a mixing bowl. Stir to mix before adding to the dry ingredients.
6. If the batter is overly thick, simply add additional boiling water or honey. If it's too moist, add additional protein powder or your preferred flour. Mix thoroughly with your hands, then press into an 8x8 baking dish lined with parchment paper. Allow bars to chill in the fridge for 1 hour or more before cutting into squares.
7. Refrigerate after opening and eat within 5 to 7 days.

Nutrition:
Calories: 273 | Carbs: 20g | Protein: 19g | Fat: 12g | Fiber: 5.2g

GRAIN-FREE GRANOLA CLUSTERS

Prep Time: 10 minutes | **Cook Time:** 25 minutes
Servings: 8

Ingredients:
- 2 cups slivered almonds
- 1/3 cup semi-sweet or dark chocolate chips (vegan) or sugar-free chocolate chips.
- 1-2 tbsp of chia or flax (optional)
- 1 tsp vanilla extract (optional)
- 1/4 tsp kosher salt
- 1/4 tsp cinnamon
- 1/4 cup pure maple syrup or raw honey

Directions:
1. Preheat the oven to 325°F.
2. Set aside a baking sheet lined with parchment paper.
3. In a mixing dish, combine all of the ingredients in the order given. To mix, stir everything together.
4. Spread the mixture evenly onto the prepared baking sheet and bake for 20 minutes.
5. Bake for 25-30 minutes at 325°F.
6. Then, take the pan out of the oven and let the granola cool on the pan. Do not make any contact! The chocolate and maple syrup should have melted together, tying everything together.
7. The granola should be ready to break into big pieces once it has cooled in the pan. Granola clusters are another name for granola clusters.
8. Keep in an airtight jar for up to two weeks.

Nutrition:
Calories: 168 | Carbs: 13g | Protein: 3g | Fat: 12g | Fiber: 5g

TOASTED COCONUT AND BERRY GRAIN

Prep Time: 10 minutes | **Cook Time:** 35 minutes
Servings: 6

Ingredients:
- 1 cup larger size whole mixed

- 1 cup raw almonds
- 1/2 cup pumpkin seeds
- 1/4 cup coconut oil
- 1/4 to 1/3 cup maple syrup
- Dash of sea salt
- 2 tbsp vanilla
- 2 tbsp cinnamon
- 1/2 tbsp ground ginger
- 2/3 cup unsweetened coconut flakes
- 1 1/2 cup to 1 1/4 cup dried berries (cranberry, blueberry, etc.)
- Optional chia seeds (2 tbsp)

Directions:
1. Preheat the oven to 325°F. Line a baking sheet with parchment paper.
2. Combine your almonds in a blender or food processor. Pulse approximately 5-8 times until the ingredients are chopped but not ground.
3. Transfer to a large mixing dish and stir in your pumpkins.
4. Combine the coconut oil, extract, and maple syrup in a separate basin. Pour this over the and toss to combine. Then add your spices and stir until evenly covered.
5. Spread the nut mixture equally on the baking sheet and top with a pinch of sea salt.
6. Bake for 15 minutes in a preheated oven.
7. Remove from the oven and toss the seeds on the tray to turn the sides. Return to the oven for another fifteen minutes of baking.
8. Remove from oven, stir seeds, and then put in your coconut. You may place the coconut on the same baking pan as the nuts and syrup or on a different baking dish. Just make sure it's evenly distributed on the tray.
9. Continue baking for another five-eight minute, or until the coconut is golden brown.
10. Remove and set aside to cool.
11. After cooling, add the coconut/nut granola to a mixing bowl and stir it around a bit more. Mix in the dried berries and toss everything together.
12. Finish with any more spices and optional chia.
13. Keep in an airtight container or gift jars.

Nutrition:
Calories: 200 | Carbs: 8g | Protein: 4g | Fat: 13g | Fiber: 5.7g

BERRY SOFT SERVE & VANILLA CHIA PUDDING PARFAIT

Prep Time: 15 minutes | **Cook Time:** 630 minutes
Servings: 2
Ingredients:
Vanilla Chia Pudding:
- 1/4 cup unsweetened plant milk
- 1/4 cup plus 1 tbsp chia seeds
- 1/2 to 2 tbsp pure maple syrup
- 2 tsp pure vanilla extract
- Berry Soft Serve
- 3 cups frozen strawberries
- 1/2 cup frozen blueberries
- 1 to 2 Medjool dates, pitted (optional to sweeten)

Topping Ideas:
- Coconut flakes
- Sliced strawberries
- Blueberries

Directions:
Vanilla Chia Pudding:
1. In an airtight jar or container, vigorously mix the plant milk, chia seeds, maple syrup, and vanilla until the chia seeds are evenly dispersed throughout the liquid. To thicken, place in the refrigerator for at least 8 hours or overnight.
2. In the morning, mix the chia pudding thoroughly. If it's too thin, add 1 tbsp of chia seeds at a time to thicken. If it's too thick, thin with additional plant milk, 1 tbsp at a time.

Soft Serve Berry:
3. Just before serving, make the soft serve. Combine the frozen strawberries, sugar, and lemon juice in a food processor. Blueberries, dates (if using) and process until smooth and sorbet-like, stopping to scrape down the sides as required. To start things rolling, you may need to add a very small amount of plant milk. To retain a thick, soft-serve texture, add 1 spoonful at a time and as little as possible.

Assemble:
4. Layer the chia pudding and soft berry serve in two jars or parfait glasses, one after the other. Serve immediately after sprinkling with preferred toppings.

Nutrition:
Calories: 296 | Carbs: 10g | Protein: 20g | Fat: 10g | Fiber: 10g

CREAMY RASPBERRY, COCONUT & CHIA SHAKE

Prep Time: 10 minutes | **Cook Time:** 10 minutes
Servings: 2
Ingredients:
- 1/2 cup frozen raspberries
- 1/3 cup full-fat canned coconut milk, chilled
- 1 cup unsweetened oat milk or almond milk
- 1/2 cup ice
- 4 soft Medjool dates, pitted
- 3 tbsp chia
- 2 tsp pure vanilla extract

Directions:
1. Combine all of the ingredients in a high-powered blender and blend until smooth.

Nutrition:
Calories: 276 | Carbs: 9g | Protein: 38g | Fat: 10g | Fiber: 7g

RAW CHERRY-APPLE PIE

Prep Time: 25 minutes | **Cook Time:** 25 minutes
Servings: 2

Ingredients:
- 3 cups fresh or thawed frozen sweet cherries, pitted and divided
- 1 large crisp apple, cored, peeled, and diced
- 4 dates, pitted
- 2 tbsp chia seeds

Topping Ideas:
- Raw almonds
- Dried mulberries
- Hemp seeds
- Cacao nibs

Directions:
1. 1 cup of the cherries, diced, should be placed in a medium airtight container with the diced apple.
2. Combine the remaining 2 cups of sweet cherries and the dates in a high-speed blender. Process or mix for 1 to 2 minutes, or until smooth, occasionally stopping to scrape down the sides. Pour the cherry sauce into the container with the chopped cherries and apple, then mix the chia seeds.
3. Refrigerate for at least an hour, if not more, before serving.
4. Divide the apple mixture into two bowls and top with raw raisins, cranberries, and hemp seeds.
5. Serve immediately and enjoy.
6. Keep any leftovers in the refrigerator.

Nutrition:
Calories: 190 | Carbs: 22g | Protein: 12g | Fat: 6g | Fiber: 8.2g

JACKET POTATOES WITH HOME-BAKED BEANS

Prep Time: 10 minutes | **Cook Time:** 90 minutes
Servings: 4
Ingredients:
- 4 baked potatoes
- 2 tbsp sunflower oil
- 1 carrot, diced
- 1 celery stalk, diced
- 400 g can haricot beans, drained
- 2 tomatoes, chopped
- 2 tbsp paprika—choose sweet or hot depending on taste
- 2 tbsp Worcestershire sauce
- 3 tbsp chopped chives, to serve

Directions:
1. Preheat the oven to 200°C/180°C fan/gas 6. Scrub and dry the potatoes thoroughly before pricking them numerous times with a fork. Bake for 1-12 hours, or until they feel soft when pressed, straight on the oven shelf.
2. After 30 minutes, heat the oil in a skillet and sauté the carrot and celery for 10 minutes, or until softened. Cook for another 5 minutes, or until the beans, tomatoes, and paprika are softened and pulpy. Cook for 5 minutes more after adding 100 ml water and the Worcestershire sauce, cover and keep heated.
3. Split the potatoes open and spoon in the beans. Serve garnished with chives.

Nutrition:
Calories: 212 | Carbs: 39g | Protein: 9g | Fat: 4g | Fiber: 11.1g

PEA & BROAD BEAN SHAKSHUKA

Prep Time: 20 minutes | **Cook Time:** 30 minutes
Servings: 4
Ingredients:
- 1/2 bunch of asparagus spears
- 200 g sprouting broccoli
- 2 tbsp olive oil
- Spring onions, finely sliced
- 2 tbsp cumin
- 1 ripe tomato, chopped
- 1 small pack parsley, finely chopped
- 50 g shelled peas
- 50 g podded broad beans
- 4 large eggs
- 50 g pea shoots
- Greek yogurt and flatbreads, to serve

Directions:
1. Clean the asparagus and slice the stalks, leaving the tips intact at the top. Finely slice the broccoli, leaving the heads intact.
2. Sauté the spring onions, tomatoes, peas, fava beans, asparagus, and broccoli with oil, cumin, cayenne pepper, parsley, and salt for 5 minutes in a skillet.
3. Make four dips with the mixture. Crack an egg into each dip, surround it with half the pea shoots, season generously, cover with a lid, and heat until the egg whites are just set. Serve with the remaining pea shoots, a spoonful of yogurt, several rolls, and, if desired, another pinch of cayenne.

Nutrition:
Calories: 172 | Carbs: 7g | Protein: 13g | Fat: 8g | Fiber: 9g

LENTIL FRITTERS

Prep Time: 15 minutes | **Cook Time:** 10 minutes
Servings: 2
Ingredients:
- 300 g leftover basic lentils
- A handful of chopped coriander
- 2 chopped spring onion
- 50 g gram flour
- 2 carrots
- 2 courgettes
- 1 handful of coriander
- 1/2 tbsp oil
- Juice of 1 lime
- 3 tbsp rape oil

Directions:
1. Combine and set aside the leftover lentils, chopped cilantro, spring onion, and wheat flour.
2. Aiding with a peeler, cut the carrots and zucchini into long ribbons, then sauté them in oil with the cilantro and lime juice.
3. Heat the oil in a frying pan. Pour in the lentil mixture, creating patties. Fry both lat until golden brown.

Nutrition:
Calories: 301 | Carbs: 39g | Protein: 18g | Fat: 12g | Fiber: 15g

SUMMER PISTOU

Prep Time: 10 minutes | **Cook Time:** 25 minutes
Servings: 4
Ingredients:
- 4 tbsp rape oil
- 2 leeks, finely sliced
- 2 large zucchini, finely diced
- 1 l boiling vegetable stock (made from scratch or with reduced-salt bouillon)
- 400 g can cannellini or haricot beans, drained
- 200 g green beans, chopped
- 4 tomatoes, chopped
- 2 garlic cloves, finely chopped
- Small pack basil
- 40 g freshly grated parmesan

Directions:
1. In a skillet, sauté the leeks and zucchini in oil for 5 minutes.
2. Pour in the broth. Add three-quarters of the haricot beans and green beans and half of the tomatoes. Cook for seven minutes.
3. Blend the remaining beans and tomatoes, basil, Parmesan, and garlic.
4. Cook for 1 minute after stirring the sauce.

Nutrition:
Calories: 162 | Carbs: 15g | Protein: 13g | Fat: 10g | Fiber: 11g

WINTER VEGETABLE & LENTIL SOUP

Prep Time: 10 minutes | **Cook Time:** 30 minutes
Servings: 2
Ingredients:
- 85 g dried red lentils
- 2 carrots, quartered lengthways then diced
- 3 sticks of celery, sliced
- 2 small leeks, sliced
- 2 tbsp tomato purée
- 2 tbsp fresh thyme leaves
- 1 large garlic clove, chopped
- 2 tbsp vegetable bouillon powder
- 2 heaped tbsp ground coriander

Directions:
1. Place all of the ingredients in a large pan. Pour in 1 1/2 liters of hot water and stir thoroughly.
2. Cook for 30 minutes, or until the veggies and lentils are soft.
3. Ladle into bowls and serve immediately, or blitz a third of the soup with a hand blender or in a food processor if you like a thick texture.

Nutrition:
Calories: 152 | Carbs: 38g | Protein: 19g | Fat: 3g | Fiber: 15g

PEA SOUP

Prep Time: 5 minutes | **Cook Time:** 25 minutes
Servings: 5
Ingredients:
- 500 g peas
- 150 g potatoes
- 2 zucchini
- 1 l vegetable stock
- 400 ml full-fat coconut milk, full-fat
- 2 tbsp coconut oil
- 1 tsp onion
- 20 g ginger
- 2 lemongrass stalks
- 1 garlic clove
- 1/2 tsp salt
- 1/2 tsp pepper

Directions:
1. Slice the zucchini. Dice the garlic, potato, ginger, and onion.
2. Add coconut oil into the pan and add potatoes to it and cook for one to two minutes. When potatoes are softened, add lemongrass, ginger, garlic, and onion and cook for one to two minutes more.
3. Add zucchini, pepper, and salt, and cook for two minutes more.
4. Then, add vegetable stock and peas and bring to a boil.
5. Lower the heat and simmer for a few minutes. Add coconut milk.
6. Place soup into the handheld blender and blend on low flame until creamy and smooth.
7. Transfer it to the bowl. Garnish with pine nuts, peas, and fresh coriander leaves.

Nutrition:
Calories: 277 | Carbs: 31g | Protein: 19g | Fat: 8g | Fiber: 15g

GUACAMOLE

Prep Time: 10 minutes | **Cook Time:** 0 minutes
Servings: 4
Ingredients:
- 2 avocados
- 1 red onion
- 1/4 cup coriander leaves

- 2 limes
- 1/4 tsp salt

Optional:
- 1 green chili jalapeño
- 1/2 cup cherry tomatoes
- 1/4 tsp pepper

Directions:
1. Let chop the coriander, chili, and onion.
2. Mash the avocados with a fork until creamy.
3. Combine the chopped veggies into the mashed avocado.
4. Add lemon juice and salt over it.
5. Combine it well.
6. Sprinkle with pepper and salt.

Nutrition:
Calories: 243 | Carbs: 16g | Protein: 4g | Fat: 15g | Fiber: 13g

CABBAGE SOUP

Prep Time: 10 minutes | **Cook Time:** 30 minutes
Servings: 8
Ingredients:
- 2 tbsp extra-virgin olive oil
- 2 cups onions, chopped
- 1 cup carrot, chopped
- 1 cup celery, chopped
- 1 cup poblano or green bell pepper, chopped
- 4 garlic cloves, minced
- 8 cups cabbage, sliced
- 1 tbsp tomato paste
- 1 tbsp chipotle chilies in adobo sauce, minced
- 1 tsp ground cumin
- 1/2 tsp ground coriander
- 4 cups vegetable broth or chicken broth, low-sodium
- 4 cups water
- 30 oz pinto or black beans, rinsed, low-sodium
- 3/4 tsp salt
- 1/2 cup fresh cilantro, chopped
- 2 tbsp lime juice

Directions:
1. Add oil into the pot and place it over medium flame.
2. Then, add garlic, bell pepper, celery, carrots, and onions and cook for ten to twelve minutes.
3. Add cabbage and cook for ten minutes until softened.
4. Add coriander, cumin, chipotle, and tomato paste and cook for one minute more.
5. Add salt, beans, water, and broth and cover with a lid. Bring to a boil over high heat. Lower the heat and simmer for ten minutes.
6. Remove from the flame.
7. Add lime juice and fresh coriander leaves.

Nutrition:
Calories: 129 | Carbs: 12.1g | Protein: 6.5g | Fat: 3.8g | Fiber: 9g

CAULIFLOWER AND POTATO CURRY SOUP

Prep Time: 10 minutes | **Cook Time:** 1 hour
Servings: 8
Ingredients:
- 2 tsp ground coriander
- 2 tsp ground cumin
- 1 1/2 tsp ground cinnamon
- 1 1/2 tsp ground turmeric
- 1 1/4 tsp salt
- 3/4 tsp ground pepper
- 1/8 tsp cayenne pepper
- 6 cauliflower, cut into small florets
- 2 tbsp extra-virgin olive oil
- 1 onion, chopped
- 1 carrot, diced
- 3 garlic cloves, minced
- 1 1/2 tsp fresh ginger, grated
- 1 red chili powder, minced
- 14 oz tomato sauce, salt-less
- 4 cups vegetable broth, low-sodium
- 3 cups potatoes, diced, peeled
- 2 tsp lime zest
- 2 tbsp lime juice
- 14 oz coconut milk

Directions:
1. Preheat the oven to 450°F.
2. Mix the cayenne, pepper, salt, turmeric, cinnamon, cumin, and coriander leaves into the bowl.
3. Toss cauliflower with one tbsp oil into the big bowl. Sprinkle with one tsp spice mixture. Spread onto the rimmed baking sheet.
4. Cook for 15 to 20 minutes. Keep it aside.
5. Meanwhile, add one tbsp oil into the pot and heat it over medium-high flame. Add carrot and onion and cook for three to four minutes.
6. Lower the heat and cook for three to four minutes more.
7. Then, add the remaining spice mixture, chili, garlic, and ginger and cook for one minute more.
8. Add tomato sauce and stir well. Let simmer for one minute.
9. Add lime zest, lime juice, sweet potatoes, and broth, and bring to a boil over high flame.
10. Lower the heat and simmer for 35 to 40 minutes.
11. Add roasted cauliflower and coconut milk and stir well.
12. Simmer until cooked well.

Nutrition:
Calories: 271 | Carbs: 31.4g | Protein: 5.3g | Fat: 11g | Fiber: 9.2g

SWEET POTATO AND BLACK BEAN CHILI

Prep Time: 10 minutes | **Cook Time:** 30 minutes
Servings: 4

Ingredients:
- 1 tbsp plus 2 tsp extra-virgin olive oil
- 1 sweet potato, peeled and diced
- 1 onion, diced
- 4 garlic cloves, minced
- 2 tbsp chili powder
- 4 tsp ground cumin
- 1/2 tsp chipotle chili, ground
- 1/4 tsp salt
- 2 1/2 cups of water
- 30 oz black beans, rinsed
- 14 oz tomatoes, diced
- 4 tsp lime juice
- 1/2 cup fresh cilantro, chopped

Directions:
1. Add oil into the Dutch oven and place it over a medium-high flame.
2. Add onion and sweet potatoes and cook for four minutes until softened.
3. Add salt, chipotle, cumin, chili powder, and garlic, and cook for a half-minute.
4. Add water and bring to a simmer. Lower the heat and cook for 10 to 12 minutes.
5. Add lime juice, tomatoes, and beans and simmer over high heat.
6. Lower the heat and simmer for five minutes more.
7. Remove from the flame.
8. Garnish with fresh cilantro leaves.

Nutrition:
Calories: 321 | Carbs: 51.7g | Protein: 13g | Fat: 7.6g | Fiber: 19g

WHITE BEAN CHILI

Prep Time: 10 minutes | **Cook Time:** 1 hour
Servings: 6

Ingredients:
- 1/4 cup avocado oil or canola oil
- 2 cups Anaheim or poblano chilies, seeded and chopped
- 1 onion, chopped
- 4 garlic cloves, minced
- 1/2 cup quinoa, rinsed
- 4 tsp dried oregano
- 4 tsp ground cumin
- 1 tsp salt
- 1/2 tsp ground coriander
- 1/2 tsp ground pepper
- 4 cups vegetable broth, low-sodium
- 30 oz white beans, rinsed
- 1 zucchini, diced
- 1/4 cup fresh cilantro, chopped
- 2 tbsp lime juice

Directions:
1. Add oil into the pot and place it over medium flame.
2. Add garlic, onion, and chilies, and cook for five to seven minutes.
3. Then, add pepper, coriander, salt, cumin, oregano, and quinoa and cook for one minute.
4. Add beans and broth and stir well. Bring to a boil and simmer for twenty minutes.
5. Add zucchini and cook for 10 to 15 minutes.
6. Garnish with lime juice and fresh cilantro leaves.
7. Top with lime wedges.

Nutrition:
Calories: 283 | Carbs: 36.7g | Protein: 19.7g | Fat: 11.7g | Fiber: 15.4g

CHICKPEA STEW

Prep Time: 10 minutes | **Cook Time:** 30-40 minutes
Servings: 8

Ingredients:
- 10 oz spinach
- 1 1/2 tbsp canola oil
- 1 onion, chopped
- 1-piece ginger, peeled and minced
- 1/2 jalapeno pepper, seeded and chopped
- 3 garlic cloves, minced
- 1 tbsp curry powder
- 3 carrots, peeled and thinly sliced
- 1/2 cauliflower head, broken into bite-size florets
- 30 oz chickpeas, low-sodium, rinsed
- 28 oz tomatoes, drained, diced, salt-free
- 1/2 cup half-and-half, fat-free
- 1/3 cup coconut milk

Directions:
1. Place spinach into the microwave-safe bowl and then add one tbsp water and cover it. Let microwave it for one to two minutes.
2. Transfer it to the colander and drain it.
3. When cooled, chop it and keep it aside.
4. Add oil into the skillet and heat it.
5. Add onion and cook for eight minutes.
6. Add curry powder, garlic, jalapeno, and ginger and cook for a half-minute. Then, add 2 tbsp water and carrots and cook for ten minutes.
7. Add cauliflower and cook for five to ten minutes more.
8. Add coconut milk, half-and-half, tomatoes, and chickpeas, and stir well. Bring to a boil. Then, lower the heat and simmer for 15 minutes.
9. Then, add reserved spinach and stir well.

Nutrition:
Calories: 249 | Carbs: 38.8g | Protein: 11.2g | Fat: 6.5g | Fiber: 18g

VEGGIE SANDWICH

Prep Time: 10 minutes | **Cook Time:** 0 minutes
Servings: 8

Ingredients:
- 2 slices sprouted-grain bread, toasted
- 1/4 avocado, mashed
- 1 tbsp hummus
- Salt, one pinch
- 4 slices cucumber

- 2 slices tomato
- 2 tbsp carrot, shredded
- 1 clementine, peeled

Directions:
1. Place one slice of bread onto the plate and spread avocado and hummus. Sprinkle with salt.

Fill the sandwich with carrot, tomato, and cucumber. Cut in half and serve with Clementine.

Nutrition:
Calories: 315 | Carbs: 48.6g | Protein: 11.4g | Fat: 10.1g | Fiber: 12.5g

BEAN AND VEGGIE TACO BOWL

Prep Time: 20 minutes | **Cook Time:** 0 minutes
Servings: 1
Ingredients:
- 1 tsp olive oil
- 1/2 green bell pepper, cored and sliced
- 1/2 red onion, sliced
- 1/2 cup cooked brown rice
- 1/4 cup black beans, rinsed
- 1/4 cup sharp cheddar cheese, shredded
- 1/4 cup pico de gallo or salsa
- 2 tbsp cilantro

Directions:
1. Add oil into the skillet and place it over medium flame.
2. Add onion and bell pepper and cook for 5 to 8 minutes.
3. Mound rice and beans into the bowl. Top with cilantro, pico de gallo, cheese, and vegetables.
4. Top with hot sauce and lime wedges.

Nutrition:
Calories: 415 | Carbs: 52g | Protein: 17.4g | Fat: 12g | Fiber: 11.6g

COBB SALAD

Prep Time: 10 minutes | **Cook Time:** 0 minutes
Servings: 1
Ingredients:
- 3 cups iceberg lettuce, chopped
- Chicken thighs diced, roasted
- 1 celery stalk, diced
- 1 carrot, diced
- 1 egg, hard-boiled, diced
- 1 tbsp blue cheese, crumbled
- 2 tbsp honey and mustard vinaigrette

Directions:
1. Place blue cheese, egg, carrot, celery, chicken, and lettuce into the salad bowl. Drizzle with dressing.

Nutrition:
Calories: 481 | Carbs: 10.6g | Protein: 30.3g | Fat: 16.7g | Fiber: 6.4g

ASPARAGUS SOUP

Prep Time: 5 minutes | **Cook Time:** 10 minutes
Servings: 4
Ingredients:
- 1 tbsp olive oil
- 1 cup shallots, chopped
- 3 garlic cloves, minced
- 2 pounds asparagus, chopped into one-inch pieces
- 6 cups vegetable stock
- 1 tsp salt

Directions:
1. Add olive oil into the pot and cook over medium flame. Add garlic and shallot and cook for three to five minutes until softened.
2. Add salt, vegetable stock, and asparagus stalks and then boil it.
3. Cover the pot with a lid and simmer on a low flame.
4. When done, transfer the cooled soup into the blender and blend until creamy.
5. Add asparagus tops and cook for five minutes until tender.
6. Serve and enjoy!

Nutrition:
Calories: 205 | Carbs: 7g | Protein: 7g | Fat: 3g | Fiber: 7g

CREAMY CARROT SOUP

Cook Time: 20 minutes | **Prep Time:** 5 minutes
Servings: 4-6
Ingredients:
- 2 tbsp olive oil
- 4 cups carrots, chopped
- 1 onion, chopped
- 3 garlic cloves, minced
- 1 tbsp curry powder
- 3 cups chicken broth
- 1 1/2 cups carrot juice

Directions:
1. Add oil into the pot and cook over medium flame.
2. Add onion and carrots and cook for six to eight minutes.
3. Then, add curry powder and garlic and cook for one minute more.
4. Add half tsp salt and broth and simmer over low flame for fifteen minutes.
5. Add carrot juice and combine well. Let's cool it. Transfer it to the blender and blend until smooth.
6. Place soup back in the pot and sprinkle with pepper and salt.
7. Add cream and combine well.
8. Serve and enjoy!

Nutrition:
Calories: 176 | Carbs: 21.7g | Protein: 6.8g | Fat: 8.3g | Fiber: 12g

MUSHROOM BARLEY SOUP

Prep Time: 5 minutes | **Cook Time:** 30 minutes
Servings: 4
Ingredients:
- 2 tbsp olive oil
- 1 cup carrots, chopped
- 1 cup onion, chopped
- 1 lb white mushrooms, sliced
- 1 1/2 cups smoked ham, chopped
- 28 oz chicken broth
- 14 oz stewed tomatoes, seedless
- 1/2 cup quick-cooking barley

Directions:
1. Add olive oil into the pot and cook over medium-high flame.
2. Add onion and carrots and cook for five minutes.
3. Add mushrooms and cook for five minutes more.
4. Add ham and cook for one to two minutes and stir well.
5. Add barley, tomatoes, and chicken broth and stir well.
6. Let boil it. Then, lower the heat and simmer for twenty minutes.
7. Serve and enjoy!

Nutrition:
Calories: 200 | Carbs: 21.8g | Protein: 5.8g | Fat: 7.3g | Fiber: 8g

BROCCOLI SOUP

Prep Time: 5 minutes | **Cook Time:** 45 minutes
Servings: 4
Ingredients:
- 2 tbsp olive oil
- 1 leek, chopped
- 1 celery stalk, chopped
- 2 garlic cloves, minced
- 3 potatoes, unpeeled, chopped
- 1/2 tsp salt
- 1 bay leaf
- 3 cups vegetable broth
- 1 1/2 cups broccoli florets

Directions:
1. Add oil to the pan and cook over medium-high flame.
2. Add bay leaf, salt, potatoes, garlic, leek, and celery, and cook until browned.
3. Add stock and boil it. Then, lower the heat and simmer for thirty minutes.
4. Add broccoli florets and simmer for fifteen minutes until tender.
5. Remove from the flame. Let it cool.
6. Discard bay leaf and then add to the blender and blend until smooth.
7. Serve and enjoy!

Nutrition:
Calories: 206 | Carbs: 23g | Protein: 12g | Fat: 11g | Fiber: 7g

CHICKEN AND ASPARAGUS PASTA

Prep Time: 5 minutes | **Cook Time:** 20 minutes
Servings: 4
Ingredients:
- 1 lb whole-wheat penne pasta
- 2 tbsp olive oil
- 1 lb chicken breast halves, boneless and sliced into strips
- 1/2 tsp poultry seasoning
- 4 garlic cloves, minced
- 1 1/2 cups asparagus, frozen, thawed, cut into 1-inch pieces
- 1 cup peas, frozen, thawed
- 1/4 cup parmesan cheese, grated

Directions:
1. Add water and salt into the pot and boil it. Then, add pasta and cook until al dente.
2. Add one tbsp olive oil into the pan and cook over medium flame. Add chicken and poultry seasoning and cook until golden.
3. Remove cooked chicken from the pan.
4. Then, add peas, asparagus, garlic, and the remaining tbsp of olive oil and cook until tender.
5. Add chicken back with asparagus mixture and cook for two minutes.
6. Add pasta to the bowl and toss with chicken mixture.
7. Sprinkle with parmesan cheese.

Nutrition:
Calories: 325 | Carbs: 19g | Protein: 24g | Fat: 11g | Fiber: 9g

RED BEANS AND RICE

Prep Time: 5 minutes | **Cook Time:** 35 minutes
Servings: 4
Ingredients:
- 1 tbsp olive oil
- 1 onion, chopped
- 3 stalks of celery, chopped
- 3 garlic cloves, minced
- 14 oz tomato sauce
- 1/2 tsp oregano
- 1/2 tbsp thyme
- 14 oz beef stock
- 28 oz red beans, drained and rinsed

- 4 cups brown rice, cooked

Directions:
1. Add olive oil into the pan and cook over medium flame.
2. Add garlic, celery, and onions and cook and stir well.
3. Add thyme, oregano, and tomato paste and stir well.
4. Add beef broth and simmer for thirty-five minutes.
5. Add red beans and cook it well.
6. Place over brown rice.

Nutrition:
Calories: 413 | Carbs: 76.3g | Protein: 29.1g | Fat: 12.5g | Fiber: 15g

BEEF STIR FRY

Prep Time: 5 minutes | **Cook Time:** 35 minutes
Servings: 2-3
Ingredients:
- 1/4 cup orange juice
- 1/4 cup low-sodium soy sauce
- 2 tbsp rice vinegar
- 1/4 cup water
- 2 tbsp canola oil
- 8 oz beef round steak, thinly sliced
- 3 garlic cloves, minced
- 6 oz peas
- 1 bunch of broccoli florets
- 1 bunch edamame, shelled
- 1 1/2 tsp cornstarch, dissolved in 1/4 cup hot water

Directions:
1. Mix the water, rice vinegar, soy sauce, and orange juice into the bowl and keep it aside.
2. Add one tbsp canola oil into the pan and cook over medium flame.
3. Add beef and cook for two minutes. Transfer the beef to another plate.
4. Add one tbsp of oil into another pan and cook over medium flame.
5. Add garlic and cook for one minute. Add edamame, broccoli, and peas, and cook for three minutes.
6. Add soy sauce mixture and cook for five minutes until tender.
7. Place sliced beef back in the pan.
8. Meanwhile, add cornstarch to the water and dissolve it. Add it to the pan and combine it well.
9. Serve and enjoy!

Nutrition:
Calories: 368 | Carbs: 41g | Protein: 37g | Fat: 12g | Fiber: 9g

BLACK BEAN NACHO SOUP

Prep Time: 10 minutes | **Cook Time:** 0 minutes
Servings: 2
Ingredients:
- 18-ounce black bean soup, low-sodium
- 1/4 tsp smoked paprika
- 1/2 tsp lime juice
- 1/2 cup grape tomatoes, halved
- 1/2 cup cabbage, shredded
- 2 tbsp cotija cheese
- 1/2 avocado, diced
- 2 oz tortilla chips, baked

Directions:
1. Place soup into the saucepan and then add paprika in it and stir well.
2. Add lime juice and stir and cook it well.
3. Place soup among two bowls and top with sliced avocado, cheese, tomatoes, and cabbage.
4. Serve with tortilla chips.

Nutrition:
Calories: 350 | Carbs: 44.1g | Protein: 10.2g | Fat: 16.9g | Fiber: 9.4g

BUTTERNUT SQUASH SOUP

Prep Time: 15 minutes | **Cook Time:** 0 minutes
Servings: 1
Ingredients:
- 15 oz butternut Squash Soup
- 3/4 cup chickpeas, rinsed
- 1 tbsp lime juice
- 1 tsp curry powder
- Pinch of salt
- 2 tbsp avocado, diced
- 1 tbsp non-fat plain Greek yogurt

Directions:
1. Add soup into the saucepan and heat it.
2. Add salt, curry powder, lime juice, and chickpeas and stir and cook it.
3. When done, top with yogurt and avocado.

Nutrition:
Calories: 302 | Carbs: 57.7g | Protein: 11g | Fat: 5.8g | Fiber: 16.4g

BROCCOLI SALAD

Prep Time: 20 minutes | **Cooking Time:** 0 minutes
Servings: 5
Ingredients:
- 1/2 cup mayonnaise
- 1 tbsp whole-grain mustard
- 1 tbsp cider vinegar
- 1 garlic clove, grated
- 1 tsp sugar
- 1/4 tsp ground pepper
- 4 cups broccoli crowns, chopped
- 1 cup cauliflower, chopped
- 1/4 cup red onion, chopped
- 3 tbsp sunflower seeds, toasted

Directions:
1. Add pepper, sugar, garlic, vinegar, mustard, and mayonnaise into the bowl and whisk it well.
2. Add sunflower seeds, onion, broccoli, and cauliflower and stir well.
3. Serve and enjoy!

Nutrition:
Calories: 246 | Carbs: 7.7g | Protein: 5.4g | Fat: 2.8g | Fiber: 9g

BEEF AND BEAN SLOPPY JOE

Prep Time: 20 minutes | **Cook Time:** 0 minutes
Servings: 4
Ingredients:
- 1 tbsp extra-virgin olive oil
- 12 oz ground beef
- 1 cup no-salt-added black beans, rinsed
- 1 cup onion, chopped
- 2 tsp chili powder
- 1/2 tsp garlic powder
- 1/2 tsp onion powder
- Pinch of cayenne pepper
- 1 cup tomato sauce
- 3 tbsp ketchup
- 1 tbsp Worcestershire sauce
- 2 tsp spicy brown mustard
- 1 tsp brown sugar
- 4 whole-wheat hamburger buns, split and toasted

Directions:
1. Add oil into the skillet and cook over medium-high flame.
2. Add beef and cook for three to four minutes until browned.
3. Transfer the beef to the bowl using a slotted spoon.
4. Add onion and beans to the pan and cook until softened for five minutes.
5. Add cayenne, onion powder, garlic powder, and chili powder, and cook for thirty seconds.
6. Add brown sugar, mustard, Worcestershire sauce, ketchup, and tomato sauce and stir well. Place beef back in the pan and simmer for five minutes.
7. Serve and enjoy!

Nutrition:
Calories: 401 | Carbs: 42.8g | Protein: 26g | Fat: 12g | Fiber: 10.4g

LEMONY MEDITERRANEAN CHICKEN

Prep Time: 30 minutes | **Cook Time:** 1 h
Servings: 4
Ingredients:
- 1 lemon, thinly sliced
- 1 red bell pepper, cut into 1-inch wide strips
- 1 red onion, cut into 1-inch wedges
- 1 tbsp dried oregano
- 1/2 tsp coarsely ground black pepper
- 1/4 cup olive oil
- 2 tbsp fresh lemon juice
- 2 tbsp fresh lemon zest
- 3/4 tsp salt
- 4 large cloves garlic, pressed
- 4 skinless, boneless chicken breast halves
- 8 baby red potatoes, halved

Directions:
1. Heat the oven to 400 degrees F.
2. In a bowl mix lemon juice, lemon zest, olive oil, oregano, garlic, salt and black pepper. Season the chicken breasts with this mixture and then arrange them in a baking dish.
3. Mix and season the red bell pepper strips, red onion, potatoes, and lemon slices with the remaining lemon juice mixture. Next, arrange them in the baking dish with the chicken.
4. Bake in the oven for about 1 h until the chicken is browned.

Nutrition:
Calories: 507 | Carbo: 61g | Protein: 31 | Fat: 15g | Fiber: 10g

DINNER

SPINACH AND ARTICHOKE DIP PASTA
Prep Time: 5 minutes | **Cook Time:** 15 minutes
Servings: 4
Ingredients:
- 8 oz whole-wheat rotini
- 5 oz baby spinach, chopped
- 4 oz cream cheese, low-fat, cut into chunks
- 3/4 cup milk, low-fat
- 1/2 cup parmesan cheese, grated
- 2 tsp garlic powder
- 1/4 tsp ground pepper
- 14 oz artichoke hearts, rinsed, squeezed dry and chopped

Directions:
1. Add water into the saucepan and boil it. Add pasta and cook it. Then, drain it.
2. Mix the one tbsp water and spinach into the saucepan and cook over medium flame. Cook for two minutes until wilted.
3. Transfer it to the bowl. Add milk and cream to the pan and whisk it well.
4. Add pepper, garlic powder, and parmesan cheese and cook until thickened. Drain spinach and add to the sauce with pasta and artichoke. Cook it well.
5. Then, serve and enjoy!

Nutrition:
Calories: 370 | Carbs: 55.1g | Protein: 17.6g | Fat: 8.1g | Fiber: 9.9g

GRILLED EGGPLANT
Prep Time: 5 minutes | **Cook Time:** 40 minutes
Servings: 4
Ingredients:
- 4 cups water
- 1 cup cornmeal
- 1 tbsp butter
- 1/2 tsp salt
- 1 lb plum tomatoes, chopped
- 4 tbsp extra-virgin olive oil
- 2 tsp fresh oregano, chopped
- 1 garlic clove, grated
- 1/2 tsp ground pepper
- 1/4 tsp crushed red pepper
- 1 1/2 lbs eggplant, cut into half-inch-thick slices
- 1/4 cup feta cheese, crumbled
- 1/2 cup fresh basil, chopped

Directions:
1. Add water into the saucepan and boil it over high flame.
2. Add cornmeal and whisk it well. Then, lower the heat and cook for thirty-five minutes until tender.
3. When done, remove from the flame. Add salt and butter and stir well.
4. During this, preheat the grill over medium-high heat.
5. Add salt, crushed red pepper, pepper, garlic, oregano, three tbsp oil, and tomatoes into the bowl and toss to combine.
6. Rub eggplant with one tbsp oil and place onto the grill, and cook for four minutes per side. Let it cool for ten minutes.
7. Chop it and add to the tomatoes.
8. Sprinkle with fresh basil leaves. Place vegetable mixture over the polenta and top with cheese.

Nutrition:
Calories: 354 | Carbs: 39g | Protein: 6.8g | Fat: 20.6g | Fiber: 10.4g

STUFFED POTATOES WITH SALSA AND BEANS
Prep Time: 5 minutes | **Cook Time:** 20 minutes
Servings: 4
Ingredients:
- 4 russet potatoes
- 1/2 cup fresh salsa
- 1 avocado, sliced
- 15 oz pinto beans, rinsed, warmed and mashed
- 4 tsp jalapeños, chopped, pickled

Directions:
1. Firstly, pierce potatoes using a fork.
2. Let microwave for twenty minutes over medium heat.
3. Place onto the cutting board and let it cool.
4. Cut to open the potato lengthwise and pinch the ends to expose the flesh and top with jalapeno, beans, avocado, and salsa.
5. Serve and enjoy!

Nutrition:
Calories: 322 | Carbs: 52g | Protein: 10g | Fat: 7.2g | Fiber: 14.1g

MUSHROOM QUINOA VEGGIE BURGERS
Prep Time: 5 minutes | **Cook Time:** 25 minutes
Servings: 4
Ingredients:
- 1 portobello mushroom, gills removed, chopped
- 1 cup black beans, rinsed, unsalted
- 2 tbsp almond butter, creamy and unsalted
- 3 tbsp canola mayonnaise
- 1 tsp ground pepper
- 3/4 tsp smoked paprika
- 3/4 tsp garlic powder
- 1/2 tsp salt
- 1/2 cup cooked quinoa

- 1/4 cup old-fashioned rolled oats
- 1 tbsp ketchup
- 1 tsp Dijon mustard
- 1 tbsp extra-virgin olive oil
- 4 whole-wheat hamburger buns, toasted
- 2 leaves green-leaf lettuce, halved
- 4 tomato, sliced
- 4 red onion, thinly sliced

Directions:
1. Add salt, half tsp garlic powder, paprika, pepper, one tbsp mayonnaise, almond butter, black beans, and mushrooms into the food processor. Blend until smooth.
2. Transfer it to the bowl. Add oats and quinoa and stir well.
3. Place it in the refrigerator for one hour.
4. During this, whisk the 1/4 tsp garlic powder, two tbsp mayonnaise, mustard, and ketchup into the bowl until smooth.
5. Make the mixture into four patties.
6. Add oil to the non-stick skillet and cook over medium-high flame.
7. Fry patties for four to five minutes.
8. Flip and cook for two to four minutes until golden brown.
9. Top burger with onion, tomato, lettuce, and sauce.

Nutrition:
Calories: 394 | Carbs: 43.9g | Protein: 12.6g | Fat: 18g | Fiber: 11.4g

SWEET POTATO SOUP

Prep Time: 15 minutes
Cook Time: 30 minutes
Servings: 6
Ingredients:
- 1/4 cup canola oil
- 4 corn tortillas, halved and thinly sliced
- 3/4 tsp salt
- 1 poblano pepper, seeded and chopped
- 1 onion, chopped
- 2 tbsp chili powder
- 4 cups chicken broth or vegetable broth
- 1 1/2 lbs sweet potatoes, peeled and cut into half-inch pieces
- 14 oz tomatoes, unsalted, pitted, diced
- 15-ounce black beans, low-sodium, rinsed
- 3 tbsp lime juice
- 3 radishes, halved and thinly sliced
- 1/4 cup pumpkin seeds, roasted, unsalted
- 1/2 cup queso fresco, crumbled
- 1 avocado, chopped

Directions:
1. Add oil into the pot and cook over medium flame.
2. Add tortilla strips and cook for five minutes until crispy.
3. Transfer it to the plate lined with a paper towel using a slotted spoon.
4. Sprinkle with 1/4 tsp salt.
5. Add half tsp salt, chili powder, onion, and poblano, and cook for two minutes until softened.
6. Add tomatoes, beans, broth, and sweet potatoes and simmer for twenty minutes.
7. Add lime juice into the soup and top with tortilla strips, avocado, queso fresco, pepitas, and radish slices. Stir well.
8. Serve and enjoy!

Nutrition:
Calories: 412 | Carbs: 45g | Protein: 13.5g | Fat: 10.6g | Fiber: 11.7g

MINESTRONE SOUP

Prep Time: 5 minutes | **Cook Time:** 25 minutes
Servings: 6
Ingredients:
- 5 garlic cloves, minced
- 3 tbsp extra-virgin olive oil
- 1 cup whole-grain rustic bread, cubed
- 1 cup leek, chopped, white and light green parts only
- 1 cup carrots, chopped
- 3 cups vegetable broth
- 3 cups water
- 3/4 tsp kosher salt
- 1 cup ditalini pasta
- 10 oz zucchini, halved lengthwise and thinly sliced
- 15 oz cannellini beans, unsalted, rinsed
- 3 cups kale, chopped
- 1 cup frozen peas, thawed
- 1/2 tsp ground pepper

Directions:
1. Preheat the oven to 350°F.
2. Add two tbsp oil and garlic and cook over medium flame for three to four minutes.
3. Add bread and toss to combine. Place mixture onto the baking sheet and bake for eight to ten minutes.
4. During this, add one tbsp oil into the pot and cook over medium-high flame. Add carrots and leek and cook for five to six minutes.
5. Add salt, water, and broth and cover with a lid and boil it over high flame. Add pasta and lower the heat to medium-high and cook for five minutes. Add zucchini and cook for five minutes until al dente.
6. Add pepper, peas, kale, and beans and stir well. Let cook for two minutes.
7. Place soup into the six bowls. Top with croutons.

Nutrition:
Calories: 267 | Carbs: 38.7g | Protein: 9.7g | Fat: 8.6g | Fiber: 9.1g

LENTIL SOUP

Prep Time: 5 minutes | **Cook Time:** 1 hour
Servings: 6

Ingredients:
- 1 onion, chopped
- 1/4 cup olive oil
- 2 carrots, diced
- 2 celery stalks, chopped
- 2 garlic cloves, minced
- 1 tsp dried oregano
- 1 bay leaf
- 1 tsp dried basil
- 14.5 oz crushed tomatoes
- 2 cups dry lentils
- 8 cups water
- 1/2 cup spinach, rinsed and thinly sliced
- 2 tbsp vinegar
- Salt and ground black pepper, to taste

Directions:
1. Add oil into the pot and cook over medium flame.
2. Add celery, carrots, and onions and cook until tender.
3. Add basil, oregano, bay leaf, and garlic, stir well, and cook for two minutes.
4. Add tomatoes, water, and lentils and stir well. Let boil it.
5. Lower the heat and simmer for one hour.
6. Add spinach and cook until wilted.
7. Add pepper, salt, and vinegar and stir well.

Nutrition:
Calories: 339 | Carbs: 41.2g | Protein: 10.3g | Fat: 9g | Fiber: 22g

GRILLED CORN SALAD

Prep Time: 15 minutes | **Cook Time:** 10 minutes
Servings: 6
Ingredients:
- 6 freshly shucked corn ears
- 1 green pepper, diced
- 2 plum tomatoes, diced
- 1/4 cup red onion, diced
- 1/2 bunch fresh cilantro, chopped
- 2 tsp olive oil
- Salt and ground black pepper, to taste

Directions:
1. Preheat the grill over medium heat. Oil the grate.
2. Place corn onto the grill and cook for ten minutes and keep it aside.
3. Let it cool. Cut the kernels off the cob and place them into the medium bowl.
4. Mix the olive oil, cilantro, onion, diced tomato, green pepper, and corn kernels and sprinkle with pepper and salt.
5. Toss to combine. Let stand for thirty minutes.
6. Serve and enjoy!

Nutrition:
Calories: 102 | Carbs: 16.7g | Protein: 4.4g | Fat: 2.5g | Fiber: 6.3g

KALE SOUP

Prep Time: 25 minutes | **Cook Time:** 30 minutes
Servings: 8
Ingredients:
- 2 tbsp olive oil
- 1 yellow onion, chopped
- 2 tbsp garlic
- 1 bunch kale, stems removed and leaves chopped
- 6 cups water
- 6 cubes vegetable bouillon
- 15 oz tomatoes, diced
- 6 white potatoes, peeled and cubed
- 30 oz cannellini beans, drained
- 1 tbsp Italian seasoning
- 2 tbsp dried parsley
- Salt and pepper, to taste

Directions:
1. Add olive oil into the pot and heat it.
2. Add garlic and onion and cook until softened.
3. Add kale and stir, and cook for two minutes.
4. Add parsley, Italian seasoning, beans, potatoes, tomatoes, vegetable bouillon, and water and stir well. Let simmer for twenty-five minutes.
5. Sprinkle with pepper and salt.

Nutrition:
Calories: 276 | Carbs: 48.9g | Protein: 10.6g | Fat: 4g | Fiber: 16.3g

PASTA FAGIOLI

Prep Time: 10 minutes | **Cook Time:** 30 minutes
Servings: 4
Ingredients:
- 1 tbsp olive oil
- 1 carrot, diced
- 1 celery stalk, diced
- 1 onion, diced, thinly sliced
- 1/2 tsp garlic, chopped
- 8 oz tomato sauce
- 14 oz chicken broth
- Ground black pepper, to taste
- 1 tbsp dried parsley
- 1/2 tbsp dried basil leaves
- 15 oz cannellini beans, drained and rinsed
- 1 1/2 cups ditalini pasta

Directions:
1. Add olive oil into the saucepan and heat it over medium flame.
2. Add onion, celery, and carrot and cook until fragrant.
3. Add garlic and cook it well. Add basil, parsley, pepper, chicken broth, and tomato sauce and simmer for twenty minutes.
4. Add salt and water into the pot and boil it. Add ditalini pasta and cook for eight minutes until al dente. Let it drain.
5. Add beans to the sauce mixture and simmer for a few minutes.

6. When pasta is done, add bean mixture and sauce and stir well.
7. Serve and enjoy!

Nutrition:
Calories: 336 | Carbs: 56.7g | Protein: 15.4g | Fat: 5g | Fiber: 12.4g

SWEET POTATO GNOCCHI

Prep Time: 30 minutes | **Cook Time:** 35 minutes
Servings: 4
Ingredients:
- 8 oz sweet potatoes
- 1 garlic clove, pressed
- 1/2 tsp salt
- 1/2 tsp ground nutmeg
- 1 egg
- 2 cups all-purpose flour

Directions:
1. Preheat the oven to 350°F.
2. Let bake for thirty minutes until softened.
3. When done, remove it from the oven and keep it aside to cool.
4. When cooled, peel and mash them and add them to the bowl.
5. Add egg, nutmeg, salt, and garlic and mix it well.
6. Add flour and combine it well.
7. Add water and salt into the pot and boil it.
8. To prepare the gnocchi: Roll the dough onto the floured surface and cut it into sections.
9. Add pieces into the boiled water and cook until they floated on the surface.
10. When done, remove and serve!
11. Top with cream sauce or butter.

Nutrition:
Calories: 345 | Carbs: 69.1g | Protein: 10g | Fat: 2g | Fiber: 7.2g

BEAN AND HAM SOUP

Prep Time: 25 minutes | **Cook Time:** 10 hours
Servings: 12
Ingredients:
- 2 sweet potatoes
- 1 garlic clove, pressed
- 1/2 tsp salt
- 1/2 tsp ground nutmeg
- 1 egg
- 2 cups all-purpose flour
- 20 oz bean mixture, soaked overnight
- 1 ham bone
- 2 1/2 cups ham, cubed
- 1 onion, chopped
- 3 celery stalks, chopped
- 5 carrots, chopped
- 14.5 oz tomatoes, diced, with liquid
- 12 fluid ounce vegetable juice, low-sodium
- 3 cups vegetable broth
- 2 tbsp Worcestershire sauce
- 2 tbsp Dijon mustard
- 1 tbsp chili powder
- 3 bay leaves
- 1 tsp ground black pepper
- 1 tbsp dried parsley
- 3 tbsp lemon juice
- 7 cups chicken broth, low-sodium
- 1 tsp kosher salt

Directions:
1. Add soaked beans into the pot, and then add water until it covers the beans. Let boil on low flame for thirty minutes. Then, drain it.
2. Add vegetable broth, vegetable juice, tomatoes, carrots, celery, onion, ham, and ham bone and sprinkle with lemon juice, parsley, pepper, bay leaf, chili powder, Dijon mustard, and Worcestershire sauce.
3. Add chicken broth and simmer on low flame for eight hours.
4. Add more chicken broth as required. Remove the ham bone and sprinkle with salt.
5. Let simmer for two hours more.
6. Discard bay leaves.

Nutrition:
Calories: 260 | Carbs: 37.9g | Fiber: 7.8g | Protein: 17.3g | Fat: 3.6g

GRILLED PEAR CHEDDAR POCKETS

Prep Time: 15 minutes | **Cook Time:** 0 minutes
Servings: 1
Ingredients:
- 2 tsp Dijon mustard
- 1/2 whole grain flatbread
- 2 slices of cheddar cheese
- 1/4 cup arugula
- 1/3 red pear, cored and cut into thick slices

Directions:
1. Spread mustard over the inner side of the flatbread pocket.
2. Place cheese slices and fold them. Then, add pear slices and arugula.
3. Place it into the skillet and cook for 3 to 4 minutes.

Nutrition:
Calories: 222 | Carbs: 27.6g | Protein: 10.3g | Fat: 8g | Fiber: 9.8g

CHICKEN AND APPLE KALE WRAPS

Prep Time: 10 minutes | **Cook Time:** 0 minutes
Servings: 1
Ingredients:
- 1 tbsp mayonnaise
- 1 tsp Dijon mustard
- 3 kale leaves
- 3 oz chicken breast, thinly sliced, cooked
- 6 slices red onion, thin

- 1 apple, cut into nine slices

Directions:
1. Combine the mustard and mayonnaise into the bowl. Spread onto the kale leaves—top with one-ounce chicken, three slices of apples, and two slices of onion. Then, roll each kale leaf. Cut in half.

Nutrition:
Calories: 360 | Carbs: 31.1g | Protein: 27.3g | Fat: 11.7g | Fiber: 9g

CAULIFLOWER RICE PILAF

Prep Time: 10 minutes | **Cook Time:** 10 minutes
Servings: 1
Ingredients:
- 6 cups cauliflower florets
- 3 tbsp extra-virgin olive oil
- 2 garlic cloves, minced
- 1/2 tsp salt
- 1/4 cup almonds, toasted, sliced
- 1/4 cup herbs, chopped
- 2 tsp lemon zest

Directions:
1. Add cauliflower florets into the food processor and blend until chopped.
2. Add oil into the skillet and place it over medium-high flame.
3. Then, add garlic and cook for a half-minute.
4. Add cauliflower rice and season with salt. Let cook for three to five minutes.
5. Remove from the flame.
6. Add lemon zest, herbs, and almonds and stir well.

Nutrition:
Calories: 112 | Carbs: 6g | Protein: 3.2g | Fat: 9g | Fiber: 5.8g

FRESH HERB AND LEMON BULGUR PILAF

Prep Time: 10 minutes | **Cook Time:** 40 minutes
Servings: 6
Ingredients:
- 2 tbsp extra-virgin olive oil
- 2 cups onion, chopped
- 1 garlic clove, chopped
- 1 1/2 cups bulgur
- 1/2 tsp ground turmeric
- 1/2 tsp ground cumin
- 2 cups vegetable or chicken broth, low-sodium
- 1 1/2 cups carrot, chopped
- 2 tsp fresh ginger, grated or chopped
- 1 tsp salt
- 1/4 cup fresh dill, chopped
- 1/4 cup fresh mint, chopped
- 1/4 cup parsley, chopped
- 3 tbsp lemon juice
- 1/2 cup walnuts, chopped, toasted

Directions:
1. Add oil into the skillet and place it over medium flame.
2. Add onion and cook for 12 to 18 minutes.
3. Add garlic and cook for one minute.
4. Then, add cumin, turmeric, and bulgur and cook for one minute.
5. Add salt, ginger, carrot, and broth and bring to a boil over medium-high flame, about 15 minutes.
6. Remove from the flame.
7. Let rest for five minutes.
8. Add lemon juice, parsley, dill, and mint into the pilaf and stir well. Garnish with walnuts.

Nutrition:
Calories: 273 | Carbs: 38.8g | Protein: 7.3g | Fat: 11.7g | Fiber: 9g

CORN CHOWDER

Prep Time: 10 minutes | **Cook Time:** 5 hours
Servings: 6
Ingredients:
- 3/4 cup yellow split peas, split
- 28 oz chicken broth, low-sodium
- 1 cup water
- 12 oz corn kernels, frozen
- 1/2 cup red sweet peppers, chopped and roasted
- 4 oz green chilies, diced
- 1 tsp ground cumin
- 1/2 tsp dried oregano, crushed
- 1/2 tsp dried thyme, crushed
- 1/2 cup cream cheese

Directions:
1. Rinse split peas underwater.
2. Mix the thyme, oregano, cumin, chilies, red peppers, corn, water, split peas, and chicken broth and cook on high heat for five to six hours.
3. Let it cool for ten minutes.
4. Transfer two cups of soup into the food processor and blend until smooth.
5. Add pureed soup into the slow cooker. Then, add cream cheese and whisk to combine—Cook for five minutes.
6. Serve!

Nutrition:
Calories: 222 | Carbs: 29.8g | Protein: 10.5g | Fat: 7.5g | Fiber: 9g

STRAWBERRY AND RHUBARB SOUP

Prep Time: 5 minutes | **Cook Time:** 30 minutes
Servings: 4
Ingredients:
- 4 cups rhubarb
- 3 cups water
- 1 1/2 cups strawberries, sliced
- 1/4 cup sugar
- 1/8 tsp salt

- 1/3 cup mint or basil, chopped
- Ground pepper, to taste

Directions:
1. Add three cups of water and rhubarb into the saucepan.
2. Cook for five minutes until softened.
3. Transfer it to the bowl.
4. Add 2-inch ice water into the bowl and keep it aside with rhubarb.
5. Place it into the fridge for twenty minutes.
6. Transfer the rhubarb to the blender. Then, add salt, sugar, and strawberries and blend until smooth.
7. Place it back in the bowl. Add basil or mint.
8. Serve!

Nutrition:
Calories: 91 | Carbs: 23g | Protein: 2.6g | Fat: 0.4g | Fiber: 5.5g

CHICKEN SANDWICHES

Prep Time: 5 minutes | **Cook Time:** 30 minutes
Servings: 4
Ingredients:
- 4 red onion slices
- 1 red sweet pepper, seeded and quartered
- 6 oz chicken breast, boneless, cut in half, horizontally
- 4 multi-grain sandwich round, split
- 2 tbsp basil pesto
- 2 tbsp kalamata olives, pitted and chopped
- 1/3 cup mozzarella cheese, shredded
- 1/4 cup feta cheese, low-fat, crumbled

Directions:
1. Grease the bell bell pepper and red onion with nonstick cooking spray and cook them in a pan for 6 to 8 minutes. Then transfer them to a bowl.
2. Coat the chicken with nonstick cooking spray and cook it in the pan for 3-5 minutes.
3. Cut the chicken into shreds. Cut bell bell pepper into strips.
4. Spread the pesto on the sandwich and add the olives. Arrange grilled onion slices, bell bell pepper strips, and chicken. Finally add feta cheese and mozzarella cheese.
5. Place the sandwich in the pan and cook both sides for 3 to 4 minutes.

Nutrition:
Calories: 296 | Carbs: 27.7g | Protein: 25.8g | Fat: 10g

TEX-MEX BEAN TOSTADAS

Prep Time: 10 minutes | **Cook Time:** 15 minutes
Servings: 4
Ingredients:
- 4 tostada shells
- 16 oz pinto beans, rinsed and drained
- 1/2 cup salsa, prepared
- 1/2 tsp chipotle seasoning
- 1/2 cup cheddar cheese, shredded
- 1 1/2 cups iceberg lettuce
- 1 cup tomato, chopped
- 1 lime wedges

Directions:
1. Preheat the oven to 350°F.
2. Place tostada shells onto the baking sheet and bake for three to five minutes.
3. Meanwhile, mix the seasoning, salsa, and bean into the bowl.
4. Mash the mixture with a potato masher.
5. Then, divide the bean mixture between tostada shells.
6. Top with half of the cheese. Bake for five minutes.
7. Top with chopped tomato and shredded lettuce.
8. Then, place the remaining cheese and lime wedges.

Nutrition:
Calories: 230 | Carbs: 33g | Protein: 12g | Fat: 6g | Fiber: 10g

FISH TACOS

Prep Time: 10 minutes | **Cook Time:** 15 minutes
Servings: 4
Ingredients:
- 1 lb tilapia fillets
- 2 tsp extra-virgin olive oil
- 2 tsp chipotle seasoning blend
- 2 cups coleslaw mix
- 2 tbsp salad dressing, ranch
- 8 whole-wheat tortillas
- 1/2 avocado, thinly sliced
- 1/4 cup cilantro leaves
- 1 lime, quartered

Directions:
1. Preheat the oven to 450°F.
2. Place fillets onto the baking dish and brush the fish with oil.
3. Sprinkle with seasoning.
4. Bake for four to six minutes.
5. Meanwhile, mix the dressing and coleslaw into a bowl. Keep it aside.
6. Flake the fish into big chunks and place them into the tortillas.
7. Top with lime, cilantro, avocado, and coleslaw mixture.

Nutrition:
Calories: 341 | Carbs: 30.5g | Protein: 29.5g | Fat: 12g | Fiber: 6.2g

CUCUMBER ALMOND GAZPACHO

Prep Time: 20 minutes | **Cook Time:** 0 minutes
Chill Time: 2 hours
Servings: 5

Ingredients:
- 2 English cucumbers
- 2 cups yellow bell pepper, chopped
- 2 cups whole-wheat bread
- 1 1/2 cups unsweetened almond milk
- 1/2 cup almonds, toasted, slivered
- 5 tsp olive oil
- 2 tsp white-wine vinegar
- 1 garlic clove
- 1/2 tsp salt

Directions:
1. Dice unpeeled cucumber and mix with half a cup of bell pepper.
2. Peel the remaining cucumbers and cut them into chunks.
3. Add remaining bell pepper, peeled cucumber, salt, garlic, vinegar, oil, six tbsp of almonds, almond milk, and bread into the blender and blend until smooth. Let's chill for two hours.
4. Garnish with the remaining 2 tbsp almonds.
5. Drizzle with oil.

Nutrition:
Calories: 200 | Carbs: 18g | Protein: 7g | Fat: 11g | Fiber: 7.3g

PEA AND SPINACH CARBONARA

Prep Time: 5 minutes | **Cook Time:** 15 minutes
Servings: 4

Ingredients:
- 1 1/2 tbsp extra-virgin olive oil
- 1/2 cup panko breadcrumbs (whole-wheat)
- 1 garlic clove, minced
- 8 tbsp parmesan cheese, grated
- 3 tbsp fresh parsley, chopped
- 3 egg yolks
- 1 egg
- 1/2 tsp ground pepper
- 1/4 tsp salt
- 9 oz tagliatelle or linguine
- 8 cups of baby spinach
- 1 cup peas

Directions:
1. Add ten cups of water into the pot and boil it over a high flame.
2. During this, add oil to the skillet and cook over medium-high flame.
3. Add garlic and breadcrumbs and cook for two minutes until toasted.
4. Transfer it to the small bowl. Add parsley and two tbsp parmesan cheese and keep it aside.
5. Whisk the salt, pepper, egg, egg yolks, and six tbsp parmesan cheese into the bowl.
6. Add pasta to the boiling water and cook for one minute.
7. Add spinach and peas and cook for one minute more until tender.
8. Save 1/4 cup of the cooking water for your next use. Drain it and place it into the bowl.
9. Whisk the reserved cooking water into the egg mixture, add to the pasta, and toss to combine.
10. Top with breadcrumb mixture and serve!

Nutrition:
Calories: 428 | Carbs: 54g | Protein: 21.2g | Fat: 12.5g | Fiber: 10.2g

SAUTÉED BROCCOLI WITH PEANUT SAUCE

Prep Time: 5 minutes | **Cook Time:** 10 minutes
Servings: 6

Ingredients:
- 8 cups broccoli florets
- 2 tbsp sesame oil, toasted
- 1 cup red bell pepper, sliced
- 1/2 cup yellow onion, sliced
- 3 garlic cloves, chopped
- 3 tbsp peanut butter
- 2 1/2 tbsp tamari, low-sodium
- 2 tbsp rice vinegar
- 1 tbsp brown sugar
- 1 tsp cornstarch
- 1 tbsp sesame seeds, toasted

Directions:
1. Add water into the pot and boil it. Then, add broccoli and cook for three to four minutes until tender.
2. During this, add oil to the skillet and cook over medium-high flame.
3. Add garlic, onion, and bell pepper and cook for three minutes.
4. Add steamed broccoli and cook for three minutes. Stir well.
5. Whisk the cornstarch, sugar, vinegar, tamari, and peanut butter into the bowl. Add vegetables and stir well.
6. Let cook for one minute. Top with sesame seeds.
7. Serve and enjoy!

Nutrition:
Calories: 153 | Carbs: 11g | Protein: 7g | Fat: 9g | Fiber: 6.4g

EDAMAME LETTUCE WRAPS BURGERS

Prep Time: 5 minutes | **Cook Time:** 25 minutes
Servings: 4

Ingredients:
- 1 cup carrots, julienned
- 3 tbsp lime juice
- 2 tsp chili-garlic sauce
- 1 1/2 cups shelled edamame, thawed
- 1 cup cooked brown rice
- 1/2 cup peanut butter powder
- 1/4 cup scallions, chopped
- 1 tbsp red Thai curry paste
- 3 tbsp peanut oil
- 2 tbsp tamari, low-sodium
- 4 leaves of bibb lettuce

- 1 cup red onion, thinly sliced

Directions:
1. Firstly, toss carrots with one tsp chili garlic sauce and two tbsp lime juice and keep it aside.
2. Add tamari, one tbsp oil, curry paste, scallions, edamame rice, and 1/4 cup peanut butter powder into the blender and blend until smooth.
3. Shape the mixture into four burgers.
4. Add two tbsp oil into the skillet and cook over medium flame.
5. Add burgers and cook for three to four minutes per side.
6. When done, transfer it to the plate.
7. During this, whisk the one tsp chili garlic sauce, tamari, one tbsp lime juice, and 1/4 cup peanut butter powder into the bowl until smooth.
8. Then, drain the carrots. Add marinade to the peanut sauce. Stir well.
9. Wrap burger in lettuce leaves and top with sauce, onions, and carrots.

Nutrition:
Calories: 309 | Carbs: 31g | Protein: 15.6g | Fat: 13.5g | Fiber: 9.6g

PIZZA STUFFED SPAGHETTI SQUASH

Prep Time: 10 minutes | **Cook Time:** 1 hour
Servings: 4
Ingredients:
- 3 pounds spaghetti squash, halved lengthwise and seeded
- 1/4 cup water
- 2 tbsp extra-virgin olive oil
- 1 cup onion, chopped
- 2 garlic cloves, minced
- 8 oz mushrooms, sliced
- 1 cup bell pepper, chopped
- 2 cups no-salt-added crushed tomatoes
- 1 tsp Italian seasoning
- 1/2 tsp ground pepper
- 1/4 tsp crushed red pepper, crushed
- 1/4 tsp salt
- 2 oz pepperoni, halved
- 1 cup part-skim mozzarella cheese, shredded
- 2 tbsp parmesan cheese, grated

Directions:
1. Preheat the oven to 450°F.
2. Add squash into the microwave-safe dish and then add water.
3. Microwave it for ten to twelve minutes until tender.
4. Then, place it into the oven and bake for forty to fifty minutes at 400°F.
5. During this, add oil to the skillet and cook over medium flame.
6. Add garlic and onion and cook for three to four minutes.
7. Add bell pepper and mushrooms and cook for five minutes more until tender.
8. Add salt, crushed red pepper, pepper, Italian seasoning, and tomatoes and cook for two minutes.
9. When done, remove from the flame.
10. Add ten to twelve pepperoni halves and cover them with a lid.
11. Scrape the squash from the shells and place it into the bowl.
12. Add salt, pepper, mozzarella, and parmesan cheese and stir well.
13. Add tomato mixture to the bowl and stir well.
14. Place squash shells onto the rimmed baking sheet and divide the filling among the halves, and top with pepperoni and mozzarella cheese. Place it into the oven and bake for fifteen minutes.
15. Let broil it for one to two minutes.
16. Serve and enjoy!

Nutrition:
Calories: 373 | Carbs: 32.2g | Protein: 16.4g | Fat: 20.6g | Fiber: 8.5g

ONE-POT DINNER SOUP

Prep Time: 15 minutes | **Cook Time:** 50 minutes
Servings: 4
Ingredients:
- 1 tbsp olive oil
- 1 cup yellow onion, chopped
- 1/2 cup carrots, peeled and chopped
- 1/2 cup celery, chopped
- 2 garlic cloves, minced
- 4 cups homemade vegetable broth
- 2 1/2 cup sweet potatoes, peeled and chopped
- 1 cup red lentils, rinsed
- 1 1/2 tbsp fresh lemon juice
- Salt and freshly ground black pepper, to taste
- 2 tbsp fresh cilantro, chopped

Directions:
1. In a large Dutch oven, heat the oil over medium heat and sauté the onion, carrot and celery for about 5-7 minutes.
2. Add the garlic and sauté for about 1 minute.
3. Add the sweet potatoes and cook for about 1-2 minutes.
4. Add in the broth and bring to a boil.
5. Reduce the heat to low and simmer, covered for about 5 minutes.
6. Stir in the red lentils and gain bring to a boil over medium-high heat.
7. Reduce the heat to low and simmer, covered for about 25-30 minutes or until desired doneness.
8. Stir in the lemon juice, salt and black pepper and remove from the heat.
9. Serve hot with the garnishing of cilantro.

Nutrition:
Calories: 471 | Carbs: 61g | Protein: 19.3g | Fat: 5.6g | Fiber: 19.7g

3-BEANS SOUP

Prep Time: 15 minutes | **Cook Time:** 45 minutes
Servings: 12
Ingredients:
- 1/4 cup olive oil
- 1 large onion, chopped
- 1 large sweet potato, peeled and cubed
- 3 carrots, peeled and chopped
- 3 celery stalks, chopped
- 3 garlic cloves, minced
- 2 tsp dried thyme, crushed
- 1 tbsp red chili powder
- 1 tbsp ground cumin
- 4 large tomatoes, peeled, seeded and chopped finely
- 2 (16-oz) cans of Great Northern beans, rinsed and drained
- 2 (15 1/4-oz) cans of red kidney beans, rinsed and drained
- 1 (15-oz) can of black beans, drained and rinsed
- 12 cups of homemade vegetable broth
- 1 cup fresh cilantro, chopped
- Salt and freshly ground black pepper, to taste

Directions:
1. In a Dutch oven, heat the oil over medium heat and sauté the onion, sweet potato, carrot and celery for about 6-8 minutes.
2. Add the garlic, thyme, chili powder and cumin and sauté for about 1 minute.
3. Add in the tomatoes and cook for about 2-3 minutes.
4. Add the beans and broth and bring to a boil over medium-high heat.
5. Cover the pan with a lid and cook for about 25-30 minutes.
6. Stir in the cilantro and remove from heat.
7. Serve hot.

Nutrition:
Calories: 411 | Carbs: 69.7g | Protein: 22.7g | Fat: 5.7g | Fiber: 18.9g

HEAVENLY TASTY STEW

Prep Time: 15 minutes | **Cook Time:** 35 minutes
Servings: 6
Ingredients:
- 1/4 cup olive oil
- 1 large yellow onion, chopped
- 8 oz fresh shiitake mushrooms, sliced
- 2 large tomatoes, chopped
- 2 tbsp garlic, chopped finely
- 2 bay leaves
- 2 tbsp mixed Italian herbs (rosemary, thyme, basil), chopped
- 1 tsp cayenne pepper
- 4 cups homemade vegetable broth
- 2 tbsp apple cider vinegar
- 1 cup whole-wheat fusilli pasta
- 1/3 cup nutritional yeast
- 8 oz fresh collard greens
- 1 (15-oz) can of cannellini beans, drained and rinsed
- Salt and freshly ground black pepper, to taste

Directions:
1. In a large pan, heat the oil over medium heat and sauté the onion, mushrooms, potato and tomato for about 4-5 minutes.
2. Add the garlic, bay leaves, herbs and cayenne pepper and sauté for about 1 minute.
3. Add the broth and bring to a boil.
4. Stir in the vinegar, pasta and nutritional yeast and again bring to a boil.
5. Reduce the heat to medium-low and simmer, covered for about 20 minutes.
6. Uncover and stir in the greens and beans.
7. Simmer for about 4-5 minutes.
8. Stir in the salt and black pepper and remove from the heat.
9. Serve hot.

Nutrition:
Calories: 314 | Carbs: 46g | Protein: 14.4g | Fat: 10g | Fiber: 12.3g

THANKSGIVING DINNER CHILI

Prep Time: 15 minutes | **Cook Time:** 45 minutes
Servings: 6
Ingredients:
- 2 tbsp olive oil
- 1 red bell pepper, seeded and chopped
- 1 onion, chopped
- 2 garlic cloves, chopped
- 1 lb. lean ground turkey
- 2 cups water
- 3 cups tomatoes, chopped finely
- 1 tsp ground cumin
- 1/2 tsp ground cinnamon
- 1 (15-oz) can of red kidney beans, rinsed and drained
- 1 (15-oz) can of black beans, rinsed and drained
- 1/4 cup scallion greens, chopped

Directions:
1. In a large Dutch oven, heat the olive oil over medium-low heat and sauté bell pepper, onion and garlic for about 5 minutes.
2. Add the turkey and cook for about 5-6 minutes, breaking up the chunks with a wooden spoon.
3. Add the water, tomatoes and spices and bring to a boil over high heat.
4. Reduce the heat to medium-low and stir in beans and corn.
5. Simmer, covered for about 30 minutes, stirring occasionally.
6. Serve hot with the topping of scallion greens.

Nutrition:
Calories: 366 | Carbs: 40.6g | Protein: 28.7g | Fat: 11.2g | Fiber: 13.4g

MEATLESS MONDAY CHILI

Prep Time: 15 minutes | **Cook Time:** 1 hour 25 minutes
Servings: 4
Ingredients:
- 2 tbsp avocado oil
- 1 medium onion, chopped
- 1 carrot, peeled and chopped
- 1 small bell pepper, seeded and chopped
- 1 lb. fresh mushrooms, sliced
- 2 garlic cloves, minced
- 2 tsp dried oregano
- 1 tbsp red chili powder
- 1 tbsp ground cumin
- Salt and freshly ground black pepper, to taste
- 8 oz canned red kidney beans, rinsed and drained
- 8 oz canned white kidney beans, rinsed and drained
- 2 cups tomatoes, peeled, seeded and chopped finely
- 1 1/2 cups homemade vegetable broth

Directions:
1. In a large Dutch oven, heat the oil over medium-low heat and cook the onions, carrot and bell pepper for about 10 minutes, stirring frequently.
2. Increase the heat to medium-high.
3. Stir in the mushrooms and garlic and cook for about 5-6 minutes, stirring frequently.
4. Add the oregano, spices, salt and black pepper and cook for about chili 1-2 minutes.
5. Stir in the beans, tomatoes and broth and bring to a boil.
6. Reduce the heat to low and simmer, covered for about 1 hour, stirring occasionally.
7. Serve hot.

Nutrition:
Calories: 346 | Carbs: 59.8g | Protein: 23.4g | Fat: 3.7g | Fiber: 16.7g

BEANS TRIO CHILI

Prep Time: 15 minutes | **Cook Time:** 1 hour
Servings: 6
Ingredients:
- 2 tbsp olive oil
- 1 green bell pepper, seeded and chopped
- 2 celery stalks, chopped
- 1 scallion, chopped
- 3 garlic cloves, minced
- 1 tsp dried oregano, crushed
- 1 tbsp red chili powder
- 2 tsp ground cumin
- 1 tsp red pepper flakes, crushed
- 1 tsp ground turmeric
- 1 tsp onion powder
- 1 tsp garlic powder
- Salt and freshly ground black pepper, to taste
- 4 1/2 cups tomatoes, peeled, seeded and chopped finely
- 4 cups water
- 1 (16-oz) can of red kidney beans, rinsed and drained
- 1 (16-oz) can of cannellini beans, rinsed and drained
- 1/2 of (16-oz) can of black beans, rinsed and drained

Directions:
1. In a large pan, heat the oil over medium heat and cook the bell peppers, celery, scallion and garlic for about 8-10 minutes, stirring frequently.
2. Add the oregano, spices, salt, black pepper, tomatoes and water, and bring to a boil.
3. Simmer for about 20 minutes.
4. Stir in the beans and simmer for about 30 minutes.
5. Serve hot.

Nutrition:
Calories: 342 | Carbs: 56g | Protein: 20.3g | Fat: 6.1g | Fiber: 21.3g

STAPLE VEGAN CURRY

Prep Time: 15 minutes | **Cook Time:** 40 minutes
Servings: 6
Ingredients:
- 10 oz whole-wheat pasta
- 1 tbsp vegetable oil
- 1 medium white onion, chopped
- 3 garlic cloves, minced
- 1 tsp dried basil, crushed
- 1 tbsp curry powder
- 1/4 tsp red pepper flakes, crushed
- 2 lb. ripe tomatoes, peeled, seeded and chopped
- 4 cups cauliflower, cut into bite-sized pieces
- 1 medium red bell pepper, seeded and sliced thinly
- 1 cup water
- 1 (15-oz) can of chickpeas, drained and rinsed
- 1 cup fresh baby spinach
- 1/4 cup fresh parsley, chopped
- Salt, to taste

Directions:
1. In a pan of salted boiling water, add the pasta and cook for about 8-10 minutes or according to the package's directions.
2. Drain the pasta well and set it aside.
3. Sauté the onion in a large cast-iron skillet over medium heat for about 4-5 minutes.
4. Add the garlic, basil, curry powder and red pepper flakes and sauté for about 1 minute.
5. Stir in the tomatoes, cauliflower, bell pepper and water and bring to a gentle boil.
6. Reduce the heat to medium-low and simmer, covered for about 15-20 minutes.
7. Stir in the chickpeas and cook for about 5 minutes.
8. Add the spinach and cook for about 3-4 minutes.
9. Stir in the pasta and remove from the heat.
10. Serve hot.

Nutrition:
Calories: 338 | Carbs: 58.4g | Protein: 15.1g | Fat: 5.9g | Fiber: 10.3g

FRAGRANT VEGETARIAN CURRY

Prep Time: 15 minutes | **Cook Time:** 1 1/2 hours
Servings: 8
Ingredients:
- 8 cups water
- 1/2 tsp ground turmeric
- 1 cup brown lentils
- 1 cup red lentils
- 1 tbsp olive oil
- 1 large white onion, chopped
- 3 garlic cloves, minced
- 2 large tomatoes, peeled, seeded and chopped
- 1 1/2 tbsp curry powder
- 1/4 tsp ground cloves
- 2 tsp ground cumin
- 3 carrots, peeled and chopped
- 3 cups pumpkin, peeled, seeded and cubed into 1-inch size
- 1 granny smith apple, cored and chopped
- 2 cups fresh spinach, chopped
- Salt and freshly ground black pepper, to taste

Directions:
1. In a large pan, add the water, turmeric and lentils over high heat and bring to a boil.
2. Reduce the heat to medium-low and simmer, covered for about 30 minutes.
3. Drain the lentils, reserving 2 1/2 cups of the cooking liquid.
4. Meanwhile, in another large pan, heat the oil over medium heat and sauté the onion for about 2-3 minutes.
5. Add in the garlic and sauté for about 1 minute.
6. Add the tomatoes and cook for about 5 minutes.
7. Stir in the curry powder and spices and cook for about 1 minute.
8. Add the carrots, potatoes, pumpkin, cooked lentils, and reserved cooking liquid and bring to a gentle boil.
9. Reduce the heat to medium-low and simmer, covered for about 40-45 minutes or until the desired doneness of the vegetables.
10. Stir in the apple and spinach and simmer for about 15 minutes.
11. Stir in the salt and black pepper and remove from the heat.
12. Serve hot.

Nutrition:
Calories: 263 | Carbs: 47g | Protein: 14.7g | Fat: 2.9g | Fiber: 12g

OMEGA-3 RICH DINNER MEAL

Prep Time: 15 minutes | **Cook Time:** 40 minutes
Servings: 4
Ingredients:
For Lentils:
- 1/2 lb. French green lentils
- 2 tbsp extra-virgin olive oil
- 2 cups yellow onions, chopped
- 2 cups scallions, chopped
- 1 tsp fresh parsley, chopped
- Salt and freshly ground black pepper, to taste
- 1 tbsp garlic, minced
- 1 1/2 cups carrots, peeled and chopped
- 1 1/2 cups celery stalks, chopped
- 1 large tomato, peeled, seeded and crushed finely
- 1 1/2 cups chicken bone broth
- 2 tbsp balsamic vinegar

For Salmon:
- 2 (8-oz) skinless salmon fillets
- 2 tbsp extra-virgin olive oil
- Salt and freshly ground black pepper, to taste

Directions:
1. In a heat-proof bowl, soak the lentils in boiling water for 15 minutes.
2. Drain the lentils completely.
3. In a Dutch oven, heat the oil over medium heat and cook the onions, scallions, parsley, salt and black pepper for about 10 minutes, stirring frequently.
4. Add the garlic and cook for about 2 more minutes.
5. Add the drained lentils, carrots, celery, crushed tomato and broth and bring to a boil.
6. Reduce the heat to low and simmer, covered for about 20-25 minutes.
7. Stir in the vinegar, salt and black pepper and remove from the heat.
8. Meanwhile, for salmon: preheat your oven to 450°F.
9. Rub the salmon fillets with oil and then, season with salt and black pepper generously.
10. Heat an oven-proof sauté pan over medium heat and cook the salmon fillets for about 2 minutes, without stirring.
11. Flip the fillets and immediately transfer the pan into the oven.
12. Bake for about 5-7 minutes or until the desired doneness of salmon.
13. Remove from the oven and place the salmon fillets onto a cutting board.
14. Cut each fillet into 2 portions.
15. Divide the lentil mixture onto serving plates and top each with 1 salmon fillet.
16. Serve hot.

Nutrition:
Calories: 707 | Carbs: 50.2g | Protein: 16.1g | Fat: 29.8g | Fiber: 12.2g

WEEKEND DINNER CASSEROLE

Prep Time: 20 minutes | **Cook Time:** 1 hour
Servings: 6
Ingredients:
- 2 1/2 cups water, divided
- 1 cup red lentils
- 1/2 cup wild rice
- 1 tsp olive oil
- 1 small onion, chopped
- 3 garlic cloves, minced
- 1/3 cup zucchini, peeled, seeded and chopped
- 1/3 cup carrot, peeled and chopped
- 1/3 cup celery stalk, chopped
- 1 large tomato, peeled, seeded and chopped
- 8 oz tomato sauce
- 1 tsp ground cumin
- 1 tsp dried oregano, crushed
- 1 tsp dried basil, crushed
- Salt and freshly ground black pepper, to taste

Directions:
1. In a pan, add 1 cup of the water and rice over medium-high heat and bring to a rolling boil. Reduce the heat to low and simmer, covered for about 20 minutes.
2. Meanwhile, in another pan, add the remaining water and lentils over medium heat and bring to a rolling boil. Reduce the heat to low and simmer, covered for about 15 minutes.
3. Transfer the cooked rice and lentils into a casserole dish and set aside.
4. Preheat your oven to 350°F.
5. Sauté onion and garlic 5 minutes in a pan with oil.
6. Add the zucchini, carrot, celery, tomato and tomato paste and cook for about 4-5 minutes.
7. Stir in the cumin, herbs, salt and black pepper and remove from the heat.
8. Transfer the vegetable mixture into the casserole dish with rice and lentils and stir to combine.
9. Bake for about 30 minutes.
10. Remove from the heat and set aside for about 5 minutes.
11. Cut into equal-sized 6 pieces and serve.

Nutrition:
Calories: 192 | Carbs: 34.5g | Protein: 11.3g | Fat: 1.5g | Fiber: 12g

FAMILY DINNER PILAF

Prep Time: 15 minutes | **Cook Time:** 1 hour
Servings: 4
Ingredients:
- 2 tbsp olive oil
- 2 garlic cloves, minced
- 2 cups fresh mushrooms, sliced
- 1 1/4 cups brown rice, rinsed
- 2 cups homemade vegetable broth
- Salt and freshly ground black pepper, to taste
- 1 red bell pepper, seeded and chopped
- 4 scallions, chopped
- 1 (16-oz) can of red kidney beans, drained and rinsed
- 2 tbsp fresh parsley, chopped

Directions:
1. In a large pan, heat the oil over medium heat and sauté the onion for about 4-5 minutes.
2. Add the garlic and mushrooms and cook for about 5-6 minutes.
3. Stir in the rice and cook for about 1-2 minutes, stirring continuously.
4. Stir in the broth, salt and black pepper and bring to a boil.
5. Reduce the heat to low and simmer, covered for about 35 minutes, stirring occasionally.
6. Add in the bell pepper and beans and cook for about 5-10 minutes or until all the liquid is absorbed.
7. Serve hot with the garnishing of parsley.

Nutrition:
Calories: 463 | Carbs: 76.7g | Protein: 18.5g | Fat: 10.1g | Fiber: 11.6g

VERY BERRY FRUIT LEATHER

Prep Time: 5 minutes | **Cook Time:** 0 minutes
Servings: 1
Ingredients:
- 4 cups berries (raspberries, strawberries, blueberries)
- 2 tbsp lemon juice
- 1/3 cup + 1 tbsp Maple syrup

Directions:
1. Preheat the oven to 170°F/75°C. Combine berries, lemon juice and maple syrup in a blender until completely smooth, about 4-5 minutes.
2. Spread the mixture onto two large baking sheets lined with parchment paper. Bake for 3-4 hours, or until the mixture is no longer sticky. Allow to cool before cutting into strips. Keep the pan closed.

Nutrition:
Calories: 56 | Carbs: 33g | Protein: 78g | Fat: 4g | Fiber: 4.6g

STRAWBERRY LEMON BARS

Prep Time: 5 minutes | **Cook Time:** 0 minutes
Servings: 9-12
Ingredients:
For The Jam:
- 2 1/2 cups fresh strawberries, hulled and quartered
- 3 tbsp lemon juice
- 1 tsp zest
- 1/4 cup maple syrup
- 3 tbsp chia seeds

For the base:
- 2 cups almond flour
- 2 tbsp coconut oil
- 1/4 tsp salt
- 1-2 tbsp water

For The Crumb:
- 1 cup walnuts
- 1/2 cup unsweetened shredded coconut
- 2 tbsp maple syrup
- 1 tsp coconut oil
- 1/4 tsp salt

Directions:
1. Bring the strawberries, lemon juice, zest and maple syrup to a simmer in a saucepan over medium-high heat. Cook until the strawberries are tender, about 10-15 minutes. Remove from heat and mash gently with the back of a wooden spoon. Remove from heat and stir in the chia seeds. Set aside to cool.
2. Preheat the oven to 350°F/180°C. Combine the almond flour, coconut oil and salt in a food processor and pulse until the texture resembles breadcrumbs. Pour in the water while the motor is running and process until the ingredients come together into a dough.
3. Using parchment paper, line a 9x9-inch baking pan with the ingredients and press firmly and evenly. Place in the oven for 10-12 minutes, or until the base is golden brown. Let cool.
4. To make the crumbs, grind the walnuts, coconut, coconut oil, maple syrup and salt in a food processor until a fine powder forms.
5. Spread the jam mixture over the cooled base and top with the crumb topping. Place in the oven for 12-15 minutes, or until golden brown on top. Allow to cool thoroughly before slicing.

Nutrition:
Calories: 80 | Carbs: 11g | Protein: 2g | Fat: 5g | Fiber: 8g

DILL POTATO SALAD WITH RADISHES AND PEAS

Cook Time: 0 minutes | **Prep Time:** 5 minutes
Servings: 4
Ingredients:
- 1 1/2 lb small (new) potatoes
- 1 tsp salt
- 8 radishes, very thinly sliced
- 1 cup green peas
- 1/4 cup dill, finely chopped

Dressing:
- 1/4 cup tahini
- 2 tbsp water
- 1/4 cup lemon juice
- 2 tbsp dill
- 2 tbsp chives
- Salt and pepper

Directions:
1. Add five centimeters of water to a medium-sized pot with a steamer basket on the stove.
2. Place the potatoes in the pot, cover and simmer for 30-40 minutes, or until tender. Drain and set aside to cool.
3. Combine the potatoes, radishes, peas and dill in a large mixing bowl.
4. Combine the tahini, water, dill, chives, lemon juice, salt and pepper in a blender to make the dressing. Pour the dressing over the salad and toss to combine.

Nutrition:
Calories: 120 | Carbs: 30g | Protein: 2g | Fat: 18g | Fiber: 14.1g

WILDFLOWER HONEY BERRIES

Prep Time: 5 minutes | **Cook Time:** 0 minutes
Servings: 1
Ingredients:
- 1 cup strawberries, hulled and halved
- 1 cup raspberries
- 1 cup wild blueberries
- 1 cup of blueberries
- 1 cup blackberries
- 2-3 tbsp wildflower raw honey

Directions:
1. Place all berries in a bowl and add the honey. Mix until coated. Serve immediately.

Nutrition:
Calories: 256 | Carbs: 33g | Protein: 16g | Fat: 13g | Fiber: 3.12g

WATERMELON SPARKLERS

Prep Time: 5 minutes | **Cook Time:** 0 minutes
Servings: 4
Ingredients:
- 1 watermelon
- Canary or 1/2 small cantaloupe melon
- 1/2 honeydew melon, small
- 1 cup fresh blueberries
- 10-12 wooden skewers
- 2 tbsp lime zest
- 2 tbsp coconut sugar

Directions:
1. Cut the watermelon into half-centimeter-thick slices. Cut the watermelon into stars using a star-shaped cutter.
2. Make balls out of the honeydew melons using a small ball popper.
3. Alternate the melon balls with the blueberries on skewers and finish with a watermelon star.
4. Simply combine the lime zest and blonde coconut sugar and sprinkle over the watermelon stars in the sparklers to form the sparklers' optional fairy dust.

Nutrition:
Calories: 180 | Carbs: 30g | Protein: 42g | Fat: 20g | Fiber: 8.2g

WILD BLUEBERRY SOUP

Prep Time: 5 minutes | **Cook Time:** 45 minutes
Servings: 2-4
Ingredients:
- 3 cups wild blueberries, fresh or frozen
- 2 cups water
- 2 tsp lemon juice
- 1/2 tsp lemon zest
- 1/4 tsp ground cinnamon or cardamom
- 2 tsp arrowroot powder mixed with 2 tbsp water
- 3 tbsp raw honey
- Mint (for garnish)

Directions:
1. Bring the cranberries, lemon juice and zest, water, cinnamon and cardamom to a simmer in a large saucepan. Cook for 8-10 minutes, or until the cranberries have softened. Mix the arrowroot powder with the cold water and add to the soup while it is boiling.
2. Cook for 2 more minutes, or until the soup thickens, then remove from the heat and let it cool for 10 minutes. Add the honey and mix well. Serve hot or cold, garnished with mint leaves. Leftovers can be stored in the refrigerator for up to three days.

Nutrition:
Calories: 140 | Carbs: 26g | Protein: 5g | Fat: 3 g | Fiber: 13.6g

BAKED ZUCCHINI TATER TOTS

Prep Time: 15 minutes | **Cook Time:** 0 minutes
Servings: 40 tots
Ingredients:
- 2 zucchinis medium-sized
- 2 russet potatoes, peeled
- 1 tsp salt
- 1 tsp dried oregano

Directions:
1. Add five centimeters of water to a medium saucepan with a steamer basket on the heat. Place the potatoes in the pot, cover and simmer for 1 hour, or until tender but still sturdy. Drain the water and let them cool completely.
2. Preheat the oven to 350°F/180°C. Place the grated potato in a mixing bowl.
3. Grate the zucchini and squeeze as much juice as possible into a clean kitchen towel. Combine with the grated potato in a mixing bowl. Mix in the salt and oregano, then roll the dough into small cylinders.
4. Place on a parchment-lined baking sheet and bake for 20-30 minutes, flipping them halfway through. Enjoy with ketchup on the side.

Nutrition:
Calories: 83 | Carbs: 9g | Protein: 6g | Fat: 4g | Fiber: 9.1g

WATERMELON STRAWBERRY GINGER LEMONADE

Prep Time: 5 minutes | **Cook Time:** 0 minutes
Servings: 4
Ingredients:
- Watermelon, cut into chunks
- 1 cup strawberries, hulled and halved
- 1 1/2 tbsp fresh ginger
- 1/3 cup lemon juice
- 1-2 tbsp raw honey (optional)
- Ice to serve
- Lemon slices, to serve

Directions:
1. Place all the ingredients in a blender and blend until smooth. Serve over ice.

Nutrition:
Calories: 84 | Carbs: 22g | Protein: 2g | Fat: 2g | Fiber: 12.1g

POTATO NESTS WITH SPINACH SALAD

Prep Time: 5 minutes | **Cook Time:** 0 minutes
Servings: 4-6
Ingredients:
For the nests:
- 1.5 lb. large russet potatoes
- 1 tbsp cassava flour
- 1/2 tsp salt
- 1/2 tsp freshly ground black pepper

Salad:
- 1 cup baby spinach, tightly packed, finely chopped
- 2/3 cup cherry tomatoes, halved
- 1/2 avocado, diced, ripe
- 1/4 cup cilantro, finely chopped
- 1 tbsp lemon juice
- Salt and pepper to taste

Directions:
1. Add five centimeters of water to a medium saucepan with a steamer basket on the heat. Place the potatoes in the pot, cover and simmer for 1 hour, or until tender but still sturdy. Drain the water and let them cool completely.
2. Preheat the oven to 350°F. Grate the potato and combine it with the cassava flour, salt and pepper in a bowl. Mix well.
3. Line a 6 or 12 muffin pan with parchment paper squares and press the mixture firmly into the pan, creating an indentation in the center. This will provide 12-16 nests. Bake for 30-45 minutes, or until the edges are golden brown and the nest is firm.
4. Prepare the salad while the nests are baking by placing the ingredients in a bowl and mixing well.
5. Remove the potato nests from the pan and serve with the salad on the side.

Nutrition:
Calories: 141 | Carbs: 30g | Protein: 3g | Fat: 2g | Fiber: 10g

GROUND BEEF & PASTA SKILLET

Prep Time: 15 minutes | **Cook Time:** 35 minutes
Servings: 4
Ingredients:
- 1 tbsp extra-virgin olive oil
- 1 pound 90%-lean ground beef
- 8 oz mushrooms, finely chopped or pulsed in a food processor
- 1/2 cup diced onion
- 1 (15 oz) can no-salt-added tomato sauce
- 1 cup water
- 1 tbsp Worcestershire sauce
- 1 tsp Italian seasoning
- 3/4 tsp salt
- 1/2 tsp garlic powder
- 8 oz whole-wheat rotini or fusilli
- 1/2 cup shredded extra-sharp Cheddar cheese

SLOW-COOKER VEGETABLE SOUP

Prep Time: 4h | **Cook Time:** 35 minutes
Servings: 8
Ingredients:
- 1 medium onion, chopped
- 2 medium carrots, chopped
- 2 stalks celery, chopped
- 12 oz fresh green beans, cut into 1/2-inch pieces
- 4 cups chopped kale
- 2 medium zucchini, chopped
- 4 Roma tomatoes, seeded and chopped
- 2 cloves garlic, minced
- 2 (15 ounce) cans no-salt-added cannellini or other white beans, rinsed
- 4 cups low-sodium chicken broth or low-sodium vegetable broth

ROASTED VEGETABLE & BLACK BEAN TACOS

Prep Time: 0 | **Cook Time:** 15 minutes
Servings: 2
Ingredients:
- 1 cup roasted root vegetables
- 1/2 cup cooked or canned black beans, rinsed
- 2 tsp extra-virgin olive oil
- 1 tsp ground cumin
- 1 tsp chili powder
- 1/2 tsp ground coriander
- 1/4 tsp kosher salt
- 1/4 tsp ground pepper
- 4 corn tortillas, lightly toasted or warmed
- 1/2 avocado, cut into 8 slices

CHICKEN & VEGETABLE PENNE WITH PARSLEY-WALNUT PESTO

Prep Time: 10 minutes | **Cook Time:** 20 minutes
Servings: 4
Ingredients:
- 3/4 cup chopped walnuts
- 1 cup lightly packed parsley leaves
- 2 cloves garlic, crushed and peeled
- 1/2 tsp plus 1/8 tsp salt

- 1/4 cup Chopped fresh basil for garnish

Directions:
1. Pour the oil into a frying pan and heat it over medium heat.
2. Add the mushrooms, beef, and onion. Cook for 10 minutes.
3. Add the tomato sauce, Worcestershire, water, Italian seasoning, garlic powder, and salt.
4. Add pasta and bring to a boil. Cover and cook for 18 minutes until pasta has absorbed the liquid.
5. Add cheese, cover, and cook for 3 minutes.
6. Garnish with basil.

Nutrition:
Calories: 580 | Fat: 19g | Carbs: 53g | Fiber: 8g | Protein: 44g

- 2 tsp salt
- 1/2 tsp ground pepper
- 2 tsp red-wine vinegar
- 8 tsp prepared pesto

Directions:
1. Add all ingredients except pesto and vinegar in a slow cooker (6-quart or larger).
2. Cover and cook on High for 4 hours.
3. Stir in vinegar and serve
4. In each serving of soup, put one tsp of pesto.

Nutrition:
Calories: 170 | Fat: 4g | Carbs: 26g | Fiber: 8.3g | Protein: 11g

- 1 lime, cut into wedges
- Chopped fresh cilantro & salsa for garnish

Directions:
1. Combine the roasted vegetables, chili powder, cumin, coriander, beans, oil, salt, and pepper in a saucepan.
2. Divide the mixture among the tortillas.
3. Serve with avocado and lime wedges.
4. Add salsa if desired.

Nutrition:
Calories: 342 | Fat: 15g | Carbs: 44g | Fiber: 13g | Protein: 8.4g

- 1/8 tsp ground pepper
- 2 tbsp olive oil
- 1/3 cup grated Parmesan cheese
- 1 1/2 cups shredded or sliced cooked skinless chicken breast (8 oz.)
- 6 oz whole-wheat penne or fusilli pasta (1 3/4 cups)

- 8 oz green beans, trimmed and halved crosswise (2 cups)
- 2 cups cauliflower florets (8 oz.)

Directions:
1. Pour water into a large pot and bring to a boil. Cook the pasta, green beans, and cauliflower in the boiling water for about 5-7 minutes.
2. Cook the walnuts in the microwave until lightly toasted. Then set them aside to cool.
3. Blend the walnuts, garlic, parsley, salt, and pepper in a food processor. Gradually add the oil through. Finally, add the Parmesan cheese and blend until combined. Pour the cream into a bowl and add the chicken.
4. Combine the drained pasta, vegetables, and pesto and chicken mixture. Serve.

Nutrition:
Calories: 510 | Fat: 20g | Carbs: 42g | Fiber: 8.9g | Protein: 32g

TURMERIC-ROASTED CAULIFLOWER

Prep Time: 20 minutes | **Cook Time:** 10 minutes
Servings: 5
Ingredients:
- 3 tbsp extra-virgin olive oil
- 1 1/2 tsp ground turmeric
- 1/2 tsp ground cumin
- 1/2 tsp salt
- 1/2 tsp ground pepper
- 2 large cloves garlic, minced
- 8 cups cauliflower florets (1 large head; about 2 pounds)
- 1-2 tsp lemon juice

Directions:
1. Heat the oven to 425 degrees F.
2. Mix oil, salt, cumin, pepper, turmeric, and garlic in a large bowl.
3. Add the cauliflower and stir.
4. Transfer cauliflower to a large rimmed baking sheet. Roast until golden brown (15 to 25 minutes).
5. Serve cauliflower with a squeeze of lemon juice.

Nutrition:
Calories: 124 | Fat: 8.8g | Carbs: 9g | Fiber: 4.9g | Protein: 4.2g

CUCUMBER AND AVOCADO SALAD

Prep Time: 15 minutes | **Cook Time:** 15 minutes
Servings: 4
Ingredients:
- 1 medium shallot, thinly sliced crosswise and separated into rings
- 3 tablespoons fresh lime juice
- 3 tablespoons extra-virgin olive oil
- 1 tablespoon thinly sliced fresh mint
- 1 tablespoon thinly sliced fresh basil
- ½ teaspoon salt
- 1 English cucumber, thinly sliced
- 1 ripe avocado, halved, pitted and sliced crosswise

Directions:
1. Add the shallot rings with the lime juice and mix in a bowl. Let stand for 10 minutes.
2. Add the oil, mint, cucumber, basil, and salt. Stir and let marinate for about 10 minutes.
3. Serve the cucumber with the avocado on a plate. Pour over the dressing.

Nutrition:
Calories: 194 | Fat: 17.8g | Carbs: 10g | Fiber: 7g | Protein: 5g

SALMON CAKES

Prep Time: 0 minutes | **Cook Time:** 45 minutes
Servings: 4
Ingredients:
- 3 teaspoons extra-virgin olive oil, divided
- 1 small onion, finely chopped
- 1 stalk celery, finely diced
- 2 tablespoons chopped fresh parsley
- 15 ounces canned salmon, drained, or 1 1/2 cups cooked salmon
- 1 large egg, lightly beaten
- 1 ½ teaspoons Dijon mustard
- 1 3/4 cups fresh whole-wheat breadcrumbs,
- ½ teaspoon freshly ground pepper
- Creamy Dill Sauce
- 1 lemon, cut into wedges

Directions:
1. Heat the oven to 450 F and coat a baking sheet with cooking spray.
2. In a skillet over medium-high heat, sauté the onion and celery for about 3 minutes with 1 1/2 teaspoons of oil. Add the parsley and remove it from heat.
3. Clean the salmon and then transfer to a medium bowl with the egg and mustard. Mix well.
4. Also, add the onion mixture, bread crumbs, and pepper; mix well. Create eight patties.
5. Cook 8 patties in a skillet with the remaining 1 1/2 teaspoons of the oil for 2 to 3 minutes.
6. Transfer the patties to the prepared pan.
7. Bake in the oven for 15 to 20 minutes. Meanwhile, prepare the creamy dill sauce.
8. Serve with the sauce and lemon wedges.

Nutrition:
Calories: 351 | Fat: 12.8g | Carbs: 24g | Fiber: 7g | Protein: 35g

GET YOUR BONUS!

Hello!

First of all, I would like to thank you for purchasing "Diverticulitis Cookbook."
I'm sure it will be very useful to improve your health. To prove my gratitude for the trust you have placed in me, I am happy to give you two of my books, "The Anti-Inflammatory Diet Cookbook" and "Mediterranean Diet Cookbook" which I am sure will make your health explode. Don't wait any longer and download the digital versions! Enjoy your reading!

Scan the QR code below!

EXTRA RECIPES READY IN 30 MINS

SMOOTHIE WITH MIXED BERRIES
Prep Time: 6 Minutes | **Servings:** 2
Ingredients:
- Dairy-Free Yogurt – ½ cup
- Frozen Mixed Berries – 12 ounces
- Honey – one tbsp

Directions:
1. Combine the water, spinach, and orange juice in a blender, and blend until smooth.
2. Blend in the peanut butter or almond butter until creamy.
3. Blend in the frozen mango and banana until smooth.
4. Finally, serve and enjoy!

Nutrition:
Calories: 265; Carbohydrates: 64g; Fat: 1g; Protein: 5g

APPLESAUCE
Prep Time: 5/6 Minutes | **Cook Time:** 20 Minutes
Servings: 4
Ingredients:
- Bramley Apples – four, peeled and cut into small slices
- Brown Sugar – four tbsp
- Dairy-Free Butter – half tbsp
- Cinnamon Powder – one pinch
- Lemon – half, juice only

Directions:
1. In a large pot, combine apple, lemon juice, and sugar. Place it on a medium-low heat source.
2. Add and stir in the cinnamon, dairy-free butter and sugar

Nutrition:
Calories: 72; Carbohydrates: 16.4g; Fat: 0.81g; Protein: 0.41g

FRUIT PUNCH
Prep Time: 10 Minutes | **Servings:** 10
Ingredients:
- Cranberry Juice – four cups
- Ginger Ale – three cups, chilled
- Lime Juice – ¼ cup
- Orange Juice – 1 ½ cups
- Pineapple Juice – 1 ½ cups

Directions:
1. In a pitcher, combine the lime juice, orange juice, cranberry juice, and pineapple juice and chill for one hour.
2. Stir in the ginger ale thoroughly

Nutrition:
Calories: 37; Carbohydrates: 11g; Fat: 0.2g; Protein: 2g

CHOCOLATE PUDDING
Prep Time: 10/15 Minutes
Servings: 7/8
Ingredients:
- Baking Cocoa – half cup
- Cornstarch – ¼ cup
- Dairy-Free Butter – 2 tbsp
- Dairy-Free Milk – four cups, almond milk
- Salt – ½ tsp
- Sugar – one cup
- Vanilla Extract – 2 tsp

Directions:
1. Into the saucepan, combine the salt, cornstarch, cocoa, and sugar. Gradually add dairy-free milk. Bring to a boil for two minutes over medium heat.
2. Take the pan off the heat. Stir in the dairy-free butter and vanilla extract well.
3. Pour the pudding into the serving bowl. Refrigerate until ready to serve!

Nutrition:
Calories: 195; Carbohydrates: 37g; Fat: 5g; Protein: 7g

SOUP WITH MUSHROOM
Prep Time: 10 Minutes | **Cook Time:** 20 Minutes
Servings: 6
Ingredients:
- All-Purpose Flour – six tbsp
- Chicken Broth – 28 ounces
- Dairy-Free Butter – 2 tbsp
- Mushrooms – ½lb, sliced
- Green Onion – ¼ cup, chopped
- Salt – ½ tsp

Directions:
1. Melt the dairy-free butter in the saucepan over medium-high flame. Sauté the green onion (just the green part) and mushrooms until soft.
2. Toss the mushroom mixture with 14 ounces of chicken broth, salt, and flour, and whisk well. Then, after two minutes, add the remaining 14 ounces of broth and bring to a boil.
3. Reduce the heat to low. Cook for fifteen minutes and stir frequently.
4. Finally, serve and enjoy!

Nutrition:
Calories: 133; Carbohydrates: 11g; Fat: 9g; Protein: 5g

SOUP WITH BROCCOLI
Prep Time: 5 Minutes | **Cook Time:** 25 Minutes
Servings: 4
Ingredients:
- All-Purpose Flour – ¼ cup
- Black Pepper – ¼ tsp
- Carrots – two, peeled and sliced

- Chicken Broth – 2 cups
- Dairy-Free Butter – one tbsp plus ¼ cup
- Fresh Broccoli – 12 ounces, chopped
- Green Onion – 1, chopped, green part only
- Mustard – ½ tsp

Directions:
1. Melt one tablespoon of diary-free butter in a Dutch oven over medium heat. Then add the green onion (just the green part) and cook for 2 to 3 minutes, or until translucent.
2. Melt ¼ cup of dairy-free butter in the Dutch oven over medium heat. Cook for two minutes after adding flour.
3. Pour in the chicken broth. Let it simmer for two minutes. Using a whisk, mix the ingredients until no lumps remain. After that, toss in the carrots and broccoli thoroughly.
4. Stir in the salt, pepper, and mustard. Reduce the fire to a minimum. Now, slowly simmer for ten minutes.
5. Now, pour the soup into a blender and reduce it to a puree until smooth. If desired, season with pepper and salt.

Nutrition:
Calories: 209; Carbohydrates: 16g; Fat: 12.1g; Protein: 11g

WONTON BROTH

Prep Time: 13 Minutes | **Cook Time:** 15 Minutes
Servings: 4
Ingredients:
- Baby Bok Choy – four, halved lengthwise and halved
- Chicken Broth – six cups, low sodium
- Fresh Ginger – one piece, sliced thinly
- Garlic – one clove, minced
- Mushrooms – 1 ½ cups, sliced
- Scallions
- Sesame Oil – one tsp
- Soy Sauce – one tbsp
- Wontons – twenty

Directions:
1. First, bring the chicken stock to a boil in a pot.
2. Using a knife, smash and cut the ginger.
3. Place it in the saucepan and cover it with a lid. Allow for five minutes of cooking time.
4. After that, add the bok choy and simmer for another five minutes.
5. Add mushrooms and wontons and continue to cook for another two to three minutes, or until they are soft and wilted.
6. Stir in the sesame oil and soy sauce well.
7. Strain the broth through a sieve.
8. Finally, serve and enjoy!

Nutrition:
Calories: 135; Carbohydrates: 21.5g; Protein: 11g; Fat: 2g

CAULIFLOWER BROTH

Prep Time: 10 Minutes
Cook Time: 20 Minutes
Servings: 8
Ingredients:
- All-Purpose Flour – three tbsp
- Butter – three tbsp
- Carrot – one, shredded
- Cauliflower – one head, broken into florets
- Celery – ¼ cup, chopped
- Cheddar Cheese – one cup, shredded
- Chicken Bouillon – two tsp
- Hot Hepper Sauce – half to one tsp, optional
- Milk – two cups
- Pepper – 1/8 tsp
- Salt – ¾ tsp
- Water – 2 ½ cups

Directions:
1. In a Dutch oven, combine the bouillon, water, celery, carrot, and cauliflower and bring to a boil. Lower the heat. Cover the Dutch oven with a lid.
2. Simmer for 11 to 15 minutes, or until vegetables are soft.
3. Add butter into the saucepan melt it over medium flame.
4. Stir in the pepper, salt, and flour thoroughly. Then, over medium heat, add the milk and bring to a boil. Cook for two minutes, or until the sauce has thickened.
5. Turn down the heat. Stir in the cheese and spicy pepper sauce well. Add cauliflower mixture and mix well.
6. Strain the broth into the basin using a fine mesh strainer.
7. Finally, serve and enjoy!

Nutrition:
Calories: 157; Carbohydrates 10.7g; Protein: 8g; Fat: 9g

GINGER JUICE

Prep Time: 20/25 Minutes | **Servings:** 7
Ingredients:
- Fresh Ginger Root – four ounces
- Fresh Mint – 14-16 leaves
- Lemons – two, juiced
- Sugar or Honey – one cup
- Water – six to seven cups

Directions:
1. Peel ginger with a knife and discard skin.
2. Break mint into the bowl with a pestle and keep it aside.
3. Chop the ginger into chunks and put it in the blender.
4. Add seven cups of water into the pot and boil it.
5. Add ginger into a blender and then add one cup water and blend until thick.
6. Add ginger paste, mint, and boiled water into the bowl.

7. Strain the contents into the basin using a sieve. Solid parts should be discarded.
8. Toss in the sugar and lemon juice, and serve.

Nutrition:
Calories: 133; Carbohydrates: 33g; Fat: 1g; Protein: 2g

LEMON TEA

Prep Time: 4 Minutes | **Cook Time:** 5 Minutes
Servings: 2
Ingredients:
- Back Tea – two tsp
- Honey – two tsp
- Lemon Juice – one tbsp
- Water – two cups

Directions:
1. Add water into the pan and heat it.
2. Let simmer it and then add tea leaves. Let steep for one minute.
3. Pass tea through a strainer into the serving cups.
4. Stir in the honey and lemon juice thoroughly
5. Finally, serve and enjoy!

Nutrition:
Calories: 22; Carbohydrates: 5g; Fat: 1g; Protein: 2g

SOUP WITH RED LENTILS AND COCONUT

Prep Time: 10 Minutes | **Cook Time:** 20 Minutes
Servings: 6
Ingredients:
- Carrot – one cup, chopped
- Cayenne Pepper – ¼ tsp
- Coconut Milk – one cup, full-fat
- Olive oil – two tbsp
- Fresh Cilantro Leaves – one cup
- Fresh Lime Juice – three tbsp
- Green Onion – one cup, chopped, green part only
- Red Curry Paste – 1/3 cup
- Red Lentils – one cup
- Salt – to taste
- Tomato Paste – three tbsp
- Water – four cups

Directions:
1. Add oil into the Dutch oven and place it over medium flame.
2. Then, add the green onion and carrot and cook for 5 minutes. Add cayenne pepper, curry paste, and tomato paste and cook for one minute until fragrant.
3. Add water, 1 tsp salt, and lentils and bring to a simmer.
4. Lower the heat to medium-low. Cover the pan with a lid. Let cook for 20 minutes until softened.
5. Remove from the flame. Stir in the lime juice and coconut milk thoroughly.
6. Sprinkle with salt if needed.
7. Garnish with fresh cilantro leaves.

Nutrition:
Calories: 265; Carbohydrates: 27g; Fat: 13g; Protein: 11g

SOUP WITH ASPARAGUS

Prep Time: 5/6 Minutes | **Cook Time:** 20 Minutes
Servings: 6
Ingredients:
- Asparagus, 2lbs, cut into 1-inch pieces
- Chicken Broth – five cups
- Dairy-Free Butter – 2 tbsp
- Dairy-Free Heavy Cream – ½ cup
- Flour – 2 tbsp
- Green Onion, 1, chopped, green part only
- Olive Oil – one tbsp
- Pepper – 1 tsp
- Salt – one tsp

Directions:
1. Add olive oil into the pot and place it over medium-high flame.
2. Add green onion and sauté for three to five minutes until tender.
3. Add flour and dairy-free butter and cook until golden brown.
4. Add asparagus and chicken broth and bring to a boil, about seven to ten minutes.
5. Puree the soup in an immersion blender until smooth.
6. Add dairy-free heavy cream and sprinkle with pepper and salt.

Nutrition:
Calories: 179; Carbohydrates: 11g; Fat: 13g; Protein: 6g

MASHED SWEET POTATOES

Prep Time: 9 Minutes | **Cook Time:** 20 Minutes
Servings: 10
Ingredients:
- Brown Sugar – one tbsp
- Cinnamon – ¼ tsp
- Dairy-Free Butter – six tbsp, cubed
- Maple Syrup – 2 tbsp
- Nutmeg – 1/8 tsp
- Sweet Potatoes – three pounds, peeled and cube

Directions:
1. Add peeled and cubed sweet potatoes into the pot and cover with water. Bring to a boil until tender. Drain and place back to the pot.
2. Using a potato masher, mash the potatoes.
3. Add maple syrup, cinnamon, nutmeg, dairy-free butter, and brown sugar and combine with a hand mixer. Finally, serve and enjoy!

Nutrition:
Calories: 191; Carbohydrates: 29g; Fat: 7g; Protein: 2g

ZUCCHINI SOUP

Prep Time: 9 Minutes | **Cook Time:** 15 Minutes
Servings: 4
Ingredients:
- Fresh Thyme Leaves – one tbsp
- Green Onion – one, green part only
- Raw Cashews – one cup
- Salt and Pepper – to taste
- Thyme Spears – three
- Zucchini – three

Directions:
1. Soak the cashews in the boiling water.
2. Cut the green onion and zucchini into big chunks.
3. Add green onion and zucchini into the pot. Cover with water. Add thyme spears and bring to a boil for fifteen minutes.
4. Pour it into a blender and puree until smooth.
5. Add pepper, salt, cashews, and one tbsp thyme leaves and blend until smooth.

Nutrition:
Calories: 179; Carbohydrates: 26g; Fat: 7g; Protein: 8g

GINGER AND MUSHROOM BROTH

Prep Time: 4 Minutes | **Cook Time:** 7 Minutes
Servings: 4
Ingredients:
- Basil – two tbsp, chopped
- Ginger – one tbsp, grated and peeled
- Green Onions – half cup, chopped
- Low-Sodium Chicken Broth – 28 ounces, fat-free
- Oyster Trimmed Mushrooms – half cup
- Soy Sauce – one tsp, low-sodium

Directions:
1. Place the ginger and mushroom in a saucepan and cook for 2 minutes over medium-high heat. After that, add the soy sauce and chicken stock and bring it to a boil.
2. Add onion and basil and heat it.
3. Strain the soup and serve immediately

Nutrition:
Calories: 71; Carbohydrates: 14.1g; Protein: 5.2g

GINGER ROOT TEA

Prep Time: 4 Minutes | **Cook Time:** 20 Minutes
Servings: 2
Ingredients:
- Fresh Ginger Root – two tbsp
- Fresh Lime Juice – one tbsp, optional
- Honey – one to two tbsp
- Water – four cups

Directions:
1. Peel the ginger, then cut it into pieces.
2. Place the sliced ginger in the pot with the water and bring to a boil for ten minutes.
3. Allow to boil for 20 minutes. When you're finished, turn off the flame.
4. Strain the tea and then add the lime juice and honey. Finally, serve and enjoy.

Nutrition:
Calories: 39; Carbohydrates: 11.2g; Protein: 0g; Fat: 0g

GUMMIES MADE WITH STRAWBERRIES

Prep Time: 9 Minutes | **Cook Time:** 6 Minutes
Ingredients:
- Strawberry Puree – one cup
- Honey – 2-3 tbsp
- Vanilla Extract – half tsp
- Water – 1/3 cup
- Gelatin Powder – four tbsp, un-flavored, grass-fed

Directions:
1. In a medium-sized saucepan, combine the vanilla essence, honey, and strawberry puree and cook for two to four minutes over medium-low heat.
2. Fill the bowl halfway with water, then add the gelatin powder. Stir everything together thoroughly
3. Turn off the flame and add gelatin mixture into the saucepan and whisk it well.
4. Place mixture into the molds and put it into the refrigerator.

Nutrition:
Calories: 6.8; Carbohydrates: 1.1g; Protein: 0.6g; Fat: 0.1g

SMOOTHIE WITH CREAMY CHERRIES

Prep Time: 4 Minutes | **Servings:** 4
Ingredients:
- Avocado – ¼, ripe
- Cherry – one
- Coconut Crème – one tbsp
- Dark Cherry Juice – 100ml
- Lecithin Granules – one tsp
- Tahini – one tsp, hulled
- Unsweetened Oat Milk – 150ml

Directions:
1. Add all ingredients into the blender. Blend until smooth.
2. Fill the glass halfway with smoothie.

Nutrition:
Calories: 269; Carbohydrates: 59g; Fat: 9g; Protein: 2g

LEMON BAKED EGGS

Prep Time: 6 Minutes
Cook Time: 9 Minutes
Servings: 1
Ingredients:
- Cheddar Cheese – 2 slices, low-fat

- Crusty White Roll – one
- Eggs – 2g
- Lemon – 1 tsp, julienned
- Parsley – 2 tbsp, chopped
- Salt – to taste

Directions:
1. Initially preheat the oven to 180 degrees C.
2. Spray the dish with olive oil.
3. Cut the cheddar cheese into three strips using a sharp knife.
4. Use cheese to line the dishes edges. In the centre of the eggs, crack them.
5. Place julienned lemon over the egg and sprinkle with fresh parsley
6. Place dish into the oven and cook for 9 to 11 minutes. Next serve with crusty white bread rolls.

Nutrition:
Calories: 232; Carbohydrates: 0.5g; Fat: 15.8g; Protein: 23.3g; Fiber: 3g

PANCAKES WITH BANANA

Prep Time: 10 Minutes | **Cook Time:** 8 Minutes
Servings: 4
Ingredients:
- Baking Powder – 1 tbsp
- Banana – 2, peeled, sliced
- Cinnamon Powder – 2 tsp
- Dairy-Free Milk – 400ml
- Firm Silken Tofu – 349g
- Flour – 250g, gluten-free
- Grapeseed Oil – 4 tbsp
- Maple Syrup
- Peanut Butter – 4 tbsp. smooth
- Sugar – 4 tbsp
- Vanilla Extract – 1 tbsp

Directions:
1. In a blender, combine the tofu, vanilla, cinnamon, and half of the diary-free milk and blend until smooth.
2. Stir in the remaining diary-free milk.
3. In a separate basin, combine the baking powder and flour. Create a hole in the center of the dry mixture and pour in the wet mixture, blending until smooth.
4. Place the pan over medium heat and add 2 tsp of oil.
5. Pour in the batter and cook for 2 minutes.
6. Flip and cook for another 2 minutes.
7. Spread the pancakes with peanut butter.
8. Finish with sliced bananas as a garnish.
9. Drizzle maple syrup over top.

Nutrition:
Calories: 191; Carbohydrates: 29.3g; Fat: 6.1g; Protein: 6g; Fiber: 3g

DEVILED EGG

Prep Time: 10 Minutes | **Servings:** 6
Ingredients:
- Eggs – six
- Mustard Powder – one pinch
- Paprika – one pinch
- Salt and Pepper – to taste
- Turmeric Powder – one pinch
- Water Cracker – one packet
- Whole Egg Mayonnaise – 3 tbsp

Directions:
1. Add eggs into the saucepan and cover with water. Place it over medium flame. Bring to a boil. When boiled, cook the eggs for four and a half minutes.
2. Take the pan off the heat. Place the eggs in cold water for one minute.
3. Finally, peel them and cut them in half lengthwise.
4. Remove the yolks from the egg white and add them into the bowl. Let mash with pepper, mustard, mayonnaise, salt and turmeric.
5. Slice a little piece of the rounded bottom of the egg white halves. Place onto the cracker or plate. Place yolk mixture into the white egg halves. Sprinkle with paprika.

Nutrition:
Calories: 121.5; Carbohydrates: 0.8g; Fat: 10.1g; Protein: 6.1g; Fiber: 2.9g

MUESLI MUFFINS WITH PEARS

Prep Time: 6 Minutes | **Cook Time:** 20 Minutes
Servings: 10
Ingredients:
- Brown Sugar – ½ cup
- Butter – 50g, melted
- Egg – one
- Milk – one cup
- Muesli – 150g
- Pears – two, thinly sliced
- Walnuts – 75g
- Wholemeal Self-Rising Flour – 200g

Directions:
1. Initially preheat the oven to 180 degrees C.
2. In a mixing dish, combine the walnuts, pears, sugar, flour, and muesli.
3. In the center of the mixture, make a well.
4. Stir together the butter, milk, and egg in the well.
5. Now spoon the mixture into the muffin tins that have been buttered.
6. Bake for 18 to 20 minutes, sprinkled with muesli.

Nutrition:
Calories: 371; Carbohydrates: 46g; Fat: 17.9g; Protein: 8g; Fiber: 5g

SHAKSHUKA

Prep Time: 10 Minutes | **Cook Time:** 15 Minutes
Servings: 2
Ingredients:
- Red Pepper 100g, drained, chopped
- Tomatoes – 800g, diced and cooked
- Tomato Paste – 2 tbsp
- Green Onion ½, minced, green part only
- Paprika – 1 ½ tsp
- Cumin – 1 tsp
- Stevia Powder – ¼ tsp
- Salt and Pepper – to taste
- Olive Oil Spray
- Eggs – six
- Parsley – 1 tbsp, chopped

Directions:
1. Place a pot over medium flame. Sprinkle with olive oil. Add green onion and cook until translucent.
2. Then, add tomato paste, red pepper, and tomatoes and combine them well. After that, add the stevia and spices to the sauce.
3. Sprinkle with pepper and lower the heat. Over the sauce, crack eggs.
4. Cover the saucepan and cook for 15 minutes on low heat. Finish by garnishing with fresh parsley leaves.

Nutrition:
Calories: 142; Carbohydrates: 18g; Fat: 10g; Protein: 9g; Fiber: 4g

SALMON FRITTER

Prep Time: 10 Minutes | **Cook Time:** 10/12 Minutes
Servings: 4
Ingredients:
- Cooked White Rice – 400g
- Egg – one
- Oats – ½ cup
- Olive Oil – 2 tbsp
- Tomato Paste – 50g
- Tuna or Salmon – 350g, drained
- Wholemeal Flour – ¼ cup

Directions:
1. Initially preheat the oven to 100 degrees C
2. Then, in a bowl, combine the salmon, rice and oats. Make a well in the center and pour in the beaten egg and tomato paste, blending until smooth.
3. Stir in the white flour, then form the mixture into eight patties.
4. Transfer to a baking tray and then bake for 5 minutes.
5. Flip and cook for another five minutes.
6. Toss with tomato sauce and serve.

Nutrition:
Calories: 301; Carbohydrates: 23.1g; Fat: 9g; Protein: 29g; Fiber: 4g

VANILLA ALMOND HOT CHOCOLATE

Prep Time: 10 Minutes
Servings: 2
Ingredients:
- Vanilla Almond Milk – 600ml
- Full Fat Coconut Cream – 30g
- Dark Chocolate – 60g
- Cocoa – 1 tsp
- Stevia – to taste

Directions:
1. Place the pan over medium heat and add the vanilla almond milk.
2. Heat the mixture with the stevia, cocoa powder, and chopped chocolate.
3. Finish with coconut cream and a sprinkling of chocolate shavings.

Nutrition:
Calories: 195; Carbohydrates: 31g; Fat: 3.8g; Protein; 8.2g; Fiber: 1.2g

FRITTATA WITH SPINACH

Prep Time: 5 Minutes | **Cook Time:** 25 Minutes
Servings: 4
Ingredients:
- Coconut Oil – one tbsp
- Eggs – eight
- Egg Whites – one cup
- Milk – three tbsp
- Shallot – one, peeled and sliced into thin rings
- Baby Bell Peppers – one cup, thinly sliced into rings
- Fresh Spinach – five ounces, chopped
- Feta Cheese – three ounces, crumbled
- Salt and Pepper – to taste

Directions:
1. Initially preheat the oven to 200 degrees C.
2. In a large mixing basin, whisk together the salt, milk, egg whites, and egg. Set it aside for now.
3. Preheat the pan over a medium-high heat. After that, pour in the coconut oil into the pan. Add sliced peppers and sliced shallot and sprinkle with pepper and salt. Let cook it for five minutes. Add chopped spinach and stir well.
4. Pour the egg mixture into the pan after whisking it. Sprinkle with the feta cheese.
5. Put it in the oven for ten to twelve minutes to cook. Set aside to cool. Finally, serve and enjoy!

Nutrition:
Calories: 241; Carbohydrates: 7g; Protein: 23g; Fat: 11g

SMOOTHIE WITH BANANA

Prep Time: 5/6 Minutes
Servings: 1
Ingredients:
- Banana – one cup, sliced
- Greek Yogurt – ¼ cup
- Milk – ¼ cup
- Vanilla Extract – ¼ tsp

Directions:
1. In a blender, combine all ingredients. Blend until smooth.
2. If necessary, add extra milk.
3. Finally, serve and enjoy!

Nutrition:
Calories: 201; Carbohydrates: 38g; Protein: 11g; Fat: 2.9g

MUFFINS WITH BANANA

Prep Time: 5 Minutes | **Cook Time:** 25 Minutes
Servings: 10
Ingredients:
- All-Purpose Flour – 1 ½ cups
- Baking Powder – one tsp
- Baking Soda – one tsp
- Bananas – three, mashed
- Butter – 1/3 cup, melted
- Egg – one
- Salt – half tsp
- Sugar – ¾ cup

Directions:
1. Initially preheat the oven to 180 degrees C.
2. Spray the muffin tins with nonstick cooking spray.
3. Strain the salt, baking powder, baking soda, and flour and keep it aside.
4. In a mixing dish, combine the melted butter, egg, sugar, and bananas.
5. Add flour mixture in it and combine it well.
6. Place mixture into the muffin pans. Bake it for 10/15 minutes.

Nutrition:
Calories: 184; Carbohydrates: 32.1g; Protein: 2.9g; Fat: 5.7g

OMELET WITH MUSHROOMS

Prep Time: 12 Minutes | **Cook Time:** 15 Minutes
Servings: 2
Ingredients:
- Cheddar Cheese – one tbsp, shredded, low-fat
- Egg – one
- Egg Whites – three
- Fresh Mushrooms – half cup, sliced
- Fresh Spinach – one cup, torn
- Fresh Tomato – half cup, diced
- Garlic Powder – 1/8 tsp
- Green Onion – ¼ cup, diced
- Ground Black Pepper – 1/8 tsp
- Ground Nutmeg – 1/8 tsp
- Olive Oil – half tsp
- Parmesan Cheese – one tbsp, grated
- Red Bell Pepper – two tbsp, chopped
- Salt – ¼ tsp

Directions:
1. First of all, in a mixing dish, whisk together the egg whites and the egg. Then, add pepper, nutmeg, garlic powder, salt, and cheddar cheese and combine it well.
2. Place the skillet over medium heat and add the oil. Add bell pepper, green onion, and mushrooms and cook for five minutes, until tender. Add spinach to the skillet. Cook until wilted.
3. Cook for 12 minutes after adding the egg mixture and sliced tomato.
4. Cut into the wedges. Serve and enjoy!

Nutrition:
Calories: 113; Carbohydrates: 5.5g; Protein: 12.9g; Fat: 4.9g

OMELET WITH ZUCCHINI

Prep Time: 16 Minutes
Servings: 2
Ingredients:
- Butter – two tbsp
- Dash Pepper
- Dried Thyme – 1/8 tsp
- Eggs – three
- Onion – two slices, separated into rings
- Parmesan Cheese – three tbsp, shredded
- Salt – 1/8 tsp
- Tomato – ¼ cup, chopped, seeded
- Water – three tbsp
- Zucchini – half cup, sliced

Directions:
1. In a skillet, first of all, melt the butter and sauté the onion and zucchini until soft.
2. In a mixing bowl, whisk together the pepper, salt, thyme, eggs, and water.
3. Place it in a skillet over medium heat and sauté it.
4. When finished, cover with cheese and tomato and broil for one to two minutes, until golden brown.
5. Serve by slicing in half.

Nutrition:
Calories: 257; Carbohydrates: 9g; Protein: 19g; Fat: 0.9g

FLUFFY PANCAKES

Prep Time: 5 Minutes | **Cook Time:** 14 Minutes
Servings: 8
Ingredients:
- All-Purpose Flour – 1 ½ cups
- Baking Powder – 3 ½ tsp
- Butter – three tbsp, melted

- Egg – one
- Milk – 1 ¼ cups
- Salt – one tsp
- White Sugar – one tbsp

Directions:
1. Combine the sugar, salt, baking powder, and flour in a mixing basin.
2. Make a well in the center and pour the egg and melted butter, mixing thoroughly.

FRENCH TOAST

Prep Time: 3 Minutes | **Cook Time:** 10 Minutes
Servings: 3
Ingredients:
- Bread – six thick slices
- Eggs – two
- Ground Cinnamon – ¼ tsp
- Ground Nutmeg – ¼ tsp
- Milk – 2/3 cup
- Salt – to taste
- Vanilla Extract – one tsp

WAFFLES WITH PEACHES

Prep Time: 3 Minutes | **Cook Time:** 20 Minutes
Servings: 6
Ingredients:
- Butter – 1/3 cup
- Sugar – half cup
- Eggs – two, big
- Flour – two cups
- Baking Powder – two tsp
- Salt – half tsp
- Milk – one cup
- Peaches – 1 ½ cups, sliced, chopped into ¼-inch pieces
- Vanilla – half tsp
- Lemon Juice – half tsp

MUFFINS WITH PUMPKIN

Prep Time: 5 Minutes | **Cook Time:** 20 Minutes
Servings: 12
Ingredients:
- All-Purpose Flour – 1 ½ cups
- Apple Juice or Water – ¼ cup
- Baking Powder – one tsp
- Baking Soda – half tsp
- Eggs – two
- Granulated Sugar – 1 ¼ cups
- Ground Cinnamon – 1 ½ tsp
- Ground Ginger – ¼ tsp
- Ground Nutmeg – half tsp
- Pumpkin – one cup
- Salt – ¾ tsp
- Vegetable Oil – half cup

COOKIES WITH PEANUT BUTTER

Prep Time: 14 Minutes | **Cook Time:** 10 Minutes
Servings: 8
Ingredients:
- All-Purpose or Plain Flour – 1 ½ cups
- Baking Powder – half tsp

3. Preheat the griddle to medium-high heat. Place the batter on the heated griddle and cook until both sides are golden brown.
4. Finally, serve and enjoy!

Nutrition:
Calories: 157; Carbohydrates: 21.6g; Protein: 4.9g; Fat: 5.1g

Directions:
1. Combine the vanilla, spices, salt, milk, and egg in a large mixing bowl.
2. Preheat the griddle to medium-high heat.
3. Dip each bread slice into the egg mixture.
4. Place on the griddle and cook for a few minutes on each side.
5. Get ready to eat!

Nutrition:
Calories: 219; Carbohydrates: 33.1g; Protein: 10.2g; Fat: 6.1g

Directions:
1. Combine sugar and butter into the glass bowl and mix it well.
2. Next, add eggs and beat them thoroughly.
3. Combine the baking powder, flour, and salt in a separate basin.
4. Then add flour mixture to the egg mixture with vanilla, lemon juice, and milk and combine well. Then, fold in the peach pieces.
5. Pour the batter into a waffle maker and bake for 20 minutes.

Nutrition:
Calories: 372; Carbohydrates: 51g; Protein: 8.9g; Fat: 13.1g

Directions:
1. Initially preheat the oven to 180 degrees C.
2. Prepare a muffin tray by lining it with paper liners.
3. Whisk together the ginger, cinnamon, nutmeg, salt, baking soda, baking powder, and flour. In the center of the mixture, make a well and set it aside.
4. Whisk together the apple juice, eggs, pumpkin, oil, and sugar in a separate bowl.
5. Using a spatula, whisk the pumpkin mixture into the flour mixture.
6. Carefully spoon the batter into the muffin tins.
7. Bake it for 20 minutes.
8. Set aside to cool.

Nutrition:
Calories: 244; Carbohydrates: 32g; Protein: 9g; Fat: 9g

- Brown Sugar – 2/3 cup
- Egg – one
- Pure Vanilla Extract – two tsp
- Salt – 1/3 tsp
- Semi Sweet Chocolate Chips – ¾ cup

- Smooth Peanut Butter – half cup
- Unsalted Butter – half cup, softened
- White Granulated Sugar – half cup

Directions:
1. Initially preheat the oven to 180 degrees C.
2. Linea baking sheets with parchment paper and set them aside.
3. Toss the smooth peanut butter and butter into the bowl and thoroughly combine.
4. Add vanilla extract, brown sugar and white sugar and beat it again until smooth. Mix with the beaten egg thoroughly.
5. Combine the salt, flour, and baking powder in a mixing bowl to make a smooth dough.
6. Mix with your hands, adding the chocolate chips (the first half).
7. Make fifteen balls out of the dough and lay them on the baking pan.
8. Bake for 10/12 minutes, or until golden.
9. Set aside to cool.

Nutrition:
Calories: 221; Carbohydrates: 25g; Protein: 6g; Fat: 9g

BARBECUE BEEF STIR-FRY

Prep Time: 4 Minutes | **Cook Time:** 25 Minutes
Servings: 4
Ingredients:
- Barbecue Sauce – ¼ cup
- Beef Broth – three tbsp, low-sodium
- Beef Sirloin Steak – one lb, boneless, cut into strips
- Carrot – one, thinly sliced
- Hot Cooked Long-Grain White Rice – two cups
- Oil – one tablespoon
- Onion – one, sliced

Directions:
1. Whisk the broth and BBQ sauce in a mixing bowl.
2. Rub on tbsp of meat and let stand for five minutes.
3. Cook over medium-high heat the vegetable, meat, and oil in the skillet for a quarter-hour.
4. Add the remaining BBQ sauce mixture and combine well. Allow cooking on low for two minutes on a medium-low flame.
5. Enjoy your meal!

Nutrition:
Calories: 301; Carbohydrates: 31g; Protein: 31g; Fat: 6g

CHICKEN SALAD

Prep Time: 5 Minutes | **Cook Time:** 5 Minutes
Servings: 4
Ingredients:
- Pulled BBQ Chicken – 200g, cooked
- Orzo Pasta – 100g
- Spinach – 150g, stalks removed
- Cheddar Cheese, 70g, cut into small cubes
- Parmesan Cheese – 30g
- Parsley – ¼ cup, chopped
- Olive Oil – five tbsp
- Red Wine Vinegar – three tbsp
- Salt - to taste
- Apricots – 1/3 cup, drained, thinly sliced
- Noodles – 1/3 cup

Directions:
1. Using a fork, shred cooked and chilled chicken.
2. Place the orzo pasta in the microwave dish after it has been cooked and cooled. Microwave for two minutes after topping with Parmesan cheese.
3. Toss together the apricots, parsley, chicken, and spinach in a mixing dish. Then drizzle red wine vinegar and olive oil over the salad, seasoning with salt. Combine everything thoroughly.
4. Add crispy noodles. Finally, serve!

Nutrition:
Calories: 340; Carbohydrates: 11g; Fat: 17g; Protein: 29g; Fiber: 11g

LEMONGRASS BEEF

Prep Time: 5 Minutes | **Cook Time:** 10 Minutes
Servings: 4
Ingredients:
- Basil – ¼ cup, chopped
- Basmati Rice – 2 packets, microwave
- Beef – 500g, minced, grass-fed
- Carrots – two, peeled and julienned
- Coconut – 2 tsp, shredded
- Cucumber – 100g, peeled and cut into chunks
- Fish Sauce – 1 tbsp
- Lemongrass Paste – 1 tbsp
- Lime – one, cut into four wedges
- Sesame Oil – 2 tbsp
- Thai Seasoning – 1 tbsp

Directions:
1. Heat the wok with sesame oil, lemongrass paste, fish sauce, and Thai seasoning. Stir in the minced meat and cook for four minutes or browned.
2. Prepare the rice separately according to package directions.
3. Stir in one tablespoon of shredded coconut.
4. In a mixing dish, combine the carrots, cucumber, rice, and minced beef.
5. Finish with a sprinkling of Thai basil and add lime wedges.

Nutrition:
Calories: 451; Carbohydrates: 40g; Fat: 15g; Protein: 29g; Fiber: 4g

VEGGIE BOWL

Prep Time: 11 Minutes
Servings: 2
Ingredients:
- Asparagus – six stems
- Cucumber – half cup, sliced
- Ginger – 2 tsp, pickled

- Green Beans – six
- Pumpkin Chunks – ½ cup, peeled and roasted
- Ripe Avocado – ¼, sliced lengthways
- Tuna – one slice
- White Basmati Rice – 100g
- Orange Juice – ½ cup, freshly squeezed
- Sesame Oil – four tbsp
- Salt, one pinch

Directions:
1. Cook the rice and thoroughly drain it.
2. Prepare the green beans by blanching them. Grill red pepper and remove skin and then dice it.
3. Cut the avocado in half lengthwise and thinly slice it. Thinly slice the cucumber.
4. Drain six asparagus stems. Drain the oil from the tuna pieces.
5. Bring the pumpkin pieces to a boil.
6. Make a pile of red pepper in the centre of the plate. Arrange all of the ingredients on the dishes in an orderly fashion.
7. Drizzle sesame oil on top. Season with salt.
8. Finally, drizzle the dressing all over the bowl.

Nutrition:
Calories: 518; Carbohydrates: 59.1g; Fat: 28.1g; Protein: 16g; Fiber: 4.9g

POMEGRANATE SALAD

Prep Time: 5 Minutes | **Cook Time:** 10 Minutes
Servings: 4
Ingredients:
- Chives – one tsp, chopped
- Dijon Mustard – 2 tsp
- Extra-virgin Olive Oil
- Pomegranate Juice – ¼ cup
- Salt – to taste
- Spinach – 100g
- Walnut Oil – three tbsp
- Zucchini – 300g

Directions:
1. Add all dressing ingredients to the bowl and whisk until a single dressing is combined.
2. Cut the zucchini into chunks and chop the chives.
3. Place a skillet over medium heat and add the chives and zucchini. Fry until golden brown. At this point, add the spinach leaves and mix well. Cook further for 3 minutes.
4. Serve and pour the dressing over the salad.

Nutrition:
Calories: 270; Carbohydrates: 14.8g; Fat: 21.1g; Protein: 9.1g; Fiber: 4g

WHITE RADISH CRUNCH SALAD

Prep Time: 5 Minutes
Servings: 2
Ingredients:
- Cucumber – 200g, shredded
- Ginger – 1 tsp, grated, steamed
- Noodles – 50g
- Nori – ¼ sheet, thinly sliced
- Radish – 200g, julienned

Directions:
1. In a bowl, combine the ginger, cucumber, and radish. Add the nori and noodles. Mix well and season.
2. Finally, serve!

Nutrition:
Calories: 81; Carbohydrates: 4.8g; Fat: 6g; Protein: 1.2g; Fiber: 3g

SPRING WATERCRESS SOUP

Prep Time: 5 Minutes | **Cook Time:** 25 Minutes
Servings: 4
Ingredients:
- Baby Arugula – four cups
- Chicken Stock – four cups
- Chives – 1 tbsp, snipped
- Greek Yogurt – 2 tbsp
- Green Onion – 1, diced, green part only
- Olive Oil – 1 tbsp
- Sea Salt – to taste
- Watercress – one bunch, rinsed

Directions:
1. Place the pot over medium-high heat and add the oil.
2. Cut the stems of the watercress into cubes place them in the pot. Set the leaves aside instead. Add the green onion together as well. Cook for 5 minutes.
3. Now add the broth. Bring to a boil. At this point, lower the heat and simmer for about 15 min.
4. Add the watercress leaves and arugula. Cook until wilted.
5. Blend everything until smooth. Then heat the soup in the pot.
6. Garnish with chopped chives. Enjoy!

Nutrition:
Calories: 173; Carbohydrates: 18g; Fat: 6.1g; Protein: 11.1g

POTATO & ROSEMARY RISOTTO

Prep Time: 2 Minutes | **Cook Time:** 25 Minutes
Servings: 3
Ingredients:
- Arborio Rice – 2/3 cup
- Butter – 1 tsp
- Chicken Stock – 3 ½ cups, low-sodium
- Green Onion – 1, diced, green part only
- Olive Oil – 2 tbsp
- Parmesan Cheese – 1 tbsp, grated
- Rosemary – 1 sprig, chopped
- Salt, to taste
- Yukon Gold Potato – 1, rinsed, peeled scrubbed, diced

Directions:
1. Heat Dutch oven to medium heat and add olive oil and rosemary.

2. Add onion and cook for 2 minutes until translucent. Then lower the heat and sprinkle with salt. Let sweat for 8 minutes.
3. Raise the heat to medium-high and then add the rice. Mix well. Cook another minute, adding the potato as well. Then finally, pour in the chicken broth and bring to a boil. Simmer until rice is cooked through.

4. With the flame off, add the butter and Parmesan cheese. Let stand.
5. Enjoy your meal!

Nutrition:
Calories: 361; Carbohydrates: 54g; Fat: 11g; Protein: 12.1g

CUCUMBER EGG SALAD

Prep Time: 10 Minutes | **Cook Time:** 16 Minutes
Servings: 4
Ingredients:
- Cucumbers – four, seedless
- Dill pickles – four
- Eggs – four
- Mayonnaise – three tbsp

Directions:
1. In the saucepan, add the eggs and cover them with cold water. Place over high heat and allow to boil.
2. Remove from flame and let eggs rest in hot water for 10 minutes. After they are peeled and chopped, then add them to the salad bowl.
3. Dice the cucumber and add it to the eggs. Also, add the mayonnaise and combine it well.
4. Refrigerate until chilled and serve.

Nutrition:
Calories: 371; Carbohydrates: 7g; Fat: 12.3g; Protein: 7.9g

LOADED PUMPKIN SOUP

Prep Time: 5 Minutes | **Cook Time:** 25 Minutes
Servings: 2
Ingredients:
- Baby Spinach – ½ cup, chopped
- Bay Leaf – one
- Carrot – one, peeled and julienned
- Celery Powder – 1 tsp
- Chicken Breast – one, precooked
- Chicken Stock Cube – 1, low-salted
- Extra-Virgin Olive Oil – 2 tbsp
- Pumpkin – 200g, peeled, boiled and cut into chunks
- Pumpkin Puree – 200g, mashed, peeled, boiled
- Salt, to taste
- Water – 200ml

Directions:
1. In the saucepan, pour the olive oil and heat. Add the water, bay leaf, celery powder, and pumpkin puree. Simmer for 10 minutes.
2. Add the pumpkin pieces and the shredded chicken. Cook 5 minutes.
3. Add the spinach and carrot. Cook 5 minutes. Retrieve the bay leaf and discard it.
4. Finally, serve!

Nutrition:
Calories: 126; Carbohydrates: 22g; Fat: 1.9g; Protein: 6g; Fiber: 5g

SIMPLE FISH STEW

Prep Time: 10 Minutes | **Cook Time:** 20 Minutes
Servings: 4
Ingredients:
- Clam Juice – one cup
- Dry White Wine – half cup
- Extra Virgin Olive Oil – six tbsp
- Fish Fillets – 1 ½ lbs, cut into pieces
- Fresh Parsley Leaves – 2/3 cup, chopped
- Garlic Cloves – three, minced
- Onion – one, chopped
- Salt – one tsp
- Tomato – 1 ½ cup, chopped
- Tomato Paste – two tsp, optional

Directions:
1. In the pot, add the olive oil and place it over medium heat. Add and sweat the onion in 4 minutes. Also, add the garlic and parsley and cook for two minutes.
2. Pour in the tomato paste and tomato. Cook for another ten minutes.
3. Add the fish, dry white wine, and clam juice. Cook for five minutes over low heat. Add salt to taste if necessary.
4. Pour the soup into bowls. Serve and enjoy!

Nutrition:
Calories: 369; Carbohydrates: 6g; Protein: 35.1g; Fat: 21g

HOMEMADE CHICKEN SOUP

Cook Time: 30 Minutes
Servings: 10
Ingredients:
- Carrots – four, halved
- Celery – four stalks, halved
- Chicken Bouillon Granules – one tsp
- Onion – one, halved
- Salt – to taste
- Water – to cover
- Whole Chicken – three pounds

Directions:
1. Add onion, celery, carrots, and chicken in a pot. Pour in cold water and simmer until chicken is tender.
2. Remove all contents from the pot and then strain through a strainer.

3. Chop onion, celery, and carrots. Remove bones from meat.
   Sprinkle with chicken broth. Add salt to taste.
4. Return the onion, chicken, carrots, and celery to the pot.
5. Stir and serve!

Nutrition:
Calories: 151; Carbohydrates: 4.1g; Protein: 13.1g; Fat: 8.9g

EASY GROUND BEEF BOWL

Prep Time: 5 Minutes
Cook Time: 20 Minutes
Servings: 4
Ingredients:
- Brown Sugar – ¼ cup
- Garlic – three cloves, minced
- Ground Ginger – ¼ tsp
- Hot Cooked White or Brown Rice – two cups
- Lean Ground Beef – one pound
- Sesame Oil – two tsp
- Sliced Green Onions and Sesame Seeds – for garnish
- Soy Sauce – ¼ cup, low-sodium

Directions:
1. In a skillet, add ground beef and then cook over medium heat until no longer pink.
2. Whisk the sesame oil, soy sauce, and brown sugar in the bowl. Place this mixture on top of the ground beef and cook slowly for five minutes.
3. Serve the hot cooked rice with the beef. Garnish with sesame seeds and green onions.

Nutrition:
Calories: 237; Carbohydrates: 31g; Protein: 24.8g; Fat: 7g

HOMEMADE PUMPKIN WAFFLES

Prep Time: 10 Minutes | **Cook Time:** 20 Minutes
Servings: 4
Ingredients:
- All Purpose Flour – two cups
- Brown Sugar – ¼ cup
- Baking Powder – one tsp
- Baking Soda – half tsp
- Salt – ¼ tsp
- Cinnamon – one tsp
- Eggs – three
- Milk – 1 1/3 cup
- Maple Syrup – ¼ cup
- Melted Butter – three tbsp
- Pumpkin – one cup

Directions:
1. In a bowl, add all dry ingredients and mix well.
2. Beat the melted butter, pumpkin, milk, and eggs in a medium bowl.
3. Combine the two preparations well together.
4. Place the mixture in the waffle maker and bake for twenty minutes. Serve with maple syrup and enjoy!

Nutrition:
Calories: 181; Carbohydrates: 22g; Protein: 7g; Fat: 6g

LEMON CHICKEN AND RICE

Prep Time: 5 Minutes | **Cook Time:** 25 Minutes
Servings: 4
Ingredients:
- Butter – two tbsp
- Carrot – one, thinly sliced
- Chicken Breasts – 1 lb, cut into strips, boneless, skinless
- Chicken Broth – 14 ounces
- Cornstarch – one tbsp
- Frozen Peas – one cup
- Garlic – two cloves, minced
- Lemon Juice – two tbsp
- Onion – one, chopped
- Salt – ¼ tsp
- Uncooked Instant Rice – one and half cup

Directions:
1. Heat a skillet over medium-high heat. Put the butter in. Add the garlic, carrot, chicken, and onion and cook for seven minutes.
2. In a bowl, mix the salt, lemon juice, broth, cornstarch, and salt. Pour the mixture into the skillet. Let cook and stir for two minutes.
3. Add the peas and rice and mix well. When cooked, remove from heat and let stand for a few minutes.
4. Serve and enjoy!

Nutrition:
Calories: 369; Carbohydrates: 41.1g; Protein: 28g; Fat: 8g

PEACHY PORK WITH RICE

Cook Time: 25 Minutes
Servings: 4
Ingredients:
- Brown Rice – one cup, cooked
- Olive Oil – two tbsp
- Peach Preserves – three tbsp
- Pork Tenderloin – 1lb, cut into 1-inch cubes
- Salsa – one cup
- Taco Seasoning – two tbsp, low-sodium

Directions:
1. In a bowl, add pork and drizzle with oil. Sprinkle with taco seasoning and mix well.
2. In a skillet, lay the pork and cook for ten minutes.
3. Add the peach preserves and salsa and mix well.
4. Serve the meat with cooked rice.

Nutrition:
Calories: 381; Carbohydrates: 41g; Protein: 26.1g; Fat: 9g

SKILLET HAM AND RICE

Prep Time: 5 Minutes | **Cook Time:** 20 Minutes
Servings: 2
Ingredients:
- Chicken Broth – half cup, low-sodium
- Green Onions – two, sliced
- Ham – one cup, fully cooked, cubed
- Mushrooms – one cup, sliced
- Olive Oil – one tsp
- Onion – one, chopped
- Parmesan Cheese – ¼ cup, shredded
- Uncooked Instant Rice – ¼ cup
- Water – ¼ cup

Directions:
1. First, place a skillet over medium heat and pour in the oil. Add mushrooms and onion and cook until tender.
2. Add the water, broth, and ham. Stir well.
3. When it reaches a boil, then add the rice and cook for 5 minutes.
4. Taste with the addition of cheese and green onions.

Nutrition:
Calories: 321kca; Carbohydrates: 37g; Protein: 24g; Fat: 7g

MANGO AND GINGER SMOOTHIE

Prep Time: 5 Minutes
Servings: 1
Ingredients:
- Carrot Juice – ¾ cup
- Fresh Ginger – one tsp, chopped
- Ground Cardamom – one pinch
- Honey – one tsp
- Ice Cubes – three cubes
- Mango Chunks – one cup, frozen
- Red Lentils – half cup, cooked cooled

Directions:
1. Add all of the listed ingredients and blend for about three minutes in a blender.
2. Serve with a cardamom garnish.

Nutrition:
Calories: 351; Carbohydrates: 78.8g; Fat: 1.2g; Protein: 12.1g; Fiber: 9.6g

SPINACH & CHERRY SMOOTHIE

Prep Time: 5 Minutes
Servings: 1
Ingredients:
- Avocado – ¼ cup, mashed
- Baby Spinach Leaves – half cup
- Chia Seeds – one tsp
- Frozen Cherries – one cup
- Ginger – ½-inch piece, peeled
- Kefir – one cup, low-fat
- Salted Almond Butter – one tbsp

Directions:
1. Add all ingredients listed and blend for about three minutes in a blender.
2. Pour mixture into a glass and enjoy with a chia seed garnish!

Nutrition:
Calories: 411; Carbohydrates: 46.1g; Fat: 19.1g; Protein: 17.3g; Fiber: 10.2g

BANANA & CACAO SMOOTHIE

Prep Time: 5 Minutes
Servings: 2
Ingredients:
- Almond Butter – ¼ cup
- Cacao Bliss – ¼ cup
- Frozen Banana – two, sliced
- Hemp Hearts – 2 tbsp
- Ice – ½ cup
- Non-Dairy Milk – 2 cups

Directions:
1. Add all ingredients listed and blend for about three minutes in a blender.
2. Pour the mixture into a glass!

Nutrition:
Calories: 511; Carbohydrates: 46g; Fat: 30g; Protein: 21.2; Fiber: 10.8g

SPINACH AND EGG SCRAMBLE WITH RASPBERRIES

Prep Time: 10 Minutes
Servings: 1
Ingredients:
- Baby Spinach – 1 ½ cups
- Canola Oil – 1 tsp
- Eggs – 2, beaten
- Kosher Salt – one pinch
- Raspberries – half cup
- Whole-Grain Bread – one slice, toasted

Directions:
1. Heat the oil in a skillet.
2. Add spinach and, over medium-high heat, cook until wilted and when cooked through, transfer to a plate.
3. Wipe out the skillet and, over medium heat, add the eggs. Cook two minutes.
4. Add the salt and spinach.
5. Stir well.
6. Serve on toast with raspberry garnish.

Nutrition:
Calories: 295.1; Carbohydrates: 20.8g; Fat: 15.6; Protein: 19.1; Fiber: 5

BLACKBERRY SMOOTHIE

Prep Time: 3 Minutes
Servings: 1
Ingredients:
- Banana – half
- Fresh Blackberries – one cup
- Fresh Lemon Juice – 1 ½ tsp
- Ginger – 1 tsp, chopped
- Honey – one tbsp
- Plain Whole-Milk Greek Yogurt – half cup

Directions:
1. Add all ingredients listed and blend for about three minutes in a blender.
2. Pour the mixture into a glass!

Nutrition:
Calories: 314; Carbohydrates: 52g; Fat: 7.1g; Protein: 14g; Fiber: 10.8g

VEGETABLE FRITTATA

Prep Time: 5 Minutes | **Cook Time:** 10 Minutes
Servings: 1
Ingredients:
- Canola Oil – one tbsp
- Cheddar Cheese – 2 tbsp, shredded
- Eggs – 2, beaten
- Mixed Veggies – one cup carrots, broccoli, and cauliflower, chopped
- Orange – 1, cut into wedges
- Salt – 1/8 tsp
- Scallions – two green and white parts separated, thinly sliced

Directions:
1. Take a skillet and, over medium-high heat, add the oil, vegetables, white shallots, and salt. Cook for five minutes until browned. Also, add the green shallots and stir well.
2. Add the eggs over the vegetables and sprinkle with cheese.
3. Remove the omelet from the flame let it rest for a few minutes.

Nutrition:
Calories: 489; Carbohydrates: 31g; Fat: 28.1g; Protein: 23g; Fiber: 6g

SMOOTHIE WITH CHOCOLATE AND BANANA

Prep Time: 4 Minutes
Servings: 1
Ingredients:
- Banana – one, frozen
- Red Lentils – half cup, cooked
- Milk – half cup, non-fat
- Unsweetened Cocoa Powder – 2 tsp
- Pure Maple Syrup – one tsp

Directions:
1. Add all ingredients listed and blend for about three minutes in a blender. Serve and enjoy!

Nutrition:
Calories: 309.1; Carbohydrates: 62.8g; Fat: 1.6g; Protein: 16.1g; Fiber: 7.5g

COCOA ALMOND FRENCH TOAST

Prep Time: 10 Minutes
Servings: 2
Ingredients:
- Unsweetened Almond Milk – ½ cup
- Egg – 1
- Ground Cinnamon – ½ tsp
- Ground Nutmeg – ½ tsp
- Almond – ¼ cup, chopped
- Non-Stick Cooking Spray
- Whole Wheat Bread – four slices
- Chocolate Syrup – 2 tbsp, sugar-free
- Raspberries – ¼ cup

Directions:
1. Beat eggs, cinnamon, and almond milk in a soup dish.
2. Divide chopped almonds among two bowls.
3. Heat griddle and coat with cooking spray.
4. Dip the bread slices first into the prepared egg mixture, then into the almonds, so they are covered on both sides.
5. Now, place these bread slices on the griddle and bake for four to five minutes until golden brown.
6. Cut the slices and arrange them on two serving plates and garnish with chocolate syrup, raspberries, and chopped almonds.

Nutrition:
Calories: 240; Carbohydrates: 28.3g; Fat: 11.1g; Protein: 16.1g; Fiber: 7.5g

MUESLI WITH RASPBERRIES

Prep Time: 4 Minutes
Servings: 1
Ingredients:
- Muesli – 1/3 cup
- Fresh Raspberries – one cup
- Milk – ¾ cup, low-fat

Directions:
1. Place muesli in a bowl and top with raspberries.
2. Serve with milk or hot water.

Nutrition:
Calories: 270; Carbohydrates: 48.3g; Fat: 6.1g; Protein: 13.1g; Fiber: 11.5g

BAKED BANANA-NUT OATMEAL CUPS

Prep Time: 5 Minutes | **Cook Time:** 25 Minutes
Servings: 10
Ingredients:
- Rolled Oats – three cups
- Low-Fat Milk – 1 ½ cups
- Bananas – two, mashed

- Brown Sugar – 1/3 cup
- Eggs – two, beaten
- Baking Powder – one tsp
- Cinnamon Powder – one tsp
- Vanilla Extract – one tsp
- Salt
- Pecans – half cup, chopped and toasted

Directions:
1. Heat the oven to 190 °C.
2. Coat muffin pan with cooking spray.
3. Mix all ingredients in a bowl.
4. Also add pecans. Fill the muffin cups with the mixture. Bake for twenty-five minutes.
5. Allow to cool for five minutes, and finally serve and enjoy!

Nutrition:
Calories: 140; Carbohydrates: 25.3g; Fat: 6.1g; Protein: 6.1g; Fiber: 3.5g

BANANA BRAN MUFFINS

Prep Time: 5 Minutes | **Cook Time:** 25 Minutes
Servings: 10
Ingredients:
- All-purpose Flour – ¾ cup
- Baking Powder – 1 ½ tsp
- Baking Soda – half tsp
- Bananas – one cup, mashed
- Brown Sugar – 2/3 cup
- Buttermilk – one cup
- Canola Oil – ¼ cup
- Chocolate Chips – half cup
- Eggs – two
- Ground Cinnamon – half tsp
- Salt
- Unprocessed Wheat Bran – one cup
- Vanilla Extract – one tsp
- Walnuts – 1/3 cup, chopped
- Whole-Wheat Flour – one cup

Directions:
1. Preheat the oven to 200 °C.
2. Using cooking spray, coat muffin cups.
3. In a bowl, beat brown sugar and eggs to smooth the mixture. Supplement with vanilla, oil, wheat bran, buttermilk, and bananas and beat again.
4. In a second bowl, mix salt, baking soda, cinnamon, baking powder, all-purpose flour, and whole wheat flour.
5. In the center of the dry ingredients, create space and pour in the wet ingredients. Mix well, adding the chocolate chips. Divide the mixture into muffin cups and decorate with nuts.
6. Bake for about twenty minutes and let cool for five minutes.
7. Finally, serve!

Nutrition:
Calories: 190; Carbohydrates: 34.3g; Fat: 6.8g; Protein: 5.1g; Fiber: 3.8g

DARK CHOCOLATE RASPBERRY OATMEAL

Prep Time: 10 Minutes
Servings: 4
Ingredients:
- Chocolate Syrup – four tsp
- Red Raspberries – one cup
- Regular Rolled Oats – 1 ½ cups
- Salt – ¼ tsp
- Unsweetened Almond Milk – three cups
- Unsweetened Cocoa Powder – two tbsp

Directions:
1. In a saucepan, add cocoa powder, oats, almond milk, and salt. Bring to a boil over high heat, stirring frequently.
2. Lower the heat and simmer for six minutes. The goal is for the mixture to thicken.
3. Allow resting for a few minutes.
4. Distribute oatmeal mixture into serving bowls. Garnish with raspberries and chocolate syrup. Finally, serve!

Nutrition:
Calories: 156; Carbohydrates: 24.3g; Fat: 4.8g; Protein: 5.3g; Fiber: 5.8g

PINEAPPLE-RASPBERRY PARFAITS

Prep Time: 5 Minutes
Servings: 4
Ingredients:
- Fresh Raspberries – half pint
- Nonfat Peach Yogurt – two cups
- Pineapple Chunks – 1 ½ cups

Directions:
1. In the four available glasses, add the pineapple, raspberries, and yogurt and finally serve!

Nutrition:
Calories: 140; Carbohydrates: 33.3g; Fat: 0.8g; Protein: 5.1g; Fiber: 2.8g

GREEN SMOOTHIE

Prep Time: 5 Minutes
Servings: 1
Ingredients:
- Avocado – ¼
- Banana – one, frozen
- Honey – one tsp
- Nonfat Plain Yogurt – one cup
- Spinach – one cup
- Water – two tbsp

Directions:
1. Add the listed ingredients to a blender and blend for two minutes until smooth. Finally, serve and enjoy!

Nutrition:
Calories: 350; Carbohydrates: 54.7g; Fat: 7.8g; Protein: 18.1g; Fiber: 6.8g

PEACH-BLUEBERRY PARFAITS RECIPE

Prep Time: 10 Minutes
Servings: 2
Ingredients:
- Blueberries – half cup
- Ground Cinnamon – ¼ tsp
- Peach – one, pitted and sliced
- Sweetener Multigrain Clusters Cereal – one cup
- Vanilla, Peach or Blueberry Fat-Free Yogurt – six ounce

Directions:
1. Divide the ingredients evenly between the two glasses. Finally, serve and enjoy!

Nutrition:
Calories: 165; Carbohydrates: 34.3g; Fat: 0.8g; Protein: 11.3g; Fiber: 6.8g

RASPBERRY YOGURT CEREAL BOWL

Prep Time: 5 Minutes
Servings: 1
Ingredients:
- Ground Cinnamon – ¼ tsp
- Mini Chocolate Chips – two tsp
- Nonfat Plain Yogurt – one cup
- Pumpkin Seeds – one tsp
- Raspberries – ¼ cup
- Wheat Cereal – half cup, shredded

Directions:
1. In a bowl, add the yogurt first. Add the cinnamon, chocolate chips, raspberries, shredded wheat, and pumpkin seeds.
2. Finally, serve!

Nutrition:
Calories: 291; Carbohydrates: 47.7g; Fat: 4.1g; Protein: 18.2g; Fiber: 6.8g

AVOCADO TOAST

Prep Time: 10 Minutes
Servings: 1
Ingredients:
- Alfalfa Sprouts – ¼ cup
- Avocado – ¼, sliced
- Extra-Virgin Olive Oil – one tsp
- Mixed Salad Greens – one cup
- Plain Hummus – ¼ cup
- Red-Wine Vinegar – one tsp
- Salt
- Sprouted Whole-Wheat Bread – two slices, toasted
- Unsalted Sunflower Seeds – two tsp

Directions:
1. Season vegetables with salt, oil, and vinegar in a bowl.
2. Spread the toasted bread slices with the hummus and top with the sprouts, avocado, greens, and spinach.
3. Garnish with the sunflower seeds as well.

Nutrition:
Calories: 491; Carbohydrates: 45.7g; Fat: 20.1g; Protein: 17.2g; Fiber: 14.1g

FULLY-LOADED PITA POCKETS

Prep Time: 10 Minutes
Servings: 1
Ingredients:
- Whole Wheat Pita – one, halved
- Low-Fat Cottage Cheese – half cup
- Walnut Halves – four, chopped
- Banana – one, sliced

Directions:
1. Fill each individual pita with walnuts, cottage cheese, and banana. Finally, enjoy!

Nutrition:
Calories: 298; Carbohydrates: 47.1g; Fat: 7.1g; Protein: 20.2g; Fiber: 10.8g

CREAMY PEA SOUP

Prep Time: 5 Minutes | **Cook Time:** 25 Minutes
Servings: 5
Ingredients:
- Coconut Oil – 2 tbsp
- Garlic – one clove
- Ginger – 20g
- Lemongrass Stalk – two
- Onion – one tsp
- Peas – 500g
- Potatoes – 150g
- Salt
- Vegetable Stock – 1 liter
- Zucchini – two

Directions:
1. Pour the coconut oil into a skillet. Add the potatoes and cook until softened. After about 2 minutes, add the lemongrass, ginger, garlic, salt, and diced onion. Cook 2 minutes again.
2. Add the zucchini. Cook for another two minutes.
3. Then add the peas and vegetable broth and bring to a boil.
4. Over low heat, cook for a few more minutes.
5. Pour the soup into an immersion blender and blend until creamy.
6. Transfer to a bowl and garnish, if desired, with pine nuts.

Nutrition:
Calories: 341; Carbohydrates: 29.7g; Fat: 21.1g; Protein: 9.2g; Fiber: 5.1g

GUACAMOLE

Prep Time: 10 Minutes
Servings: 4
Ingredients:
- Avocados – two
- Red Onion – one
- Coriander Leaves – ¼ cup
- Limes – two
- Salt

Directions:
1. First, using a fork, mash the avocados until creamy.
2. Chop the coriander and onion and add to the mashed avocado.
3. Add the lemon juice and salt.
4. You can store the guacamole in the refrigerator for up to 2 days.

Nutrition:
Calories: 181; Carbohydrates: 16.7g; Fat: 11.1g; Protein: 3.2g; Fiber: 8g

CABBAGE SOUP

Cook Time: 30 Minutes
Servings: 8
Ingredients:
- Cabbage – eight cups, sliced
- Carrot – one cup, chopped
- Celery – one cup, chopped
- Chipotle Chilies in Adobo Sauce – 1 tbsp, minced
- Cilantro – half cup, chopped
- Olive oil – 2 tbsp
- Garlic – four cloves, minced
- Ground Coriander – half tsp
- Ground Cumin – one tsp
- Lime Juice – 2 tbsp
- Onions – 2 cups, chopped
- Pinto or Black Beans – 30 ounces, rinsed, low-sodium
- Poblano or Green Bell Pepper – one cup, chopped
- Salt
- Tomato Paste – one tbsp
- Vegetable Broth (or Chicken Broth) – four cups, low-sodium
- Water – four cups

Directions:
1. In a saucepan, add the oil and place over low heat.
2. Add the garlic, bell pepper, carrots, celery, onions, and salt and cook for ten minutes.
3. Add the cabbage. Cook until softened (about 7 minutes).
4. Add the cilantro, chipotle, cumin, and tomato paste. Cook for one more minute.
5. Add the beans, water, and broth. Cover the pot and bring it to a boil. Then over low heat, simmer for 13 minutes.
6. After adding the lime juice and fresh cilantro leaves, then serve!

Nutrition:
Calories: 161; Carbohydrates: 26.7g; Fat: 3.1g; Protein: 6.2g; Fiber: 7g

THE BEST VEGGIE SANDWICH

Prep Time: 10 Minutes
Servings: 8
Ingredients:
- Avocado – ¼, mashed
- Carrot – 2 tbsp, shredded
- Clementine – one, peeled
- Cucumber – four slices
- Hummus – one tbsp
- Salt
- Sprouted-Grain Bread – two slices, toasted
- Tomato – two slices

Directions:
1. Using a fork, spread avocado and hummus on a slice of bread. Fill sandwich with tomato, carrot, and cucumber.
2. Add salt to taste. Close the sandwich and serve with Clementine.

Nutrition:
Calories: 311; Carbohydrates: 46.1g; Fat: 8.1g; Protein: 11.2g; Fiber: 11.9g

QUICK VEGGIE TACO BOWL

Prep Time: 10 Minutes
Servings: 8
Ingredients:
- Bell Pepper – half, cored, and sliced
- Black Beans – ¼ cup, rinsed
- Cilantro – 2 tbsp
- Cooked Brown Rice – half cup
- Olive Oil – one tsp
- Red Onion – half, sliced
- Sharp Cheddar Cheese – ¼ cup, shredded

Directions:
1. Add the oil to the skillet and set it over medium-low heat.
2. Add the onion and bell pepper and cook for 8 minutes.
3. In a bowl, place rice and beans. Cover with cilantro, cheese, and vegetables.

Nutrition:
Calories: 433; Carbohydrates: 56g; Fat: 12.1g; Protein: 18g; Fiber: 9.7g

COBB SALAD

Prep Time: 10 Minutes
Servings: 1
Ingredients:
- Carrot – one, diced
- Celery – one stalk, diced
- Cheese – one tbsp, crumbled

- Chicken Thighs – one, diced, roasted
- Egg – one, hard-boiled, diced
- Honey and Mustard Vinaigrette – 2 tbsp
- Iceberg Lettuce – three cups, chopped

Directions:
1. Place all the ingredients in the salad bowl and drizzle with dressing.

Nutrition:
Calories: 473; Carbohydrates: 66g; Fat: 15.1g; Protein: 18.9g; Fiber: 12.7g

CREAM OF ASPARAGUS SOUP

Prep Time: 5 Minutes | **Cook Time:** 20 Minutes
Servings: 4
Ingredients:
- Asparagus – two pounds, chopped into one inch pieces
- Garlic – three cloves, minced
- Olive Oil – one tbsp
- Salt – one tsp
- Shallots – one cup, chopped
- Vegetable Stock – six cups

Directions:
1. Add the olive oil, garlic, and shallots to a saucepan and cook over medium heat for three minutes until softened.
2. Add the asparagus stalks, salt, and vegetable broth. Cover the pot and bring to a boil, then simmer.
3. At the same time, in a frying pan, quickly sauté the tops of the asparagus with the oil until tender.
4. Transfer the soup to a blender and blend until creamy.
5. Combine the soup with the two preparations and serve!

Nutrition:
Calories: 203; Carbohydrates: 16g; Fat: 5.1g; Protein: 8.9g; Fiber: 12g

CARROT SOUP

Prep Time: 5 Minutes | **Cook Time:** 20 Minutes
Servings: 4
Ingredients:
- Carrot Juice – 1 ½ cups
- Carrots – four cups, chopped
- Chicken Broth – three cups
- Garlic – three cloves, minced
- Olive Oil – two tbsp
- Onion – one, chopped

Directions:
1. In a saucepan over medium heat, add the oil, onion, carrots, and salt and cook for eight minutes. Cook one minute with the garlic as well.
2. Pour in the broth and cook for fifteen minutes on low heat.
3. Add the carrot juice. Once cooled, transfer to a blender and blend until smooth.
4. Serve and enjoy!

Nutrition:
Calories: 173; Carbohydrates: 16g; Fat: 5g; Protein: 8g; Fiber: 5.7g

MUSHROOM-BARLEY SOUP

Cook Time: 30 Minutes
Servings: 4
Ingredients:
- Carrots – one cup, chopped
- Chicken Broth – 28 ounces,
- Fresh Mushrooms – 1lb, sliced
- Olive Oil – two tbsp
- Onion – one cup, chopped
- Quick Cooking Barley – half cup
- Smoked Ham – 1 ½ cups, chopped
- Stewed Tomatoes – 14 ounces, seedless

Directions:
1. In a saucepan over medium-high heat, add the olive oil, onion, and carrots and cook for about five minutes.
2. Also, put in the mushrooms and cook for another five minutes.
3. Add the ham, barley, tomatoes, and stir. Cook two minutes.
4. Pour the hot chicken broth into the pot and let it come to a boil. Then let simmer for 20 minutes.

Nutrition:
Calories: 201; Carbohydrates: 26g; Fat: 7.1g; Protein: 7g; Fiber: 3.9g

PENNE WITH CHICKEN AND ASPARAGUS

Prep Time: 5 Minutes
Cook Time: 20 Minutes
Servings: 4
Ingredients:
- Asparagus – 1 ½ cups, thawed, cut into 1 inch pieces
- Chicken Breast Halves – 1lb, boneless and sliced into strips
- Garlic – four cloves, minced
- Olive Oil – two tbsp
- Parmesan cheese – ¼ cup, grated
- Peas – one cup, thawed
- Penne (Pasta) – 1lb
- Poultry Seasoning – half tsp

Directions:
1. Boil water with salt in a pot. Drop in the pasta and cook until al dente.
2. In a skillet over medium heat, cook chicken with half the oil and poultry seasoning until golden brown. Transfer the cooked chicken to a bowl.
3. In the skillet, add the peas, asparagus, garlic, and remaining olive oil and cook until soft. Add the

chicken back in and cook all together for two minutes.
4. Drain the pasta and toss it with the chicken mixture.

RED BEANS AND RICE RECIPE
Cook Time: 30 Minutes
Servings: 4
Ingredients:
- Olive Oil – one tbsp
- Onion – one, chopped
- Celery – three, chopped
- Garlic Cloves – three, minced
- Tomato Sauce – 14 ounce
- Oregano – half tsp
- Thyme – half tbsp
- Beef Stock – 14 ounce
- Red Beans – 28 ounce, drained and rinsed

BLACK BEAN NACHO SOUP
Prep Time: 15 Minutes
Servings: 2
Ingredients:
- Avocado – half, diced
- Black Bean Soup – 18 ounce, low-sodium
- Cabbage – half cup, shredded
- Grape Tomatoes – half cup, halved
- Lime Juice – half tsp
- Smoked Paprika – ¼ tsp

BEST BUTTERNUT SQUASH SOUP
Prep Time: 15 Minutes
Servings: 1
Ingredients:
- Butternut Squash Soup – 15 ounce
- Chickpeas – ¾ cup, rinsed
- Lime Juice – one tbsp
- Salt
- Avocado – two tbsp, diced
- Nonfat Plain Greek Yogurt – one tbsp

EASY BROCCOLI SALAD
Prep Time: 25 Minutes
Servings: 5
Ingredients:
- Bacon - ½ cup crumbled
- Broccoli Crowns – four cups, chopped
- Cider Vinegar – one tbsp
- Clove Garlic – one, grated
- Fresh Cauliflower – one cup, chopped
- Mayonnaise – half cup
- Mustard – one tbsp
- Red Onion – ¼ cup, chopped
- Sunflower Seeds – three tbsp, toasted

BEEF & BEAN SLOPPY JOES RECIPE
Prep Time: 25 Minutes
Servings: 4
Ingredients:
- Black Beans – one cup, rinsed
- Brown Sugar – one tsp
- Garlic Powder – half tsp
- Ground Beef – 12 ounce

5. Finally, serve and add parmesan cheese to taste!
Nutrition:
Calories: 601; Carbohydrates: 74g; Fat: 3.1g; Protein: 39g; Fiber: 8.9g

- Brown Rice – four cups, cooked

Directions:
1. In a skillet over medium heat, pour the olive oil and add the garlic, celery, onions, thyme, and oregano. Cook and stir well.
2. Add the tomato paste and red beans and stir.
3. Add the hot beef broth and simmer for 25 minutes. Serve this dressing over brown rice.

Nutrition:
Calories: 411; Carbohydrates: 74.1g; Fat: 2.1g; Protein: 22g; Fiber: 9g

- Tortilla Chips – two ounce, baked

Directions:
1. Pour the soup into a saucepan. Add paprika, lime juice, and stir.
2. Ladle soup into bowls, add sliced avocado, tomatoes, cabbage, and serve with tortilla chips.

Nutrition:
Calories: 351; Carbohydrates: 43g; Fat: 13g; Protein: 11g; Fiber: 9.1g

Directions:
1. Heat the soup in a saucepan.
2. Add the salt, lime juice, and chickpeas. Stir and cook.
3. Serve by adding the yogurt and avocado.

Nutrition:
Calories: 401; Carbohydrates: 66g; Fat: 7.1g; Protein: 18g; Fiber: 11g

Directions:
1. Take a bowl and whisk garlic, vinegar, mustard, and mayonnaise well.
2. Add the sunflower seeds, onion, and bacon. Also, add the broccoli and cauliflower and mix well (They don't usually need to be blanched, but you can do it. ½ minutes or so).
3. Serve and enjoy!

Nutrition:
Calories: 245; Carbohydrates: 5g; Fat: 1.9g; Protein: 20g; Fiber: 20g

- Olive Oil – one tbsp
- Onion – one cup, chopped
- Spicy Brown Mustard – two tsp
- Tomato Sauce – one cup
- Whole-Wheat Hamburger Buns – four, split and toasted

Directions:
1. Place a skillet over medium-high heat. Add the oil and beef and cook for four minutes until golden brown. Then transfer to a bowl.
2. Put the onion, garlic, and beans into the skillet and cook for five minutes until softened.
3. Add the brown sugar, mustard, and tomato sauce and mix well. Transfer the beef to the skillet and simmer for five minutes.
4. Serve on sandwiches and enjoy!

Nutrition:
Calories: 365; Carbohydrates: 35g; Fat: 13g; Protein: 26g; Fiber: 3.1g

PEANUT SOUP WITH SWEET POTATO

Prep Time: 10 Minutes | **Cook Time:** 20 Minutes
Servings: 5
Ingredients:
- Beans – 15 ounce, rinsed
- Canola Oil – two tbsp
- Fresh Cilantro – ¼ cup, chopped
- Garlic – one tbsp, minced
- Ginger, one tbsp, minced
- Lime Juice – two tbsp
- Onion – 1 ½ cups, diced
- Salt – ¾ tsp
- Sweet Potatoes – 1lb, peeled and cubed
- Unsalted Dry-Roasted Peanuts – ¾ cup
- Water – three cups

Directions:
1. Take a pot and, over medium heat, add the oil and onion and cook for minutes until softened.
2. Add ginger and garlic. Stir and cook for one minute. Pour in water and sweet potatoes and bring to a boil. Then lower the heat and simmer for 12 minutes.
3. Pour the soup into a blender and, adding the peanuts and salt, blend until smooth. Transfer it back to the pot.
4. Add the beans. Stir and bring to a boil.
5. When cooked, let stand and add the lime juice and fresh cilantro leaves.

Nutrition:
Calories: 295; Carbohydrates: 23g; Fat: 9.9g; Protein: 13g; Fiber: 8g

CHEDDAR & PEAR PANINI

Prep Time: 15 Minutes
Servings: 1
Ingredients:
- Arugula – ¼ cup
- Cheddar – 2 slices
- Mustard – 2 tsp
- Red Pear – 1/3, cored and cut into thick slices
- Whole Grain Flatbread – half

Directions:
1. On the inside of the flatbread pocket, spread mustard.
2. Insert the cheese slices and fold them over. Also, add the arugula and pear slices.
3. Place them in the pan and cook for 4 minutes.

Nutrition:
Calories: 222; Carbohydrates: 27g; Fat: 7g; Protein: 13g; Fiber: 5.1g

CHICKEN & APPLE KALE WRAPS

Prep Time: 15 Minutes
Servings: 1
Ingredients:
- Apple – one, cut into nine slices
- Chicken Breast – three ounces, thinly sliced, cooked
- Kale Leaves – three
- Mayonnaise – 1 tbsp
- Mustard – 1 tsp
- Onion – six slices, thin

Directions:
1. On the cabbage leaves, spread the mustard and mayonnaise.
2. Add the chicken, apples, and onion. Then, roll up each cabbage leaf and enjoy.

Nutrition:
Calories: 355; Carbohydrates: 33g; Fat: 11g; Protein: 28g; Fiber: 5.9g

EASY CAULIFLOWER RICE PILAF

Prep Time: 10 Minutes | **Cook Time:** 12 Minutes
Servings: 1
Ingredients:
- Almonds – ¼ cup, toasted, sliced
- Cauliflower Florets – six cups
- Extra-Virgin Olive Oil – three tbsp
- Fresh Herbs – ¼ cup, chopped
- Garlic – two cloves, minced
- Lemon Zest – 2 tsp
- Salt – half tsp

Directions:
1. Chop cauliflower florets in a food processor or with a knife.
2. In a skillet, add the oil and garlic and place over medium-high heat for 30 seconds.
3. Then, add the cauliflower rice and salt. Cook five minutes on medium heat.
4. At the end of cooking, add the lemon zest, fresh herbs, and almonds. Finally, serve!

Nutrition:
Calories: 115; Carbohydrates: 5g; Fat: 10g; Protein: 4.1g; Fiber: 2.9g

STRAWBERRY & RHUBARB SOUP

Prep Time: 5 Minutes | **Cook Time:** 25 Minutes
Servings: 4
Ingredients:
- Basil – 1/3 cup, chopped
- Rhubarb – four cups
- Salt – 1/8 tsp
- Strawberries – 1 ½ cups, sliced
- Sugar – ¼ cup
- Water – three cups

Directions:
1. In a saucepan, add the water and rhubarb. Cook until softened (5 min). Transfer to the refrigerator in a bowl with cold water for 20 min.
2. Blend rhubarb with salt, sugar, and strawberries in a blender until smooth.
3. Serve in the bowl with the addition of basil.

Nutrition:
Calories: 98; Carbohydrates: 23.2g; Fat: 1g; Protein: 1.8g; Fiber: 3.3g

CHICKEN PESTO SANDWICH

Prep Time: 5 Minutes | **Cook Time:** 25 Minutes
Servings: 3
Ingredients:
- Basil Pesto – 2 tbsp
- Chicken Breast – six ounces, boneless, cut in half, horizontally
- Feta Cheese – ¼ cup, low-fat, crumbled
- Kalamata Olives – 2 tbsp, pitted and chopped
- Mozzarella Cheese – 1/3 cup, shredded
- Multi-Grain Sandwich Round – four, split
- Onion – four slices

Directions:
1. Heat the skillet with the oil and, over medium heat, cook for four minutes the onion.
2. Add the chicken to the skillet and cook for five minutes. Transfer the chicken and shred it.
3. To assemble the sandwiches: spread the pesto and add the olives. Place grilled onion slices and chicken on top. Add feta and mozzarella cheese.
4. Place sandwich in skillet and cook 2 minutes per side and serve!

Nutrition:
Calories: 295; Carbohydrates: 28g; Fat: 9.8g; Protein: 24.1g; Fiber: 5.9g

BEAN TOSTADAS

Prep Time: 15 Minutes | **Cook Time:** 10 Minutes
Servings: 4
Ingredients:
- Tostada Shells – four
- Beans – 16 ounces, rinsed and drained
- Salsa – half cup, prepared
- Cheddar Cheese – ½ cup, shredded
- Salad – 1 ½ cups
- Tomato – one cup, chopped
- Lime Wedges – one

Directions:
1. First, heat the oven to 350 F°.
2. Place tostada shells on a baking sheet and bake for three minutes.
3. In a bowl, mix the salsa and beans and mash this mixture with a fork.
4. Spread the bean mixture between the tostada shells and add half of the cheese. Cook for 5 minutes.
5. Add the chopped tomato and lettuce.
6. Finally, before enjoying, put the remaining cheese and lime wedges.

Nutrition:
Calories: 231; Carbohydrates: 31g; Fat: 5.9g; Protein: 13.1g; Fiber: 5.9g

PERFECT FISH TACOS

Prep Time: 10 Minutes | **Cook Time:** 15 Minutes
Servings: 3
Ingredients:
- Avocado – half, thinly sliced
- Cilantro Leaves – ¼ cup
- Coleslaw Mix – 2 cups
- Lime – one, quartered
- Olive Oil – 2 tsp
- Salad Dressing – 2 tbsp, ranch
- Tilapia Fillets – 1lb
- Whole Wheat Tortillas – eight

Directions:
1. Heat the oven to 450 F°.
2. Bake the fillets for 5 minutes. The fillets should be brushed with oil and placed in a baking dish. Add the seasoning.
3. Simultaneously, mix the dressing and coleslaw in a bowl.
4. The fish should be, at the end of cooking, cleaned of bones and put in the tortillas.
5. To complete the dish add lime, avocado, and coleslaw mixture.

Nutrition:
Calories: 331; Carbohydrates: 31g; Fat:11.9g; Protein: 31g; Fiber: 15.9g

EASY PEA & SPINACH CARBONARA

Prep Time: 10 Minutes | **Cook Time:** 15 Minutes
Servings: 4
Ingredients:
- Egg – one
- Egg Yolks – three
- Fresh Parsley – three tbsp, chopped
- Fresh Spinach – eight cups
- Garlic – one clove, minced

- Linguine – 9 ounce
- Olive Oil – 1 ½ tbsp
- Panko Breadcrumbs – half cup
- Parmesan Cheese – eight tbsp, grated
- Peas – one cup
- Salt

Directions:
1. In a pot, boil water and cook the pasta, spinach, and peas in it for two to three minutes.
2. At the same time, in a frying pan, toast the breadcrumbs with garlic and oil for 2 minutes over medium heat and transfer to a small bowl. Also, add parsley and two tablespoons of Parmesan cheese.
3. In another bowl, whisk the egg, egg yolks, salt, and six tablespoons of Parmesan cheese.
4. Drain the pasta and vegetables from the pot. Keep and store cooking water in a cup.
5. Whisk the appropriate amount of the saved cooking water into the egg mixture. The result should be creamy.
6. Add the pasta to the cream and stir to combine.
7. Top with breadcrumbs and serve!

Nutrition:
Calories: 431; Carbohydrates: 51g; Fat: 15.9g; Protein: 23.1g; Fiber: 7.9g

BROCCOLI WITH PEANUT SAUCE

Prep Time: 6 Minutes | **Cook Time:** 10 Minutes
Servings: 4
Ingredients:
- Broccoli Florets – eight cups
- Brown Sugar –one tbsp
- Cornstarch – one tsp
- Garlic – three cloves, chopped
- Peanut Butter – three tbsp
- Rice Vinegar – two tbsp
- Sesame Oil – two tbsp, toasted
- Sunflower Seeds – one tbsp, toasted
- Tamari – 2 ½ tbsp
- Onion – half cup, sliced

Directions:
1. Boil water in a pot. Cook broccoli for 3 minutes until tender.
2. At the same time, heat a skillet with garlic and oil.
3. Add broccoli and cook for 3 minutes.
4. Whisk the cornstarch, vinegar, sugar, tamari, and peanut butter in a bowl. Add this sauce to the broccoli and cook for about one minute.
5. Serve with added sunflower seeds.

Nutrition:
Calories: 151; Carbohydrates: 12.1g; Fat: 9.9g; Protein: 7g; Fiber: 2.9g

SPINACH ARTICHOKE DIP PASTA

Prep Time: 10 Minutes | **Cook Time:** 15 Minutes
Servings: 4
Ingredients:
- Whole-Wheat Rotini – eight ounce
- Fresh Spinach – five ounce, chopped
- Cream Cheese – four ounce, low-fat, cut into chunks
- Parmesan Cheese – half cup, grated
- Garlic Powder – two tsp
- Artichoke Hearts – 14 ounce, rinsed, squeezed dry and chopped

Directions:
1. Boil water in a pot. Drop in the pasta, cook, and drain.
2. In a saucepan, cook spinach over medium heat until wilted. You can add some pasta cooking water. When cooked, move the spinach to a separate bowl.
3. Transfer them to the bowl. Add the milk and cream to the saucepan and whisk well.
4. In the pan, melt the cream cheese. Then add the garlic powder and Parmesan cheese. Cook until thickened.
5. Add the spinach to the sauce. Add the pasta and artichokes. Heat everything together for a few minutes and serve.

Nutrition:
Calories: 359; Carbohydrates: 52.1g; Fat: 9.2g; Protein: 17g; Fiber: 6.9g

STUFFED POTATOES WITH SALSA & BEANS

Prep Time: 8 Minutes | **Cook Time:** 20 Minutes
Servings: 4
Ingredients:
- Avocado – one, sliced
- Fresh Salsa – half cup
- Jalapeños – four tsp, chopped, pickled
- Pinto Beans – 15 ounce, rinsed, warmed and mashed
- Russet Potatoes – four

Directions:
1. Using a fork, pierce the potatoes. Cook them in the microwave for 20 minutes. Then let them cool a little.
2. Cut the potatoes, but not all the way through. Remove some of the pulp and fill them with beans, jalapeños, avocado, and salsa.

Nutrition:
Calories: 321; Carbohydrates: 52.9g; Fat: 7g; Protein: 10g; Fiber: 10g

CLASSIC MINESTRONE SOUP

Prep Time: 5 Minutes | **Cook Time:** 25 Minutes
Servings: 6
Ingredients:
- Cannellini Beans – 15 ounce, unsalted, rinsed
- Carrots – one cup, chopped
- Ditalini (Pasta) – one cup

- Peas – one cup, thawed
- Garlic – five cloves, minced
- Kale – three cups, chopped
- Salt – ¾ tsp
- Leek – one cup, chopped
- Olive Oil – three tbsp
- Vegetable Broth – three cups
- Water – three cups
- Whole-Grain Bread – one cup, cubed
- Zucchini – ten ounce, thinly sliced

Directions:
1. Toast bread with oil and garlic for 2 minutes in the oven at 350 F°.
2. In a saucepan, pour one tablespoon of oil and salt. Cook carrots, leek, peas, cabbage, and beans for 8 minutes over high heat.
3. Pour in the water and broth. Cover with a lid and bring to a boil. Toss in the pasta and zucchini and cook for five minutes.
4. Pour soup into bowls. Top with croutons.

Nutrition:
Calories: 269; Carbohydrates: 38.1g; Fat: 9.1g; Protein: 10g; Fiber: 6.9g

VEGAN CARROT CAKE ENERGY BALLS

Prep Time: 20 Minutes
Servings: 20
Ingredients:
- Carrots – 2, finely chopped
- Chia Seeds – ¼ cup
- Ground Cinnamon – ¾ teaspoon
- Ground Ginger – ½ teaspoon
- Ground Turmeric – ¼ teaspoon
- Oats – ½ cup
- Pecans – ¼ cup, chopped
- Pitted Dates – 1 cup
- Salt
- Vanilla Extract – 1 teaspoon

Directions:
1. Grind dates, pecans, chia seeds, and oats in a food processor.
2. Also, add the carrots, cinnamon, vanilla, ginger, turmeric, and salt and grind until paste forms.
3. With this mixture, then create small balls. Help yourself with a spoon.

Nutrition:
Calories: 49; Carbohydrates: 8.1g; Fat: 1.2g; Protein: 1g; Fiber: 1.9g

SKILLET LEMON CHICKEN WITH SPINACH

Cook Time: 25 Minutes
Servings: 4
Ingredients:
- Olive Oil – 2 tablespoons
- Chicken Thighs – 1 pound, boneless, skinless, cut into bite-size pieces
- Red Bell Pepper – 1 cup diced
- Salt – ½ teaspoon
- Garlic – 4 cloves, minced
- White Wine – ½ cup dry
- Cornstarch – 1 teaspoon
- Lemon – 1, zested and juiced
- Fresh Spinach – 10 cups lightly packed
- Parmesan Cheese – 8 teaspoons, grated

Directions:
1. Take a large skillet, add chicken, bell pepper, salt, and stir. Cook over medium-high heat for 9 minutes, until chicken is cooked through.
2. Then also, add garlic and cook for 1 minute.
3. Separately, whisk the wine and cornstarch together in a bowl. Add lemon juice and zest to this mixture to the pan. Bring to a boil.
4. Before serving, add the spinach and cook the last 2 minutes. Finally, garnish with Parmesan cheese.

Nutrition:
Calories: 316; Carbohydrates: 12.1g; Fat: 16g; Protein: 26g; Fiber: 3.9g

TOMATO BASIL PASTA

Cook Time: 30 Minutes
Servings: 4
Ingredients:
- Baby Spinach – 6 cups
- Basil – ½ cup
- Chicken broth – 2 cups
- Garlic Powder – ½ teaspoon
- Grated Parmesan Cheese
- Italian Seasoning – 1 ½ teaspoons
- Olive Oil – 2 tablespoons
- Onion Powder – ½ teaspoon
- Salt – ½ teaspoon
- Tomatoes – 1 (15 ounce) can no-salt-added, diced
- Water – 1 cup
- Whole-Wheat Rotini – 8 ounces

Directions:
1. In a large pot, place the water, broth, pasta, tomatoes, Italian seasoning, onion powder, and salt. Over high heat, bring to a boil.
2. Next, lower the heat and simmer for 10 minutes. Stir frequently.
3. Add the spinach and cook until the liquid part is absorbed. (About 7 minutes more).
4. Also, add the basil. Serve with Parmesan garnish.

Nutrition:
Calories: 329; Carbohydrates: 55.1g; Fat: 9.2g; Protein: 12g

30 DAYS MEAL PLAN

DAY	BREAKFAST	LUNCH	DINNER
1	Peach-Blueberry Parfaits	Creamy Raspberry, Coconut & Chia Shake	Spinach and Artichoke Dip Pasta
2	Southwest Breakfast Quesadilla	Raw Cherry-Apple Pie	Grilled Eggplant
3	Raspberry Yogurt Cereal Bowl	Strawberry-Watermelon Refresher Juice	Stuffed Potatoes with Salsa and Beans
4	Bean & Bacon Breakfast Tacos	Blueberry Bircher Pots	Mushroom Quinoa Veggie Burgers
5	Peanut Butter & Fig Crispbreads	Jacket Potatoes with Home-Baked Beans	Turkey Meatballs
6	Avocado & Caper Flagel	Pea & Broad Bean Shakshuka	Sweet Potato Soup
7	Strawberry-Ricotta Waffle Sandwich	Lentil Fritters	Minestrone Soup
8	Make-&-Take Breakfast Sausage Sandwich	Summer Pistou	Lentil Soup
9	Loaded Pita Pockets	Winter Vegetable & Lentil Soup	Grilled Corn Salad
10	West Coast Avocado Toast	Baked Sweet Potatoes & Beans	Kale Soup
11	Mango Raspberry Smoothie	Pea Soup	Pasta Fagioli
12	Peanut Butter & Chia Berry Jam English Muffin	Guacamole	Sweet Potato Gnocchi
13	Green Eggs & Ham Bagel Breakfast Sandwich	Cabbage Soup	Bean and Ham Soup
14	Pumpkin Pie Smoothie	Cauliflower And Potato Curry Soup	Grilled Pear Cheddar Pockets
15	Peanut Butter-Chocolate Chip Overnight Oats with Banana	Sweet Potato and Black Bean Chili	Chicken and Apple Kale Wraps
16	Baked Banana Cups	White Bean Chili	Cauliflower Rice Pilaf
17	Peanut Butter-Banana English Muffin	Chickpea Stew	Fresh Herb and Lemon Bulgur Pilaf

18	White Bean & Avocado Toast	Veggie Sandwich	Corn Chowder
19	Berry-Almond Smoothie Bowl	Bean and Veggie Taco Bowl	Strawberry and Rhubarb Soup
20	Avocado Toast with Burrata	Cobb Salad	Chicken Sandwiches
21	Baked Oatmeal	Asparagus Soup	Tex-Mex Bean Tostadas
22	Homestyle Pancake Mix	Creamy Carrot Soup	Fish Tacos
23	Multigrain Pancakes	Mushroom Barley Soup	Cucumber Almond Gazpacho
24	Cinnamon–Oat Bran Pancakes	Broccoli Soup	Pea and Spinach Carbonara
25	Whole-Wheat Buttermilk Pancakes	Chicken and Asparagus Pasta	Sautéed Broccoli with Peanut Sauce
26	Cornmeal Pancakes	Red Beans and Rice	Edamame lettuce wraps burgers
27	Oven-Baked Pancake	Beef Stir Fry	Pizza stuffed Spaghetti Squash
28	Baked Pancake	Black Bean Nacho Soup	One-Pot Dinner Soup
29	Wheat Waffles	Butternut Squash Soup	Heavenly Tasty Stew
30	Oatmeal Waffles	Broccoli Salad	Thanksgiving Dinner Chili

CONCLUSION

You've finally finished the Diverticulitis Cookbook! Thank you for all of your efforts. Now, if you managed to follow all of the instructions in this recipe book, I think you can safely assume that you are qualified enough to make a delicious and nutritious meal for yourself or even for a family member.

Diverticulitis is a common illness that occurs when there is an irritated, inflamed pouch in the colon. The most common victims are people over the age of 50 and children under the age of four.

I want to give one last set of suggestions to better manage this type of inflammation as the symptoms of diverticulosis can be avoided or reduced by taking the following measures:

- Eat smaller meals more often than three times daily, like 6-7 times per day or less.

- Avoid fatty, fried, and processed foods.

- Reduce or eliminate coffee, alcohol, and caffeinated drinks like tea, coffee, and soft drinks.

- Avoid simple sugars (sugar, honey) as much as possible. Instead, eat fruit or 100% whole grain bread that is high in fiber. Choose whole grains instead of refined grains such as white bread or white rice. Eat foods that are high in fiber, such as fruits that have skin on them to add fiber. If you prefer something without skin, peel the fruit before consuming it but don't consume too much fiber at a meal because it can cause bloating and abdominal pain.

- Eat more vegetables, beans, and whole grains as they are high in fiber, which helps with constipation.

- Practice a healthy, balanced diet. High-fiber foods such as fruits and vegetables are excellent for your digestive system.

- Drink plenty of fluids (eight to ten glasses per day) to prevent constipation. If you tend to drink coffee or caffeinated drinks, have a glass of water after drinking the beverage. Avoid fizzy drinks like soft drinks and carbonated water because they can cause gas, bloating, or diarrhea which can be painful, especially if you have diverticulitis.

- Eat plenty of low-fat protein foods because they are good for your body. You can get protein from foods such as eggs, fish, or chicken. If you prefer vegetarian protein sources, use tofu as it is a good source of protein.

- Exercise regularly to increase your muscle strength and improve muscle function. If you do not exercise or already have weak muscles, it can lead to diverticulosis symptoms like constipation and bloating.

- Eat the right meal sizes and exercise regularly to maintain a healthy weight. Create an activity regimen that is perfect for you with the help of your doctor.

- Keep a healthy balance of water and fiber and reduce unhealthy fats in your diet.

- Use flaxseed oil to help regulate bowel spasms and constipation problems. It also reduces the risk of diverticular disease. To use flaxseed oil, mix one tbsp with juice or yogurt daily until the bowels start moving normally again.

I hope that you found this recipe book helpful and can continue to have a healthy life. If there are any recipes that you haven't found in the cookbook and think would be helpful to others with Diverticulitis, please share them with me. Thanks again to all the people who have written to me, and thank you all for your support!

Printed in Great Britain
by Amazon